THE
TEN-LETTER
COUNTRIES

MORE ZANY ADVENTURES

OF THE

ALPHABET TRAVELLER

THE TEN-LETTER COUNTRIES

MORE ZANY ADVENTURES

OF THE

ALPHABET TRAVELLER

DAVID JENKINS

Matador
9 Priory Busines Park
Wistow Road
Kibworth Beauchamp
Leicester LE8 0RX, UK
Tel: 0116 279 2299
Email: books@troubador.co.uk
Web: www.troubador.co.uk/matador

ISBN 978 1780880 754

British Library Cataloguing in Publication Data.
A catalogue record for this book is available from the British Library.

Typeset by Troubador Publishing Ltd, Leicester, UK

Matador is an imprint of Troubador Publishing Ltd

Printed and bound in the UK by TJ International, Padstow, Cornwall

ACKNOWLEDGEMENTS

To Paul the Poet and Sue the Solicitor: love and thanks, you are top siblings and the best marketing team any man could wish for.

To Alistair and Lizzie: a big thank you for giving your time, advice and expertise so generously.

To all at the office in UK and South Africa: none of this could happen without your great support and dedication. A job well done, always. Thank you.

To Victoria and Milly: a kiss from your uncle who isn't always as mad as you think.

To Joycey and the team at The Inn on the Park: you've done St Albans proud. Thanks for all your help mate.

To the many people I have had the privilege to travel, laugh and drink with in the course of this journey: you are too many to mention by name but your friendship and humour will be remembered long after the places have been forgotten.

And of course to Katharine: for more patience, encouragement, love and support than any one man deserves. I can never thank you enough.

1 BANGLADESH
2 LUXEMBOURG
3 TAJIKISTAN &
3ᵦ KYRGYZSTAN
4 KAZAKHSTAN &
4ᵦ UZBEKISTAN
5 MAURITANIA
6 MOZAMBIQUE
7 AZERBAIJAN
8 MONTENEGRO
9 SEYCHELLES
10 MADAGASCAR

THE TEN-LETTER COUNTRIES

CONTENTS

Introduction..xi

1. Bangladesh..1

2. Luxembourg...37

3. Tajikistan & Kyrgyzstan...................................63

4. Kazakhstan & Uzbekistan.............................97

5. Mauritania...133

6. Mozambique..161

7. Azerbaijan..187

8. Montenegro..211

9. Seychelles..233

10. Madagascar..257

To my Mum, Joan Jenkins

*Thank you for your love, friendship, sense of
humour and unwavering resolve to
look on the bright side of life.*

INTRODUCTION

You probably remember the moment when Steve Redgrave crossed the line for his fourth consecutive Olympic gold. Triumphant yet tortured, he slumped breathlessly in his boat and immediately announced to the world that he would rather be shot than attempt to do it all over again. But of course he did, he went on to win a fifth in Sydney and the following year was deservedly knighted for one of the greatest sporting achievements of all time.

Well, we have quite a lot in common, Sir Steve and I. Not so much in stature - I'd have to stand on my tiptoes to ruffle the hair of a man 6ft 5ins tall - nor, I suppose, in terms of athletic prowess. No, I was thinking more about our shared desire to cross new boundaries, our common quest to go places no man has journeyed before. Two men in our prime, focused, pushing it to the absolute limit.

OK, I know what you're thinking, my journey to the four-letter countries was never really up there with the bagging of five Olympic golds. But I can empathise with Steve because I too had been the breathless man in the boat, temporarily craved a "normal" existence, felt a longing to return to the world of the ordinary geezer. To step on to the streets without a map in hand or a bottle of water stuffed into a daypack, to get up for a pee in the night and not walk into a wardrobe.

Trouble is with me and Steve, we just never know when to stop. Where does a man go after the excitement and terror of the four-letter countries? Fives, sixes, sevens and eights are, well... ten-a-penny, too numerous to be in the hunt and I realised with some surprise that I'd already chalked off most of the nines. Spooky indeed. Could it be that deep in my subconscious I'd *always* been an alphabet traveller?

And then I saw the list, the ten-letter countries, a dozen* delightful destinations that few people ever get the chance to visit. Unusual, exotic, the world's richest and poorest, largest and smallest, another outrageous combo of deserts and jungles and mountains and islands. And places I'd never even heard of, couldn't possibly spell or pronounce, let alone point out on the globe. The adrenalin was pumping once again.

What do you think, Steve?

* *No disrespect to multi-worders. New Zealand, South Sudan, Ivory Coast etc....you are in a league of your own.*

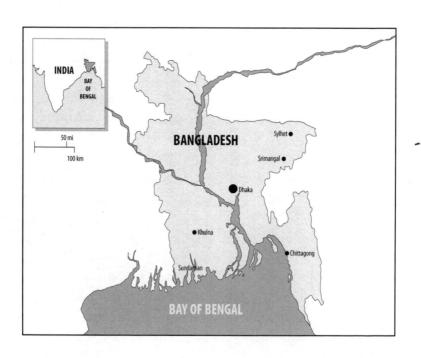

Bangladesh

There I was amongst an army of commuters emerging from St Albans City station, a mass of grey faces, grey coats, grey suits and grey briefcases leaning forward as one into the teeth of a howling gale. The poor buggers. Not only do they have to confront this misery on a daily basis but every year they have to face the sartorial disruption of a bright red paper flower foisted upon their pin-striped lapels. Has nobody ever thought to produce a nice, grey, commuter-friendly poppy?

It was that time of year. Random fireworks were already letting rip somewhere in the distance, the sun was setting earlier than the Countdown Conundrum and the hardy folk of Great Britain were about to plunge headlong into five months of wintry gloom. What I needed more than anything was a hearty helping of TLC. But which of the twelve TLCs would I head for?

I consulted Mr Collins – who is to maps what Kipling is to cakes – and learned that four and a half of the world's ten-letter countries sit inside the tropics, those handy lines of latitude that separate the permanently warm and sunny destinations from the sometimes cold and damp ones. Forking out one's hard-earned dosh to explore some dodgy corner of the globe is one thing but freezing one's nuts off in the process is simply a step too far.

Mauritania, Mozambique and Madagascar, ten-lettered and almost fully tropical, all sounded magical, mysterious and mighty appealing but I wasn't yet ready to head back in the direction of Africa. Seychelles, maybe? Don't be silly, what sort of an adventure kicks off with G + Ts on the beach and a cruise through an archipelago of palm-fringed islands? So that was it really; by process of elimination the decision was made. I was to head east, the furthest east a man can travel in the TLC world.

The Tropic of Cancer runs right across the middle of Bangladesh, a land that was once a part of India and which later became the eastern half of Pakistan. I stared long and hard at the map and at the triangular shape of the sub-continent in particular. Here was a region that provoked only thoughts of war, disease, famine, and unspeakable catastrophe. Not to mention over-population and desperate poverty. Was I really up for this?

Bangladesh. It seemed a strange place to go, an odd thing to do. I needed someone to say everything would be OK, it would be fun, so I groped around on the internet and found encouragement from the most reliable and unbiased of sources. The official website of the Bangladeshi government offered an assurance that theirs was a place of natural beauty, a country where tigers roamed the jungle, people lived off the land and a fascinating culture remained entirely unblemished. "Get here before the tourists arrive" implored their catchy, if somewhat optimistic slogan. And it was rather to my own astonishment, that purely in the spirit of alphabet travelling, I was about to do just that.

* * * * *

Dhaka International, far from being held together with bamboo poles and sheets of plastic, looked a rather more polished airport than most. It was early evening, a quiet time, the air outside was surprisingly cool, and the fifteen minute taxi ride from the terminal to the northern suburb of Gulshan not at all what I'd expected. The Crystal Garden Hotel (booked on-line) turned out to be a pristine guest house on a leafy lane surrounded not by squalour and chaos but by houses from Hampstead and smart cars from Germany. Ironically it was the cycle rickshaws parked outside these gated mansions that looked out of place. So far so good.

Twelve hours later I jumped out of bed like a kid at Christmas and threw back the curtains for that moment of magic. Waking up to a big sun and a bright blue sky is one of the delights of travel and how I just love that feeling of warmth and cheeriness, a perfect start to a day and the best

2

possible introduction to any new country. Except that it was raining like hell.

Not just raining but teeming in a way that looked as though there was little else in prospect for a long time to come. But hold on a minute, this was the dry season, the reason I had timed my visit with such care and precision. There had obviously been some sort of mistake and so, in the interest of getting the problem sorted as quickly as possible, I would demand an explanation from reception before going through to take breakfast.

As it turned out, the TV in the lobby was ready with all the answers and the staff had gathered in a semi-circle around it on account of Bangladesh making the BBC World headlines. Cyclone Sidr was gathering pace, heading towards the Bay of Bengal and would be crashing into the south of the country later that day. Oh no. Oh dear. Oh shit.

I joined the huddle of anxious viewers, all silent and wide eyed and more used than I to satellite images of such foreboding. It was like watching a ship about to collide with an iceberg knowing that a disaster was imminent but uncertain as to the scale of the devastation and demise that would follow. After much debate the news story moved on and everybody calmly returned to their respective duties (me included); there was nothing else we could do except wait... and pray.

* * * * *

"Do you have a map of Dhaka please?" I asked of reception, more in hope than expectation.

'Certainly sir,' answered the obliging gent, simultaneously jerking his head towards his right shoulder – Bangladeshi for OK – and then nodding to one of his colleagues who was standing behind me. Whereupon the assistant disappeared round the corner and returned a few seconds later with a beaming smile and an enormous country map unhooked from the wall of the restaurant. Not quite as pocketable as I'd hoped but a lovely gesture and a wonderful moment.

Dhaka sits plumb in the centre of Bangladesh, a country not dissimilar in shape to Scotland though twice its size and, incredibly, housing forty times its population. (Can you imagine a world of 158 million Jocks?). From what I could make out the dangerous south coast was about 200kms away, the cyclone wasn't expected to strike with full venom for another twelve hours and so for me to take a few paces forward from the centre of the lobby to the other side of the main door would not be subjecting myself to any unnecessary risk. I thanked the staff for their help and, brave as a lion, stepped outside.

The rain descended in straight lines and was clearly destined to do so for the rest of the day. Could I take it like a man and climb up onto the seat of the three-wheel cycle taxi parked at the door or would I return inside to sit and contemplate my misfortune? I sheltered and I pondered, watching water pour from the dark sky onto the head of the hapless rickshaw wallah, then clambered up on to his brightly painted chariot as though that decision had been taken by somebody else. The young lad leapt into action with a Colgate white smile from beneath his small black moustache and proffered a crumpled plastic sheet with which to protect my legs and upper body from the elements. He tucked me in like a mother would her child and started cycling through the puddles as fast as he could.

There is something very unpleasant about being wet, I decided. Pools of fresh rainwater had quickly formed where the sheet folded on to my lap so we had barely completed a hundred metres before the first lukewarm surge permeated my thin cotton trousers. At least this was an adventure, I tried to convince myself, knowing deep down the same could be said of open heart surgery. Cowering beneath that pathetic bit of plastic I started to wonder why I was there and to contemplate just how very unhappy I was quickly becoming. All I could see through the spray was the sodden shirt on the back of my rider, a spindly young lad standing upright on his pedals, drenched to the bone and pumping away for all he was worth. This was his day, all day, every day, and would be for the rest of his life. It was time to stop feeling so bloody sorry for myself.

He dropped me at the side of a busy road in what was evidently "downtown" Gulshan. The lack of a common language had given him the initiative in deciding my destination but it was broadly what I'd hoped for and 20 Taka (15p) seemed such a small price to pay for his efforts. The rain now seemed even heavier than before and, unless it was my imagination, had developed a teasing slant that met me full on, right between the eyes, Manchester-style. I was saturated, trying my best not to be miserable but already looking forward to getting back to the hotel. Or better still, the airport.

This was obviously the posh end of town with several rows of glass-fronted shops competing amidst the open stall variety, a distinction that usually separates the third world from the first (whatever happened to the second world by the way?). With head down and shoulders hunched I splashed along the pavement, trying to hurdle the larger puddles, but a series of gaping, man-sized holes kept forcing me back into the road. The prospect of dying is always bad enough but disappearing into the Bangladeshi sewage system would be a most unsatisfactory finale.

Meanwhile an endless procession of rickshaw cyclists crawled the kerb and pinged their old-fashioned bells to tout for custom, undaunted by the vile conditions and the vast army of motorised three-wheeler taxis swerving around them. As with the more conventional, and usually more bashed-up, four-wheel taxis, these green machines competed for customers and road space by using their horns: a beep-beep to register every desired manoeuvre, announce an impending one or simply to vent frustration at not being able to make one at all. An estimated toot tally, I later calculated, of one per vehicle every twenty seconds. Yes, this was more like it. Proper chaos. Chalfont St Giles to central Kolkata in the space of ten minutes.

Rusty buses and smoky trucks cranked up the danger levels another notch while pedestrians and the occasional cow profited from the many moments of gridlock to paddle from one side of the road to the other. A very normal everyday scene to millions, probably even billions, of people. Their lives had to go on despite the weather, I silently philosophised (never one to miss the bleedin' obvious) as I waited pre-scamper on the wrong side of Gulshan Circle, a sort of Bangladeshi Piccadilly Circus. My target was the HQ of a company that came with high recommendations and with whom I'd been in contact before leaving home. They own three passenger boats and run trips into the Sundarbans, the jungle wilderness of the Ganges Delta that was about to be ravaged by the cyclone. When the tourists do finally arrive this World Heritage site will be their first port of call, so I decided to book early to avoid disappointment.

Following e-mailed directions, I found the office by climbing up a concealed spiral stairwell in the middle of a ramshackle indoor market. As though that wasn't weird enough, the power to the building failed as I walked through their door so the negotiations about a journey into the disaster zone had to be conducted in a dark room across a desk illuminated by only a candle. No matter, the lady spoke good English, seemed serious and professional in her work and a deal was struck for me to join one of their vessels in the southern town of Khulna two weeks hence.

Happy with my morning's work I plucked twenty grand from an ATM (Taka is worth rather less than sterling), boarded another ricky back to the Crystal Garden and sat on my lovely dry bed to make some phone calls. The first of which was to a local gentleman name of Albert Biswas, a name given to me by some good friends who had recently left Bangladesh after an eight-year stint. During their time in the country they had raised finance from folks back in the UK to fund the setting up of two small medical clinics close to Albert's home village and it was some years earlier that I'd made my humble contribution to it.

Albert knew my name, was extremely grateful for the tiny part I'd played in helping to realise his dream and he spoke with the warmth of an old family friend. He was keen to show me the clinics in action so we agreed to make the trip together at the end of the following week – he would hire a car for the seven hour journey and, as it was in the same direction, I could then continue on to Khulna to pick up my boat.

Cyclone aside, things seemed to be falling nicely into place. My next call, following a Lonely Planet tip, was to a man known as Razu whose

6

speciality was arranging cycle trips around the tea estates up in the hillier north-east of the country. He would send a car to pick me up on Sunday and whisk me across the country for a lower price than I'd just paid one of his countrymen to get me from home to Heathrow airport! So job done, itinerary sorted, I could get on and enjoy the delights of Dhaka, or at least hunker down until Mother Nature had done her worst.

* * * * *

Andrew speaks Welsh because he comes from Llanelli, and English because…well, because he's Welsh. He learnt Bangla after a couple of years in Dhaka, Chinese when he used to live in China and Czech during his days in Prague. If you think that's impressive then wait till you hear that he can chat fluently in ten other languages and in his spare time dashes around the world to play the saxophone alongside one of Asia's top musicians. Thanks to the input of my now-departed friends Rob and Jacqui (still alive and kicking, just living elsewhere) this friendly stranger had e-mailed me an invitation to dinner and was even kind enough to bring along a bottle of wine to the restaurant to mark the occasion.

It was a wonderful evening and fascinating to see the other side of Bangladeshi life. The venue offered sophisticated international food, tasteful lighting and gentle jazz music courtesy of Andrew himself and his friend on the piano. This could have been Paris or Manhattan except that, in keeping with the rules of Islam, the locals would have to drink orange juice while the ex-pats were allowed to pay a few Taka in corkage and sip on a delicious burgundy. It was a rule that struck me as extremely unfair and I made a mental note to ask the Prophet Mohammed for a bit of leeway on this if and when he does re-appear. Who knows, perhaps he'll even have a PM's Question Time?

As Andrew played the sax I talked to his friend Mahmoud, an interesting and knowledgeable man who had fled the country with his parents during the War of Liberation in 1971 and had lived in the USA ever

7

since. He had come back for a year to write a book about the Bangladesh of today compared to the memorised version of his boyhood and how embarrassed I suddenly felt to know so little of the history of his homeland. The next day I would have to put that right.

The rickshaw that took us home was as brightly and ornately hand painted as all the others I'd seen during the course of the day. What made this one a little different was the Welsh dragon across its rear and the word Finland painted in enormous letters above it. Fortunately Andrew had already told us the story: he had come to know and trust a decent young lad who worked as a taxi cyclist but who would never be able to afford a rickshaw of his own. Like most of the others he would work all day to take 150 Taka (£1) then pay half his earnings to the wealthy owner of the machine. So Andrew had invested £120 in a brand new rickshaw, promised him a fixed salary of Tk 3000 a month to ride it and even presented him with a mobile phone to take bookings. Now the Welshman has his own chauffeur when required and gives his man the chance to earn extra dosh as a freelancer the rest of the time. A lovely story don't you think? But …Finland? Such was the gratitude and respect of the lad that he'd wanted to paint his master's country name across the dragon that he'd been given to copy. He didn't know how to spell Wales but – the next best thing – at least he knew how to spell England. Or so he thought.

* * * * *

I woke up for a few minutes during the night and heard the ferocious winds bending the trees as the cyclone headed north across the city of Dhaka. And then I turned over and went straight back to sleep.

How lucky was I compared to the fishermen and farmers who lived with their families down on the coast. They may have heard the news of what was about to happen, might even have abandoned their boats or attempted to barricade their simple homes, but when the wind comes through at over 200 kph and the water levels rise as much as ten metres, decisions on matters of survival or death are entirely in the lap of the gods. Thousands of innocent people were crushed by falling trees or simply swept away in the rampaging rivers that night, a horrendous death count and one which will never be accurately known. As though the country didn't have enough to contend with, here was yet another catastrophe in the sad history of Bangladesh.

I woke again five hours later, safe and sound. Everything looked pretty normal except that the mains power had gone off and the hotel generator called into action, something that happened several times a day anyway by all accounts.

It seemed rather appropriate that today was my Bangladesh history day, if only to understand more of what happened in 1971. There is an excuse for being vague on events from a few hundred years ago isn't there, but something definitely not right about completely missing a war that happens in your own lifetime. I tried to think back to those mischievous schoolboy days but my only recollection of that particular year was Manchester City losing to Chelsea in our defence of the European Cup Winners Cup. (In case you've forgotten, we'd lifted the trophy on April 29th the previous year, pulverising Gornik Zabrze 2-1 on a wet night in Vienna with goals from Neil Young in the 12th minute and a trademark Frannie Lee penner on 43. I don't remember who scored for Gornik, but that's not really relevant is it?)

It was Friday, the first (and, often only) day of the Muslim week-end. The streets would be a little quieter than usual during the morning, shops would open later or not at all, but according to my information The Liberation Museum would welcome visitors from 10am onwards. The map announced its location down in the heart of the city proper, a few miles but a world away from my mollycoddled existence on the tree-lined avenues of Gulshan. I ordered up some scrambled eggs for breakfast and, in preparation for the day ahead, turned the pages to the history section of my guidebook.

* * * * *

Britain officially ruled the sub-continent from 1858 but had already been there in some shape or form for two hundred and fifty years. India's Hindu majority was largely happy to co-operate under the Raj (as this regime was known) but the significant Muslim population felt they were being pushed aside and were determined to protect their religion and culture at all costs. They refused to play ball. Throughout the years they lobbied for an independent state – especially in Bengal which had always been a Muslim stronghold – and in 1947, in what turned out to be one of the final acts of the British government in India, their ultimate wish was granted. Lord Mountbatten declared that a large part of the states of Punjab in the north-west and Bengal in the north-east would no longer be part of India but together would form the new Islamic country of Pakistan.

Fifteen million people relocated according to their religion, the new (but divided) country came to be known as West and East Pakistan and, crucially, the western part governed both states. Separated by a thousand miles of India, this was never going to be easy. The Bengalis shared little in common with the Urdu speakers from the Punjab so when the (already despised) government in the west decreed that Bengali (Bangla) would no longer be recognised as an official language, you can guess what hit the fan.

That was 1952. Riots broke out on the streets of Dhaka (then spelt Dacca), the government sent the army in from the west and its soldiers killed five students for trying to protect the right to use their own language. Incredibly the country of two halves limped along for another two decades but in 1970, when the government failed to help after a massive cyclone had struck the east, resentment spilled over once again. The campaign for an independent "Land of the Bangla Speakers" gathered momentum and by the following year it was outright civil war.

In the carnage and chaos that ensued as many as ten million people from East Pakistan fled over the border into India. Those that stayed and survived suffered nine months of genocide and brutality at the hands of their own government before India eventually sent in its own troops to settle the issue once and for all. Within ten days the powerful neighbour had forced the Pakistani army to surrender and in December 1971 the War of Liberation had finally been won. The new, independent country of Bangladesh was born but how many lives had been lost in achieving that goal? It was time to head off to the museum.

* * * * *

Not sure of how far one could reasonably expect to travel on a cycle rickshaw I made what I though was a pretty good train impersonation and hoped to be taken to the nearest station. Twenty Taka got me to a railway line (well done, Jenks) but having dismounted, paid and smugly waved off my rider I realised there was in fact no train, station or even platform in sight (not so well done after all, Jenks). In fact there were hundreds of people wandering along the track, including a blind man swishing his white stick from side to side. For his sake if nothing else, I found myself praying there was no train due for quite some time.

It was time to test ride a motorised three-wheeler, in some countries a tuk-tuk but known to all in Bangladesh as a CNG after the fuel that powers it. I had a stab at pronouncing the name of a park allegedly close to the museum and earned myself a twenty minute white-knuckle ride through alleyways of cyclists and pedestrians who were forced to swerve or dive for cover. Yet another unmissable experience and one that came to an end when I was instructed to alight alongside a main road teeming with buses. There was no park, certainly no museum and unfortunately not a single word of a common language to explain what was happening.

In the absence of a better plan, I started walking. The streets were named on my guidebook map but not on the streets themselves, not even in Bangla, and nothing at all corresponded to the page on which I'd pinned such hope. In fact it might as well have been a tourist guide to Beijing. My humble approaches to shopkeepers and passers-by proved equally useless as nobody spoke any English or understood the words of Bangla I'd randomly selected. So I just kept going and hoped that something good might happen.

Walking alongside a dual carriageway is not a great deal of fun, particularly on a Friday in Dhaka. Half an hour of futile pacing convinced me of this and the mood was bleakening somewhat (sorry, I know it's not a proper word) when an instantly recognisable sound emerged from behind. There is something entirely unambiguous about the gathering of phlegm, the most repulsive of all human habits that in one split second relegates our species to the lowest level of the animal kingdom. I turned and saw the man with the puffed-out cheeks, rolling the contents of his mouth as one might savour a vintage wine and wobbling his head in anticipation of the impending despatch. Just a question now of finalising the unloading strategy and from what I would later observe, he had three options from which to select:

Think about taking a free kick on the edge of the penalty box. You can float the ball up and over the top of "the wall" applying just the right pace and trajectory to make it land perfectly in the bottom corner of the net. Or you can blast it, hard and low, a torpedo, Stuart Pearce style. In the world of expectoration the former tends to pose the bigger threat in that a bolus upwardly projected from a shop doorway can easily, given unfortunate timing, make an unwelcome appearance on the face or clothing of an innocent passer-by. We'll call these options 1 and 2.

To my slight relief the man that I found myself snarling at had actually gone for number 3: The Stroke-Victim's Drool. Perhaps the most pathetic technique of all, the slight stoop forward, the downward tilt of the head, the slow, stringy, vertical drip that eventually forms a sticky puddle just in front of the right toe.

So where do you stand on public throat-clearing? Do you respect the culture and habits of a foreign land and take it entirely in your stride? Literally. Is it right to malign people for acting in a way that to them is perfectly normal everyday behaviour? Tricky. I have thought long and hard about this and would like to put forward for your consideration what I see as a reasonable compromise: any person caught gobbing in the street, anywhere in the world, should be picked up by the ankles, lobbed into a truck, offered a meal of their choosing, two telephone calls to relatives and then, as the sun goes down, lowered slowly into a pit of pre-menstrual crocodiles. On second thoughts, forget the meal.

The easiest way to the museum was to give the actual address to a taxi driver and, had I noticed three hours earlier that it was written in my book alongside the words "The Liberation Museum", I reckon that would have been my initial approach. It turned out to be an understated building that offered an arrowed walking tour from one small room to the next and whilst the presentation was basic the message could not have been more effective: "This is what the Pakistanis did to 3 million of our people." And then, as if to prove the point, there was a room piled up with skulls and bones. It wasn't done distastefully – in fact it was a great tribute to those that had fought to achieve independence – and the other exhibits, mostly newspaper articles from 1971, poignantly detailed the individual stories of triumph and torture. This was their holocaust, a tragedy on an enormous scale and, to my great shame, I hadn't known the first thing about it.

* * * * *

The morning newspapers brought photographs of the devastation in the delta and a death toll that would multiply each day. Estimations of the fatalities seemed to vary greatly according to source and, as with the war in 1971, the political agenda of the author. The main direct impact on Dhaka itself was the loss of electricity and also a huge chunk of its workforce that had headed south in search of their stricken families. Fortunately for me, I was about to go north.

Mr Razu arrived as agreed to collect his dollars, proudly introduce his chauffeured minibus and explain that the driver would need to stop for fuel shortly after leaving Dhaka. All being well we would be in Srimangal five hours later, he confirmed, but "all being well" is a mighty big expression in the not so developing world. Sure enough it took two hours to get through the madness of the capital and a further two to search for, and wait at, a filling station that was blessed with both petrol and sufficient electricity to power the pumps. And that was the best part of the journey.

The road was of normal width for two vehicles, flanked by dusty pedestrian pathways and – as is always the case in poorer countries – packed with people transporting cargo by hand, head, cart and animal. The flat, semi-waterlogged fields stretched as far as the eye could see in all directions though only on the rarest of occasions did my eye, either of them for that matter, stray from the road ahead.

In case you've never been there, be warned that the system of driving in Bangladesh is very different from anywhere else in the world. It is so utterly flawed and absolutely terrifying that every second of every journey is dominated almost entirely by thoughts of impending disaster. The crux of the problem is that the driver of an overtaking vehicle transfers the responsibility of death-avoidance to all other motorists upon the sounding of his horn, thus pulling out at high speed in front of an oncoming bus then becomes the bus driver's headache. Or limb amputation. Or funeral. It's a philosophy that gives the approaching vehicle a real incentive to brake as hard as possible and, when that doesn't quite do the trick, swerve through cyclists and pedestrians to create that extra bit of space.

My taxi travelled faster than most other northbound vehicles so I got to see more than a fair share of buses and trucks moving at pace towards my forehead. Not very manly, I know, but I couldn't prevent the release of a gasp-cum-whimper with each manic manoeuvre, nor could I stop the reverse body thrust – arms and legs fully outstretched – that would extend my life by 0.2 of a second. The frequent sight of crumpled wrecks in the paddyfields, often part submerged, did little to lighten the mood and it was only when darkness had fallen and we swung into the driveway of the Tea Resort that my fists and teeth and buttocks finally became unclenched.

It had probably been the most terrifying afternoon of my life. I felt sick. I felt more exhausted than if I'd crawled from Dhaka on my hands and knees. I felt angry that I had been stupid enough to choose a car instead of letting the train take the strain. I felt cheated that a whole day had been wasted. Yes, I felt pissed right off, as they say in Manchester. (And possibly one or two other places).

A scruffy man led me down a corridor where several million flying insects had gathered around a dangling light bulb. Then he handed me a key and walked away. No wonder. The room was so damp and smelly and utterly disgusting in every detail that I couldn't even bring myself to sit on the sagging bed with its repulsive floral eiderdown, or touch the shabby moth-eaten curtains or even look in the bound-to-be-revolting en-suite bathroom. Resort! They actually had the temerity to call this a fucking resort! What a stinking, festering, God-forsaken dump. Alphabet travelling? Bollocks to it. Enough is enough. Pissed right off. Right?

And then I lay down and fell asleep, the first of my three nights at the Tea Resort.

* * * * *

I woke up to a bright blue sky, gorgeous lush surroundings and a very much nicer person than the miserable old git of the night before. The room was still horrid (I didn't mention the dried blood on the sheets did I?) but the bathroom was OK and all things considered I have probably slept in a whole lot worse. Just that then I would have been twenty years younger and no doubt considerably less sober.

My guide arrived after breakfast as Razu had promised and together we cycled the few kilometres to the Lawachara National Park. Set in a tranquil forest this is home to the rare Hoolock Gibbon (no, I hadn't either, but they are the second largest in the world) and an eerie display of spiders' webs, hundreds of them, enormous and perfectly symmetrical, tilted upwards like satellite dishes between the branches of the trees. All so very peaceful, no peeping of car horns, just the occasional rustling as the family of monkeys played high above us. Absolutely lovely.

Though I hadn't been in Dhaka for very long, this country outing already felt like a much needed breath of fresh air. The weather was settled now, a gorgeous twenty something degrees, and what a treat it was to pedal through the gently rolling hills of the tea estates and watch the brightly-dressed ladies plucking handfuls of leaves and filling the baskets on their backs. They waved and posed excitedly for photos and laughed when I showed them their faces on the camera. The pictures were a feast of colour: beautiful brown skin, white smiles (the one's that had teeth) and colourful wrap-around saris set against the shiny green of the tea plants and a cloudless blue sky.

Those ladies, indeed all the staff on the estate, will almost certainly live there from cradle to grave. Considered amongst the lowest of the castes they earn next to nothing but are given on-site accommodation, basic medical support and schooling for their children, most of whom will also go on to live and work there. A self-contained, isolated world with little in the way of danger but no dreams or ambitions either. I looked around again at the glorious scenery and thought of the city slums and the millions who eke out an existence in filthy, squalid conditions. At least this was poverty with a measure of style.

We weaved through the low spiky bushes of the pineapple plantations – did you know each bush yields just one fruit? – and on into the relative darkness of the forest. The men had already tapped the rubber trees early that morning, leaving a skilled diagonal cut across each of the boughs and we got there just as the ladies were going round to empty the pots that had filled up as a result. They zig-zagged from tree to tree, transferring the sap into a bucket, and took away a day's work of the milky white stuff that would one day become a tyre or a condom.

It was time for a relaxing break and what better idea than to stop for a nice cup of tea. And not just any old tea but a Five Colour Tea, a secret recipe closely guarded by the entrepreneurial owner of this particular café who it seemed had managed to draw in the crowds from far and wide with his magic brew. It was whilst looking for a chair that I got my first sighting of this house speciality, a glass with five very different coloured liquids, one hoop on top of the next, each tier maintaining its own identity. I'll have one of those please.

It didn't take very long to realise that the customers, perhaps forty in number, had one thing only on their minds. Their interest was in no way subtle or disguised, indeed most of them moved closer to get a better view of the alien and a complete circle formed very quickly with yours truly sitting alone at its centre. It didn't stop at that. A group of teenagers, evidently from wealthy families, moved in with mobile phones and fought for position, paparazzi-style, to get the best close-up photograph of the foreigner, only to be outdone by a chap with a video camera who was diligently filming every minute of my visit. What a treat his family and friends were in for that evening.

The crowd seemed entirely unthreatening and in the main were too busy staring to offer anything else in the way of facial expression. Dialogue was zero, even amongst themselves. I did my best to look relaxed and cheerful but in truth felt anything but. What the hell are you *supposed* to do when eighty eyes are fixed directly upon you? My inane smiling and gesticulating elicited absolutely zilch by way of a response so in a few test cases I returned the glare and waited to see what might happen. Nothing. Not a sausage. It was almost as if I didn't really exist. They stared on and on, and in most cases, on, though some finally did get bored and wandered back to their chairs and their cold cups of tea. A very peculiar experience and now I know exactly how that lion feels in the Serengeti when the tourist jeeps turn up and park alongside.

* * * * *

Srimangal the town is nothing more than a busy street of shops and market stalls crossed by a railway line that links Sylhet in the north (original home of most of Britian's "Indian" restaurant owners) with the cities of Dhaka and

Chittagong further south. I opted for the first of the three daily trains back to the capital and arrived on the platform in plenty of time for both locals and fellow passengers to assemble for another serious session of eyeballing. This time with constant begging, sleeve tugging and prodding from elderly women and snotty-nosed children who wouldn't take no for an answer. It was all starting to get a little uncomfortable when a policeman appeared and launched a one-man attack with baton drawn, evidently a tried and tested tactic, that saw them scattering quickly from the station.

A first class ticket to Dhaka costs £1.50 which is pretty good value if you're not travelling on a derailment day (though even a derailment has to beat a road smash). It brought five hours of pure pleasure enlivened by a constant flow of vendors each with a single product to offer...tea, lemons, dates, water, towels, juices, nuts.... I could keep going... and even a wandering trio of folk musicians came along to do a little turn. But my mind soon switched off from all the in-train activity, I kept face-in to the breeze from the open windows and just watched the incredible landscape roll by like a National Geographic documentary. Only then did I really start to appreciate what a fascinating and beautiful country this is.

Most of Bangladesh is entirely flat and little more than a few metres above sea level. As vulnerable as a sleeping baby in the shadow of an elephant, it sits at the foot of the highest mountain range on the planet and sees more water flowing through it than does the whole of Europe. Quite an incredible piece of trivia that, isn't it, considering the country is barely a quarter the size of France? The Ganges and Brahmaputra pour out of the Himalayas from the north-west and north-east respectively and create an enormous Y that dominates the map, its confluence in the centre of the country just to the west of Dhaka. Those mighty rivers feed a vast network of smaller ones and eventually fresh water meets salt when they hit the Indian Ocean in the Bay of Bengal.

In the wet summer season the view from the train window will be nothing more than a vast lake. Even now, four months later, a significant number of fields were still under water, a glorious scene with much of the surface covered by the dense leaves and striking purple flowers of the water hyacinth. The wide, open panorama changed little but was always pleasing on the eye and the rattle of the train never failed to elicit smiles and waves from the people working the land and the groups of children who should have been at school. There were few towns or cities to disrupt the tidy rural picture so when the slums, garbage and graffiti announced our arrival on the outskirts of Dhaka it came as something of a shock to the system. Tea break over, it was time for me to get back to work.

* * * * *

An independent traveller turning up in Bangladesh is an opportunity no tour operator would ever want to miss, hence the irrepressible Mr Razu's call to offer me a room at the Sheraton for a price (he felt was) too good to refuse. There were a couple of good reasons to accept his deal. This hotel chain had been the first of the big guns to come to Dhaka and was right in the heart of the city, unlike the later arrivals that opted for the fancier northern suburbs closer to the airport. I wanted to be down there in the thick of it for a couple of days and the added bonus of an ice-cold beer (booze is available to foreigners in international hotels) or a glass of wine, or most likely both, made it all seem like a pretty good idea. It *was* a very low dollar rate, more like the price of a room in a pub, and so, feeling more Del Boy than at any time in my life, I had the three-wheeler drop me off in front of the revolving doors.

The Sheraton Hotel, Dhaka is an ugly sprawling edifice. The grim, over-chilled lobby has more in common with a major railway terminus and the convention centre tacked on to its side generates an endless flow of human traffic. My room smelled of damp, overlooked an ugly dual carriageway and relied on the TV to drown out the cacophony of horns that blasted away all day and most of the night. I'd wanted to be in the thick of it and in that respect I had succeeded. What an idiot you are Jenkins. I love you, Gulshan.

Dhaka for beginners is a triangle with the airport and posh suburbs at the top, the old city bottom left and the business district away to the right. My starting point was now somewhere in the middle and the plan was to get down to the river that flows through the historic old part of the city. I asked the hotel to get me a cab and after a mere forty minutes it arrived.

The driver's English was good enough to convey that he wasn't prepared to go to Old Dhaka but it wasn't up to explaining the reason why. "Oh please mate, I'll give you loads of Taka" I pleaded like a spoiled public schoolboy desperate to buy a conker. In the end he succumbed, we agreed on a price and he nosed his wreck of a motor forward into the traffic jam from hell. And that was just the hotel driveway.

Real proper hell was once we got into the old city itself. The roads narrowed, men pulled carts piled high with all manner of produce and several hundred thousand cycle rickshaws battled against the green motorised three-wheelers for what little space remained. Sweat-soaked pedestrians criss-crossed at will through this stalemate of honking vehicles but trucks, cars and taxis stood no chance at all. The very point that my driver was trying to make as he repeatedly mumbled messages to Allah and threw his non-honking arm up in the air.

We crawled past the post that denotes the geographical centre of the country and it was agreed that we'd gone as far as we could. It would take the poor guy another hour to fight his way back through the chaos, the reason he'd originally declined the fare, so a few extra Taka and an apologetic shrug was the least he deserved. He accepted the bundle of scruffy notes with a solemn – almost gracious – nod of the head, as though acknowledging that the struggle against stifling heat and absurd traffic was his destiny, he would just have to get on and make the best of a bad job. I looked again into his sad face. It didn't seem fair that I could just bail out and melt away into the crowd.

* * * * *

The narrow old streets oozed personality, each one specialising in the sale of a given product and bringing together all the competing vendors side by side. I wandered along past all the bicycle shops, then a line of stonemasons chipping away at the roadside, then a row of printers, then buckets and pans, religious artefacts, oranges...and finally to the river. I'd reached Sadarghat, the boat terminal, the main transport hub for the city of Dhaka.

The Buriganga looks nothing on the map, just one of many mere tributaries, but still it is half a kilometre wide as it winds across the city, twice the girth of the Thames flowing under London Bridge. It delivers a mind-boggling volume of people and produce from near and far, as well as the city's most desperate folk who hang around the shabby dock buildings in search of shelter or a change of fortune. It did feel strangely intimidating so when a friendly English-speaking guy approached with the offer of a half-hour cruise in his rowing boat I went through the motions of a haggle and jumped eagerly on board.

The busy channel reminded me of Hong Kong's harbour with vessels of all shapes and sizes moving at different speeds along the length and breadth of the river. Sadly though, that is where the comparison ends. No state-of-the-art skyscrapers here, just dour and derelict buildings on both sides reflecting the plight of a country that gets kicked to the ground every time it tries to stagger to its feet. The only exception was the beautiful Pink Palace that had been restored in the late 80s but when I got to it later that day even that had been abandoned, the gates locked and the gardens left to run wild. In truth it all painted a rather depressing, hopeless picture and after another short walk and yet another wild rickshaw ride, I was more than ready for that very expensive and oft-dreamt-about tiny little can of Heineken.

* * * * *

What do you do in a city if you hate shopping, get grumpy in traffic and have had more than your fill of pacing the streets in search of dubious places of interest? Simple really. You go for a nice long walk in the park, read your

21

book and then slip into a cosy little bar. Thus was my challenge for the new day.

By a quirk of good fortune Ramna Park was just a ten minute stroll from the Sheraton. It was entirely unremarkable as parks go but, as you might expect on a warm sunny day, well stocked with young couples enjoying their few hours of privacy. A typical scene in most parts of the world but apparently groundbreaking stuff for Bangladesh, as Andrew had explained on my first night out. Tradition has always dictated that women never be left alone with men from outside the immediate family and so, for most, courtship and romance is rarely more than a schoolgirl fantasy. Parents arrange their marriage to whomever they deem suitable – cousins are a particular favourite – and refusal to co-operate often results in violence and even death.

There are many unfortunate souls for whom death would no doubt have been a blessing. The unluckiest women fall victim to acid attacks, usually sulphuric acid poured over their faces and bodies by men whose advances have been rejected. This most barbaric of acts not only inflicts a lifetime of physical and mental torture – it melts the skin and often causes blindness – but these poor ladies then find themselves excluded from society for having been mutilated in this way. The brave charity known as Acid Survivors Foundation (www.acidsurvivors.org) offers support where it can and the government has pledged to bring the perpetrators to justice but the sad reality is that witnesses rarely come forward. To the minds of many men these attacks are a justifiable form of revenge. Is it possible, I wonder, that the human race can sink any lower than this?

Back at the hotel, the doors to the lift were generously held apart by none other than a besuited and bebadged (another made up word) gentleman name of Mr Trevor McDonald. Not the Caribbean newsreader we all know and love but the Australian general manager who seemed genuinely matey and was curious to know which company or charity I represented in Dhaka. My "just a visitor" response produced an extraordinary reaction, a level of bemusement that caused his eyebrows to move up and down with dramatic style and deep furrowed lines to appear across his forehead. Then slowly, and very deliberately, he asked me to confirm his understanding that I was, in fact, a *tourist* in Bangladesh.

Trevor had been the boss at the Sheraton for five years and was nearing the end of his contract so it came as quite a revelation when he announced that I was the first tourist he'd ever met in his hotel. Such was his dismay he suggested we meet for coffee the next morning when he hoped to have the opportunity to introduce me to his wife. What a thrill that would be for Mrs McDonald.

The next phase of the current day, the reading of my book, went pretty much according to plan. Short of falling off the bed and crushing my skull or finding that the pages had dislodged and drifted through an open window it was never likely to throw up the same level of complication as the final challenge: the locating of a decent bar. Islamic countries vary considerably on the booze front from the Dubai "drink in our mock Irish bars if you can afford it" approach (my personal favourite) to the enforced removal of body parts or public hanging in Saudi Arabia. So I asked around, as you do, and from what I could gather Bangladesh had found a happy medium somewhere between the gallows and Paddy McGinty's by allowing ex-pat communities to form their own private, alcohol-licensed clubs. Needless to say the Brits, along with the Dutch and Americans, were quick to climb on board and the only question for me was whether my novelty tourist visa would get me through the doors.

It would entail a manic three-wheeler ride back up to Gulshan but I was genuinely curious to see what the British Club was all about. What on earth could one expect in the crazy, dusty world just north of downtown Dhaka? Would I be greeted at the door by a Mr Tomkinson-Smythe sporting a cravat and a monocle? Led along a red carpet to the timbered walls of the majestic snooker room? Cucumber sandwiches on the floodlit lawn? (Why *do* posh people eat cucumber sandwiches?)

The bloke that signed me in was called Mike, he was hobbling around from an afternoon of touch rugby and still dressed in a pair of tatty shorts (must have removed his monocle when donning his jockstrap). He led me through a room that reminded me of a village hall, almost empty except for a scattering of children's toys and posters on the walls advertising forthcoming events. And thence upstairs to the small bar that was almost empty and, in truth, it wasn't difficult to see why.

I ordered a beer and, purely out of politeness, accepted the menu. Why was I there? I read it anyway and found more interest in the pricing policy – everything quoted in sterling – than the dishes on offer. Did I really want to eat Fish and Chips or Shepherd's Pie in Bangladesh? Shouldn't I just leave, go and get a tasty curry? The waiter was back, and for reasons I can't explain, we agreed on cheeseburger and chips. The beer wasn't going down as it should have, this all felt too contrived.

I sat there quietly, unlike the lady with a very strong Manchester accent who talked non-stop at four males huddled around an adjacent table. She sounded like a United fan, I decided, one of the few that doesn't come from Norway or Ireland or Weston-Super-Mare, and she was only marginally less boring than the food that was heading my way. At that point Mike left with a limp and a wave and some twenty minutes later, having managed three bites of the very dodgy burger, I too was back aboard a rickshaw.

* * * * *

It was quite cool standing in front of the Sheraton at 05.50 that Saturday morning. Albert had suggested we make an early start so as to reach his village by lunchtime and, true to his word, the minibus hired for the occasion pulled up just as the sun was starting to rise. He and his brother, James, had put aside two days to make this journey for me (they had taken Sunday, a working day in Bangladesh, as annual leave) and after the introductions and handshakes we all set off for Khagbari in the province of Gopalganj.

There is something a little strange about spending a week-end in a remote primitive village with people you don't know. This was the gist of my silent one-man conversation, the secret and somewhat dark contemplations from the back seat of the vehicle. So what if it *is* strange, I persisted? Does that really matter? Isn't that what the world of exploration is all about? How did real men like David Livingstone go on, setting out into the depths of the African jungle where no white man had ever been before? The train of negative thought came screeching to an abrupt halt when James flashed his wide handsome smile, produced a Tupperware container of cauliflower curry and proudly unwrapped the chapattis he'd made himself the night before. It was time to stop behaving like a wuss. I tucked into the spicy breakfast.

It took some time to leave the city behind but the roads were not congested and our driver seemed more eager than most of his fellow professionals to go about his work in a civilised manner. The sun was bright now, shoppers were already flooding the markets in the outlying suburbs, a dense mass of buildings had given way to trees and fields and a fresh landscape of rich, vibrant colour. Yes, this was how adventures were supposed to be.

Our destination lay to the south-west of Dhaka, just short of Khulna in fact where I'd be dropped off the next day to join up with the boat. Not a great distance when you look at the map but this is a country of over 700 rivers and, as a consequence, few road journeys are ever in a straight line. I noticed the sun was right behind us now, we were heading due west to the point just below the junction of the big Y, where, if our luck was in, a ferry would be waiting to take us across.

It was and it did. And it was a cherished experience to stand up on deck with a glass of hot, sweet tea and look down at the Meghna river weaving as far as the eye could see like a huge fat snake sprawled across a lawn. She would swell and burst in the summer but lose depth in the drier months, hence the machine away to my left pumping sand from the riverbed to keep the channel open. This was real Bangladesh, thought Jenkins The Philosopher, the interminable juxtaposition of land and water and man's endless fight for survival against the extremes of nature.

The drive south took on a new dimension with tall, elegant trees lining the roads in a scene from rural France. Behind them, as always, the patchwork quilt of paddyfields, many under water. Ladies in beautiful saris brought colour to the streets, men cycled rickshaws and pulled trailers stacked with produce. This was everything that my car journey "up north" had not been, death even seemed a very distant concept and I was in no hurry at all for the journey to come to an end.

The further we travelled, the more charming our surroundings became and it wasn't until we closed in towards Albert's home village that we saw the first signs of devastation. The trees that had been most exposed to the cyclone now leaned into the road, many with branches completely sheered off or dangling precariously, crippled by the strength of the winds. Walls and fences lay crumpled and broken, some of the simple houses had lost their roofs and one or two looked to have been destroyed completely. This had been one of the least affected areas of the south but that would offer no consolation to the poor folk whose lives had been torn apart.

The village of Kaligonj is built around a single street, the sort of place you see in a cowboy movie. Within the row of basic shops is the clinic, a room of no more than five metres by five, the rear quarter of which is divided by a curtain in order to create, at least in theory, a private space for doctor and patient. The remaining area is given over to a table, several chairs for the waiting customers and a large ancient cabinet from which medication is dispensed.

The most innocuous of buildings but instantly recognisable on a Saturday afternoon. This is the day that the doctor makes his weekly visit and those people lined up outside in the midday sun, mostly women holding their babies, were just the visible tail of a formidable queue. All heads turned at once as the Biswas brothers arrived, the local lads who had gone away to the big city but never stopped fighting the cause of the folks back home. Thanks to these heroes, the villagers no longer had to walk miles across the fields to get a simple wound dressed or to find a paracetemol to numb their pains. There were smiles, waves, happy faces. Whispers exchanged. Hold on though, who was that funny white bloke sitting between them?

The crowd willingly moved aside, chairs were hastily rearranged and the three of us joined the doctor at his desk. A nurse then drew the curtain around us and stood waving a large wand to keep the flies off the VIPs: that a consultation was in progress mattered not, the nervous lady with the crying baby would simply have to reveal their medical problems to five onlookers instead of one. It was a scene from a black comedy and the urge to burst out laughing was tempered only by the seriousness of the faces around me.

The baby had earache, as did three of the next four. Probably infections caused by the water since the cyclone, was the doctor's best guess, though he didn't have an otoscope to reach a proper diagnosis. The same likely cause was offered in response to complaints of nausea, rashes and respiratory problems but again, without any resources to check patients out, he was working almost entirely in the dark. In our privileged world the doctor would generally urge patience and resist medication or, in more serious cases, encourage further investigation. But in Bangladesh, as with most developing countries, a course of antibiotics is the only avenue open to the doctor and the patient would be disappointed to leave the clinic with anything less.

The doctor spoke good English and explained with a certain sadness that the locals could barely afford the tablets he'd prescribed. These simple rural folk, with an hourly income equal to 5p at best, would buy the medication on a day by day basis then stop at the first sign of improvement, only to see the sickness return a week later. Such is the dangerous cocktail of ignorance and poverty and it didn't take long as an outsider to realise how better education could significantly help their cause. Nobody had ever told the residents of Kaligonj that eating food off the floor is a health risk, that dirty water should not be used for drinking or pouring into the ears of their children, that hands should be washed after using (whatever passes for) the toilet. Simple things we take for granted and assume that everybody else does too.

Albert and James had long since recognised that the teaching of such basics is fundamental to the healthcare of the villagers and they introduced me to three beautiful ladies, impeccably dressed in matching purple saris, whose role was to do just that. The dream of the Bizwas boys was to employ more of these healthcare workers and, perhaps, some day in the future, enable the clinic to offer free medication to the poorest of the poor. If only they had some money.

Remarkably, the two clinics, eight staff and visiting doctor manage to keep going on a total income of less than £1500 per month but as only 20% of this sum is generated from consultation fees (15p per visit) and the sale of drugs, they depend heavily on donations from overseas just to hold their own. To think that my mates Rob and Jacqui had brought this support to a community of 20,000 people was something quite remarkable and I felt an enormous sense of pride in their efforts and, dare I say, my own very small contribution. I made the decision there and then that I wanted to help some more.

It took just a few minutes to move on to Khagbari, the slightly larger of the two clinics and the village that was home to the Biswas family. We attended more consultations, all strikingly similar to those in Kaligonj, mostly female patients arriving and departing without so much as a word of greeting or thanks (not uncommon in Bangladesh) but many of them bending to transfer kisses from their hands to our feet in the ultimate gesture of respect.

Our bags were transferred by boat along one of the many narrow waterways, known as khals, to where Albert and James' parents were waiting to receive us. As our luggage was punted upstream we walked along a parallel series of paths through the forest and across a terrifying bridge that resembled a fallen ladder with five out of every six rungs damaged or missing. The cyclone devastation was all too clear now, many large trees had come crashing down and it had clearly just been a matter of luck whether you or your house had been beneath one of them at the time. We stopped to witness the sad, pathetic sight of a lady and her small children sitting on the ground amidst the ruins of what had been their home. There was nothing left, no roof, no walls, only a few clothes and old pans scattered amongst the debris. She was motionless, shell-shocked I suppose, just staring in silence at the destruction all around her, powerless to offer any form of response.

* * * * *

Dinner, as lunch, was vegetable curry with rice and a small portion of fish, prepared on a wood-burning stove in front of the house. I was warmly welcomed by this most Christian of families and as we took our seats at the long table the charming Mrs Biswas presented a fork in deference to my foreign status. The Bangladeshi method of eating generally requires no cutlery, just a mixing and scooping with the right hand followed by a series of upward thrusts aimed somewhere between nose and chin. This is not the prettiest of sights. The food that makes it into the mouth first time round is rotated like laundry in a washing machine, whilst residual bits attach to various parts of the face until the forces of gravity dump it back onto the plate for inclusion within the next load.

Albert's guided tour of his village offered a unique insight into rural life. There had been no electricity since the cyclone so we walked through the forest by torchlight and stopped at several of the houses to shake hands with the people inside. Most homes were no larger than the size of a double garage; kitchen on one side, family bedroom the other and a tiny living room area in the middle where parents and children of all ages would sit in a rectangle around the light of a candle. It seemed such a primitive and hopeless existence: did they spend every night like this or was it just a post-cyclone lull? What else could they do anyway? I didn't like to ask.

Khagbari is a small village but nonetheless physically divided according to the religious communities: Muslim, Hindu and Christian. Unlike the country as a whole, which is 83% Muslim and less than 1% Christian, here there is an equal three-way split and everybody gets along in an atmosphere of tolerance and harmony. Until, that is, two people from different camps are unlucky enough to fall in love. That's when the preaching goes out of the window, prejudice and bigotry come to the fore and the glaring hypocrisy we've seen from Belfast to Beirut is yet again so crudely exposed.

* * * * *

We sat in front of the house and watched the reflection of the moon on the surface of the shallow water. All was silent except for the constant background whirring of the cicadas when suddenly a splash came out of the darkness and we could just make out the shape of a small boat moving towards us. There were two men on board, both standing, preparing their powerful lights and primitive harpoons in the hope that by morning they would have some fish to take home to the family.

Incredible to think that every year, from the same flooded fields, they produce two crops of rice and, in between, a single harvest of jute. It was jute season and though I hadn't known what it was, I'd seen the pale brown bundles of stringy, woody fibre tied together wigwam-style at the side of the road. This was their life, fishing and farming, their ongoing battle for survival. Hard, painstaking work, whether it be searching for dinner with spotlights or collecting fibre to weave into hessian mats and sacks for sale on market stalls around the world. Twenty first century it may be but a sad reminder of how tough life is for the vast, silent majority.

The next day, straight after breakfast (a sort of vegetable curry), we continued the journey south through the town of Gopalganj and on to Khulna. Again a gorgeous, tranquil, green and watery landscape and, as always seemed to be the case, as flat as the proverbial pancake. So are there any mountains in Bangladesh, you must now be curious to know?

The answer is yes. A few. The country is surrounded by India on three sides with the shores of the Bay of Bengal to the south. On the eastern side, in the bottom right hand corner of the map, it also shares a border with Burma (Myanmar, as its nasty dictators prefer to call it) in an upland region known as the Chittagong Hill Tracts. It's an area almost twice the size of Cumbria where a plaque on the mountain of Keokradang claims it to be the country's highest peak at 1230 metres. Alas, not so. Subsequent studies have shown that the top of the range is actually a different peak and even this one is still only just over 1000m above sea level. Still, it's not a bad effort. No part of England makes it into four figures and we are justly proud of Scafell Pike and the wonderful Lake District aren't we?

* * * * *

There wasn't a great deal to do in Khulna so 48 hours there to wait for a boat demanded a visit to the two main hotels. Both boasted a huge, brightly-lit, chrome and glass restaurant, both had the same upholstery and both were kitted out with enormous TV screens and an excessive number of a/c machines lining the walls. They were identical to a T, as was the mind-boggling multi-paged plastic menu divided into Bangladeshi, Chinese and Thai specialities. In the bad-taste competition the creator of these eateries, presumably one and the same, had left not a single box unticked.

It was Hobson's choice (a Cambridge horse trader you can tell your friends, died in 1631) or at least a double-Hobson and so I spent one evening in each. And believe it or not, the experiences were almost identical. Both had seating for two hundred, were almost empty and had fifteen waiters for every guest. One to bring the menu, one to take your water order, one to ask if you were happy with everything so far, one to *deliver* the said water, one to come and take the top off the water bottle, one to come and ask if you were enjoying the water, one to bring the bread, one to ask if the bread was OK....Please stop now you are thinking. And so was I. But I couldn't allow myself to get rattled, this was the highlight of my day.

The Hotel Castle Salem, where I was staying, had been the second of the two dining adventures. Here it was essential to keep body parts moving to fend off the threat of A/C-induced frostbite and of course the TV was also turned up as high as it would go. This was their culture I told myself, their country, and they had absolutely every right to make it as cold and loud and bright and utterly uncomfortable as they saw fit.

I recall looking up from the menu in search of some respite, grasping for just a moment of happiness, when it came to my attention that the food-order waiter had taken up a semi-permanent position about five centimetres from my right shoulder. Now you will probably have heard of the term "personal space", indeed subconsciously seek it out and apply it as appropriate on most days of your life. You never really give it a thought, at least not until you are on an empty bus and somebody decides to share your seat. The expression, and this concept of politeness, is as automatic to you and me as the act of breathing but in Asia, home to over 60% of the world's population, the idea quite simply does not exist. You will be leaned on in the queue, trodden on in the lift, interrupted in mid-conversation and stared at by anybody who wants to do some staring. None of this is considered rude, it is normal everyday life. So when I looked at the waiter, indicated that I might be some time, of course he just smiled and stayed exactly where he was.

The food when it came was delivered by a posse of white-shirted young men who emerged in a procession from the kitchen like leafcutter ants assembling a new nest. They laid out the dishes on an adjacent table then battled amongst themselves for the kudos of executing the final transfer. By now I was enjoying the show and the steaming pot of hot and sour soup was exactly what the doctor ordered to counter an air temperature more readily associated with Lapland. In fact all the food was superb and, had it not been for a fellow diner clearing his throat loudly into a nearby washbasin, there would not have been any further Meldrew Moments.

I chilled mentally, unchilled physically and sat there reading my Lonely Planet guide to Bangladesh. An excellent source of information as always but one thing concerned me. Who else would buy a tourist guide to a country that attracts no tourists? And come to think of it, who could I expect to find aboard a tourist boat? All very mysterious, and with that thought, and really for the first time, my mind turned to the upcoming voyage.

* * * * *

Elisabeth has a Swiss father, an American mother and a Bangladeshi husband. She is a beautiful, intelligent and articulate lady with an unrivalled passion for, and knowledge of, the wildlife of Bangladesh. For eleven months of every year she works at her desk in Dhaka as CEO of the Guide Tour Company but by a stroke of good fortune she had decided to guide this particular trip herself. I joined her on board for dinner where I was introduced to the rest of the team.

By pure coincidence there were two other ladies from Switzerland: one a student of dolphins, the other attached to the embassy and responsible for channelling her country's funds towards the development of third world nations. Does life get any more diverse than that?! Added to the intriguing mix was a Swedish eye doctor, called Sven of course, two American lads making a documentary about the country, and an English man who lived in France and was carrying out some research for a book. I was interested to know more.

"Well, it's a sort of guide," Stuart revealed a little sheepishly.

"A ..well..er…a travel guide," he conceded when pressed further.

We'd been on the boat for ten minutes and would be living together for the next three days. Far too long to get away without spilling the beans so he smiled in defeat and introduced himself as the author of the next edition of the Lonely Planet for Bangladesh.

* * * * *

We were sailing south towards the Sundarbans, pronounced locally as Shonderbon, 6000 sq kms of mangrove forest and dense jungle that stretches across the country's south-western border with India and down to the shores of the Bay of Bengal. This remote and largely forgotten corner of the world is home to wild pigs, deer and many exotic species of bird but, rather more significantly, it is the last remaining habitat of the Bengal tiger.

A third of the national park is made up of rivers and channels, a dense network of wavy blue lines running down the map like the veins on a lump of cheese. Two weeks earlier the cyclone had forced the water levels up by as much as ten metres, the Indian Ocean attacking parts of the jungle that had managed to survive the winds but would not cope with the massively increased amount of salt. It was the first time I'd ever realised the damage caused to plants and animals by a change in the chemical balance of water as opposed to merely a fluctuation in its volume. Does this mean that one day a freak tide in Liverpool could contaminate the Mersey and ultimately wipe out the natural wildlife of Stockport?

As we sailed down a river perhaps half a mile wide, the devastation to the trees on both banks was all too evident. Only the most exposed had succumbed to the power of the wind but the influx of sea water had left them discoloured and in poor state of health. It could have been a lot worse but it had been low tide when the cyclone had struck and, being so early in the dry season, there was still plenty of fresh water in the rivers to dilute the salty surge. It was all so calm but a little eerie to see the endless rows of brown, spent trees, once proud and resourceful but now so sad, rejected and seemingly with no useful purpose left to serve.

Our eight-cabin vessel was a comfortable home and the catering would have done justice to the QEII. We did little to merit the consumption of three buffet meals a day *and* snacks in between but it was all too tasty to say no and, an ever-ready excuse for gluttony, we didn't consume a single drop of alcohol. Our activity came twice a day, just ahead of sunrise and sunset, when we left the boat to explore the narrower waterways by canoe and traverse the more open jungle areas on foot. The total silence was quite magnificent and the prospect of catching a glimpse of a tiger, remote though it was, kept everybody's interest alive.

In terms of wildlife we saw very little but learned a lot. The Bengal tiger, the bewildering and beautiful animal that evokes so many emotions, always prompted the most exciting discussions. It terrifies the farmers and fishermen of the countryside whose communities lose a hundred lives a year to this creature, yet to the rest of us we feel nothing but admiration for its ability to have survived this far and great pity that its inevitable demise is just around the corner.

Just how many are left in Bengal nobody can really say, though "a few hundred" seems the most popular guess. We listened intently as the experts talked us through the story. The survival of a male depends on its good fortune as a cub in not being eaten by an adult tiger and then its ability to claim its own territory without being killed by a rival. Assuming phases one and two are successfully negotiated, food then has to be hunted. Big lumps of meat come in the form of animals that wander in packs, most of whom defend as a team and can move rather faster in a long chase than the solitary tiger. So patience and cunning is very much the order of the day but sometimes, many times, hunger wins over and the battle is lost.

We walked through the muddy jungle and across open savannah, stopping frequently for Elisabeth to identify the animal footprints clearly visible on the surface. Mostly deer, wild pigs and small leopards but she did find one set belonging to a tiger and male claw marks gouged onto a nearby tree to let everybody know that this was his manor. We spotted eagles and kingfishers, a sign that the birds were returning to the area, and watched a python swimming in the river, its small head protruding above the surface but its long body carefully obscured from view. After a couple of hours the path brought us out on to a deserted beach, a vast expanse of sand with the waves of the Indian Ocean lapping up on one side and the dejected mass of badly broken trees on the other.

This was it, as far as I could go. There was something symbolic about reaching the Bay of Bengal, a sort of confirmation that I'd travelled the length of the country and now it was time to go home. I walked up to the top of the beach and, as a final mark of respect, stood amidst the carnage at the very point Cyclone Sidr had struck her first blow. Then I turned around and kept walking, throwing off my shirt and kicking away my sandals as I went, until the warm salty water of the Indian Ocean came up to my knees.

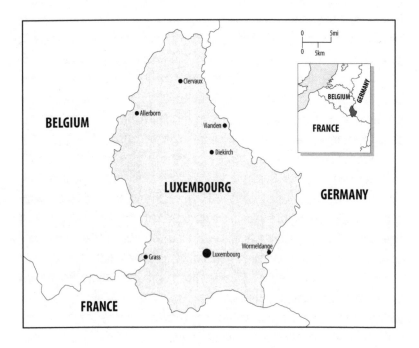

LUXEMBOURG

The first steps in pursuit of a new country tend to follow pretty much the same pattern. Journey to the airport, the queue to check in, an even longer one to pass through security and passport inspection. Hours of waiting in line, a tedious ritual that just seems to get worse year on year. Coats off, belts off, shoes off. Sorry madam can you just slip your bra off. Where is it all going to stop?

Back in my four-letter days, Mali had been the closest of the ten destinations to the UK and no person in his right mind would seriously consider travelling there, or to any other of the FLCs, by anything other than air. So what a mouth-watering prospect it was when the penny dropped, for the first time in my life, that we have a TLC just down the road at next door but one. I could jump in my own car, bomb down to the white cliffs, head south for 250 miles and, without giving any thought to visas, x-ray machines or any form of official molestation I would, with a following wind, find myself in the ten letter enigma known curiously as the Grand Duchy of Luxembourg.

But isn't Luxembourg just a one-horse town in the middle of Europe, somewhere that people might stop for ten minutes to stretch their legs and fill up with petrol? That certainly seemed to be the view amongst my more cynical friends when presented with the news that I was about to spend a whole week there. Wouldn't that be like popping a Polo mint into your mouth on a Monday morning and trying to make it last until Sunday lunch arrives? I must admit, it didn't sound too promising, until I unearthed the more encouraging news that the country of Luxembourg, rather than just its capital city of the same name, is a mighty 50 miles long and, in some places, 32 miles wide. More or less the size of Derbyshire, a county where three quarters of a million people (albeit mostly strange ones) and many generations before them have spent their entire lives. Surely just a week wouldn't be too much of a challenge?

It cost me £75 to fill the car up, a tenner for the petrol itself and a heartily begrudged sixty plus notes to the government. "Just where does all this tax revenue go?" I was mumbling to myself as grumpy people do, enjoying the comparison between the tight squeeze of the lead-free nozzle and that of the chancellor upon one's scrotum. And then a smile with the realisation that the money goes towards feeding the insatiable monster known simply as "Europe" and the bevy of faceless politicians who prosper by its very existence. It was time to go and pay them a visit.

* * * * *

I had never knowingly been to a Grand Duchy or devoted much time to wondering what one is. The explanation, I discovered, lies with the Head of State, who would be the king or queen in the case of a kingdom, the president of a republic or a prince ruling over his principality. But in Luxembourg, unlike anywhere else in the world, the Head of State just happens to be a Duke, and a Grand one at that.

Grand Duke Henri took over the job when his father abdicated in October 2000. His full name is actually Henri Albert Gabriel Felix Marie Guillaume but if you want to drop him a line to ask him how he feels about a girl's name being slipped in you would be advised to observe protocol and use his correct title: *His Royal Highness Henri, by the Grace of God, Grand Duke of Luxembourg, Duke of Nassau, Count Palatine of the Rhine, Count of Sayn, Konigstein, Katzenelnbogen and Diez, Burgrave of Hammerstein, Lord of Mahlberg, Wiesbaden, Idstein, Merenberg, Limburg and Epstein.* I suggest you get a fairly big envelope, though I suppose "Luxembourg" will suffice by way of an address.

Whenever I find myself sitting in the car-wash claustrophobia of the Eurotunnel I always vow that next time I'll go back to crossing the Channel by ferry. There is something uniquely invigorating about standing up on deck clutching a cup of tea, wind in face, watching the white cliffs fading away into the distance. It just isn't the same sitting there in that container, squirming as the man with the ferocious Cockney accent tries to announce the safety procedures over the tannoy in French.

Noon brought re-acquaintance with daylight and the empty motorways of Calais. I headed east along the E40 through the unmistakeable flatness of France's top right corner, an unchanging picture of bright green fields and red-roofed farmhouses and funny-shaped Citroen vans parked out front. Within half an hour the road-signs had given way to Flemish, by two o'clock the Brussels ring road had steered me to the south-east of the city and an hour later the motorway was rolling up and down through the gentle hills of the Belgian Ardennes. It could have been a pleasant ride but it was a wet, grey Sunday afternoon and by the time the first Luxembourg signs appeared the traffic had dissolved to barely a trickle.

The forests and the undulating greenery tempted me to switch to smaller roads earlier than anticipated and a glance at the map confirmed that by snaking cross country to the town of Bastogne I would put myself within striking distance of the border with Luxembourg. A name that requires clarification. You see, not only is Luxembourg a ten-letter country with Luxembourg (City) as its ten-letter capital but it is also the name of the southern-most of the ten provinces of the small-but-ever-so-confusing country of Belgium. In fact, it's even the largest of the provinces despite… and I promise to stop now…having the smallest population of the lot.

So, ignoring the motorway signs pointing Luxembourg to the south, I drove eastwards through the countryside of Luxembourg towards the border with Luxembourg. This was the Ardennes, hills rather than mountains and forests rather than jungles but nonetheless a comfortable, pleasing, orderly little corner of the globe. It was still raining between occasional bursts of sunshine; there were incredibly few cars and even fewer people.

The small towns and villages seemed entirely deserted and most houses were in darkness as though this was a country in mourning. Think "lunchtime" in rural France and you'll get the general idea. I was prepared to find Bastogne in a similar state of repose but to my astonishment, as I second-geared alongside the central square and peered through the drizzle, the place was absolutely rocking. The shops and restaurants on the other three sides were open and buzzing away, pedestrians were wandering around in groups despite the cold and rain and kerb-crawling motorists were hunting spaces in the huge rectangular car park. And not just any old car park but one with a trendy glass tourist information office at its centre and a huge tank parked in the corner. What on earth was going on?

The name of the square, I noticed, was Place McAuliffe and the parking space that came free was directly in front of the Hotel Collin. Five minutes later I was looking out over the town from an upstairs room, the Grand Duchy just a few kilometres away. This would do me very nicely for today.

* * * * *

Ignorance is nothing to be proud of but it does occasionally contribute to unexpected pleasures. I should have known that the Battle of the Ardennes, also known as the Battle of the Bulge, was one of the most significant of World War II and that it was the gritty defence of Bastogne, against all the odds, that ultimately turned the war in the Allies favour. By pure chance I had stumbled across one of the greatest stories of European history.

It was December 1944 and there were 70,000 American soldiers stationed in the cold, snowy Ardennes having liberated Belgium and Luxembourg from four years of German occupation. The Brits had moved in to northern France in huge numbers during that summer and everybody was now hopeful that the war was reaching its end. But it wasn't to be, at least not just yet. Hitler surprised everybody by sending 200,000 men and a thousand tanks on the rampage to try to recapture the Low Countries. The Americans, shocked, overwhelmed and totally unprepared for the savage winter conditions, suffered more casualties than they had throughout the entire conflict. They were down and almost out but thanks to their great

40

courage and the support of the local people who offered food, blankets and shelter against the bitter cold, they managed to cling on for dear life to the town of Bastogne. The Gerries had them surrounded and called for a surrender but the US General Anthony McAuliffe was having none of it and in his fury responded with the first word that came to mind. "Nuts!"

Perhaps not the expression you or I would plump for when half your comrades have been slaughtered, you're getting shelled from all points of the compass and it's 23 degrees below zero. But come on, it was 1944. It certainly confused the German officers who called for a translator and then had to explain to the poor, disenchanted Adolf that he was being told, in no uncertain terms, to fuck off.

And when the allied planes finally arrived on the scene, that's exactly what he did. His quest to take Bastogne and drive northwards to capture the port of Antwerp had failed, the Germans were forced to retreat and by 1945 the war was over. The Battle of the Ardennes had left 19,000 Americans dead and 60,000 seriously injured or taken as prisoner. German casualties were even greater: up to 100,000 of their men were killed or maimed, many young lads barely out of school forced to march in the snow into a battle they would never understand. What a tragic, pointless waste of human life.

I read all this over dinner – a typical Belgian offering of tasty beer, delicious meat and a truckload of fresh chips – and decided that next morning I would follow the story with a visit to the Historical Centre on the edge of the town.

It was to be a poignant experience. I sat and watched the grainy film from six decades earlier: hundreds and hundreds of German tanks rolling across the hillsides, frightened people helplessly standing in front of their houses, dead bodies lying in fields with pools of blood staining the snow even on the old black and white footage. A sickening, shocking, reminder of the brutality of war.

The American victory had been masterminded by the famous General Patton who died a year later, ironically as a result of a car accident when on a shooting vacation in Germany (this time just for pheasants). His body was laid to rest in the American Cemetery just outside Luxembourg City along with five thousand other men who had never made it home. I resolved to pay them a visit later that week.

The Ardennes had taken on a very different meaning now, never more would I think of these rolling hills and their pretty villages with the same sense of innocence as I had just twenty four hours earlier.

* * * * *

There isn't very much difference to report between the landscape of south-east Belgium and that of north-west Luxembourg. The blue EU sign with its 12 yellow stars welcomed me into TLC number 2 and my first thought was that it *was* quite similar to Derbyshire after all. A scene so calm and reassuring that I parked up in the first village of Allerborn to sit and gaze at the lush green countryside, the random clusters of dark trees and just the occasional flash of silver grey where a paved country lane ducked between the fields. This could easily have been Lyme Park, those miles of rolling hills on the edge of the Peak District where I spent so many years as a kid.

Allerborn was evidently a community of very few people, not one of whom had yet taken to the street on this particular Monday. It appeared I was the only living soul, in fact, come to think of it, I'm not sure I had yet seen a person in Luxembourg at all. I would make that my challenge for the day.

A few more miles of silent, empty roads led me to the small town of Clervaux, now almost at the top of the country. Luxembourg is shaped like the head of a howling dog, nose in the air, and this little place is nestled in a valley somewhere around the left nostril. I drove through the main street, realised that's all there was, so turned round and went back again. This was a valley in the true sense, a V with steep, wooded sides, a road and railway line running along the bottom. If I was going to try to spot a human, I decided it would make sense to park up and take a stroll.

In fact I went one better. Not one but two ladies were perched behind the counter in the post office (no customers though) and seemed somewhat bemused, even a tad stern, when I enquired about the town's internet facilities. It yielded a blank but at least prompted a conversation between themselves, my first ever exposure to the peculiar Flemish/German mix that is Luxembourgish, or as they would say, Letzebuergesch. This is the language used in school, though everybody in the tiny country also speaks French and German from such an early age that they are pretty much trilingual by the time they grow up. And then comes English, a distant fourth.

The neat, and strikingly spotless, pedestrianised shopping arcade offered little in the way of pedestrians but a surprising number of pleasing hotel-cafés. I slipped inside for a piping hot "potage du jour" and a croque monsieur, otherwise known as soup of the day and posh cheese toastie, the latter presented with a small gherkin finely sliced lengthways. Its multiple incisions and overall aesthetic beauty occupied my attention for quite some time and when my trance was finally broken I couldn't help but wonder whether this was a measure of the fun one could expect to have in the Grand Duchy.

With that in mind I opted not to bother with the castle high up on one side of the valley but instead to drive up to the Benedictine Abbey on the other. I'd read that the monks in there were famed worldwide for their peculiar style of Gregorian chanting and that was exactly the sort of post-gherkin experience I had in mind. But how would I recognise this chant as being different from the norm? Come to think of it, what exactly is a Gregorian chant anyway? It mattered not.

The large spooky-looking abbey up in the forest was absolutely silent and I'm not ashamed to admit I even crept round the gardens at the back to listen out for any monks having a crafty one. I was well in the mood for adventure and the sleepy valleys of northern Luxembourg were already starting to look (and sound) decidedly tame. So, feeling positively reckless, I pointed the motor along a few more winding lanes and on to the N7, the motorway that is the spine of the country. The world was my oyster; I would head south towards the city of Luxembourg. There was nothing stopping me now.

* * * * *

You won't be surprised to learn that a motorway bimble through the world's richest country shares little in common with a north/south traverse of Bangladesh. No ragged people pulling carts at the roadside, trucks billowing black smoke, buses keeling over with the collective weight of their human load. This is Luxembourg: green, spotless, immaculate in every sense. Houses are large and square and sturdy, dotted here and there and painted in bright and cheery colours like a scene from a children's crayoning book. Nobody is walking anywhere, cars tootle along at an inoffensive pace and road rage is still a concept from another planet. I see little connection with the real world except for tiny, orderly industrial estates occasionally appearing on the outskirts of towns, usually sporting a fleet of shining vehicles parked outside neat rows of highly polished warehouse doors. The rest is rolling hills, and to complete the fantasy, most have a castle perched on top.

It took less than an hour to drive most of the length of the country, a disappointing achievement with six days still to go. The metropolis was looming before me now, was I ready to adjust to the urban pace? Could I cope with a city of 90,000 people, almost the population of Chesterfield? The image of that dismal town with its funny crooked spire brought negative thoughts, as did the bleak possibility of completing the adventure within thirty six hours of arrival. And so I turned left without entering the capital and headed east towards Germany and, more importantly, towards the Moselle.

As you probably know, this is a river, a little beauty that rises in the Vosges mountains of eastern France and eventually joins the Rhine at the city of Koblenz over three hundred miles further north. The good news for me was that roughly half way along its course it travels along the boundary of south-eastern Luxembourg and actually forms the border with Germany for a stretch of around 25 miles. I knew that both the north and the south of the Moselle (Mosel in German, Musel in Luxembourgish) valley were regions well known for their vineyards, but what about the bit in the middle?

When was the last time you cracked open a bottle of Luxembourgish wine? The journey east along the N1 was best remembered for the two men in orange boiler-suits who were evidently employed to scour the motorway embankments in search of litter. Recruited for their powers of vigilance and patience, they obviously worked in pairs to keep up morale and create a sense of competition, desperate to be the first to find a discarded item worthy of spiking into the empty plastic sack. Just what is the life of a garbage man in a country so untainted by the vulgarities of the modern world? What would constitute a "good day at the office"? I pictured them entertaining their wide-eyed kids around the dinner table with outrageous stories handed down from their forefathers, the great Luxembourgish refuse collectors of yesteryear. "Come on Dad – tell us the one about the crumpled crisps packet and the rusty Coke can".

For me this was still Toytown, a storybook place where only happy events could unfold. A land of decent people who wear smart clothes, live in nice houses, drive unscratched cars and don't have to wait till pay day to go out for a pizza. Would the local folk ever have been exposed to the idea of thieves or rapists or politicians who drop their pants in public toilets? My mind continued along that track. Would there even be a prison in Luxembourg? For no good reason at all I made a mental note to find out.

I was soon brought back to reality (Luxembourg, *reality?*) by a road sign depicting a bunch of grapes and an arrow pointing the way to the town of Wormeldange. Happy days. No way would I be missing out on a Wormeldange. So I took the exit ramp and followed the country lane across the fields until it came to a T junction offering Grevenmacher left and Remich right. I'd landed smack in the middle of Luxembourg's Moselle valley and as I turned right (flip of the coin job) and headed south, I realised the river was right there along the side of the road.

Daylight was fading now but there was no mistaking the perfect rows of the grapevines sloping down on both sides of the river. I'd missed the delights of downtown Wormeldange (I knew I should have turned left) but tomorrow would be another opportunity and anyway driving through a village with the wonderful name of Stadtbredimus proved adequate compensation. Next came Remich, a place that looked as though it might have some charm outside hours of darkness so I pulled off the main drag and found myself climbing up a steep hill that led quickly to the top of the town. And then the town ended.

Logic dictated a U-ey if I was going to find a hotel but a stubborn refusal to retrace my steps sent me left along a road running high up across the top of the valley. Curiosity alone compelled me to keep going so it was an unexpected bonus when out of the blue, or dark grey as it was by then, I spotted the sign introducing "Hotel des Vignes". I took the last room they had available which was a surprisingly shabby offering considering a) the hotel's tidy exterior and b) Luxembourg's status as richest country in the world. But it had been a long day, I was too tired to start getting fussy and the prospect of a bar, restaurant and bed all under one roof was just too good to resist.

* * * * *

The room faced east and the morning sun poured in through the enormous "tilt and turn" window (my favourite type of window, by the way). This brightness gave my new abode a pleasing dimension and the views over the vineyard to the river below and Germany beyond were far more attractive than anything I could have hoped for. I was in love with the hotel now: the fish dinner and the bottle of white wine (all the way from Wormeldange) had gone down a treat the night before and today I could sit here in the sunshine, admire the views and link my computer to the net to continue my research. And with that the first decision of the day was in the bag – I would stay a few nights, make this my base and explore the country from this south-eastern corner.

Research? I heard someone titter. Well, at least I can now tell you that there *is* a prison in Luxembourg and it goes by the ugly, mean, locked-in-a-dungeon-with-your-genitals-wired-up sounding name of Schrassig. From what I could work out it was located in a village of that name and the web seemed to indicate it wasn't so very far away from where I was sitting.

Nothing in Luxembourg was. It was time to get out for some air.

It was crisp and cold and sunny and altogether perfect conditions for a drive through the Moselle valley. The road was empty – March still had over a week to run – and the trees that formed a perfect line along the river had produced a spectacular white blossom in contrast to the grey and murky water. The wineries were open for business and invitations to enter their *caves* hung hopefully at the roadside but the season had yet to get going. There was nobody around.

It took only a few minutes to reach Wormeldange, a community of 742 people. The *cave* on the waterfront was the size of a Tesco superstore and it stood to reason that this imposing establishment would rank as one of the village's major attractions. So I parked up in the empty car park and headed for the revolving door.

This was Les Caves Crémants Poll-Fabaire, a rather grand building and one of four vineyards owned by the largest producers in the region. Judging by the exhibits in their impressive entrance hall their wines had won numerous awards and this display of silverware was something akin to the trophy room of a successful football club (think Manchester City 1968-71. Vintage years). The room to my right was effectively a large warehouse with thousands of bottles of wine produced from different grapes, from different years, using different processes.

A friendly assistant, Daniel Cardoso introduced himself and offered to show me around, the language quickly switching from English to Portuguese once I'd commented on his name and reminisced about my years of living in Brazil. He seemed proud of the fact that 15% of Luxembourg's citizens originally came from Portugal and that they made up the largest immigrant group, even outnumbering the ubiquitous Italians.

And so to a presentation of Luxembourgish wine given in Portuguese, not an experience I ever imagined would come my way. The specialities of the house were the Crémants, the sparkling wines that cannot legally be called champagne but which are produced using the identical method. So how does real bubbly differ from cheap, pretend fizz, you might be wondering? Well, it's all a question of carbon dioxide apparently. In champagne the bubbles occur naturally in the bottle during the final fermentation whereas other fizzy drinks, wine included, have it pumped in artificially at the end. Here the crémants differed according to the grape used, or in some cases a blend of different varieties, or the same grapes but not necessarily harvested in the same year (hence the undated bottles). I'd never thought of that one.

The tour took me through those grapes that flourish in the relatively cool climate, one of the northernmost locations in terms of the world's major wine producing regions: Pinots Blanc, Gris and Noir (the only red in the region), Riesling, Rivaner (part of the Riesling family), Auxerrois, Gewurztraminer and finally Elbling, a lower grade variety specific to the Moselle. A vast array and a mind-boggling display of still and sparkling permutations. But who drinks them all? Where do they go? According to Daniel these wines had traditionally been exported to the neighbouring countries but now – increasingly – they are sold to the world's newest and fastest growing market. China, of course. Its middle classes are emerging so quickly and they can't be expected to drink snakes blood and that horrid green tea for ever.

I was eager to put all this alluring produce to the test but it was far too early in the day for such a potentially damaging confrontation. And so I thanked my new friend for his time and patience and headed back towards daylight with the promise that I would return, next time with credit card in hand. This was all starting to be quite enjoyable, I think I was even having fun.

So I got back in the car and drove for twenty minutes to the outskirts of the capital, parked alongside the two other vehicles on the edge of the forest, and braced myself for an experience that would quickly wipe the smile off my face. From the neat rows of plants in the vineyards I walked into the silence of the American Cemetery and the startling, sobering sight of 5076 white marble crosses, again in neat rows, spread evenly across 50 acres of immaculate lawn. Each marked the grave of a young man, save for one solitary female nurse, and twenty two double graves where brothers lie

Luxembourg

side by side. It doesn't come any sadder than that, does it?

I walked slowly between the crosses, stopping to read the names, regiments, states of origin and the dates that these short lives had come to an end. Most had fallen within the space of two months, December 1944 or January 1945. The Battle of the Ardennes. Just sixty something years ago, I couldn't help thinking that some of these men could still have been living today had it not been for the lunacy of war. I kept looking up to take in the whole picture, the striking contrast of white on green like a cue ball on a billiard table, an enormous, cherished expanse of land surrounded by lovely spruce and oak trees. What a solemn, yet strangely beautiful place. And such an eerie silence except for the birds twittering in the surrounding woods and, a little further away, the planes taking off from the city's airport.

The US flag flies from the terrace overlooking the graves and two large stone memorials tell the story of the war and list the names of those other poor souls that were never recovered. All deeply disturbing and to think that for every single grave here, three dead bodies were sent back home to their families. An appalling tragedy and, what makes it worse, as we now know, there would be many more in the decades to follow.

* * * * *

Easter was approaching, the earliest for many years. My plan was to stay for the week and leave the country on Sunday, even though Easter Monday is by all accounts an auspicious day in the Luxembourgish calendar. It heralds a celebration known as Emaischen when tradition has it that the menfolk go to market to purchase a small earthenware bird for the women they love. What had originally started out as a festival of whistles was apparently taken a step further by the villagers of Nospelt around the middle of the last century. This tiny place had become famous for its handcrafted pottery – a potter's village you could say – and from there evolved the Peckvillchen, a special whistle in the form of a small bird. Nowadays it only appears for sale once a year in the old part of the capital, or back home in

Nospelt, and that is on the morning of Easter Monday.

Having read this wonderful tale I felt an urge to seek out this mysterious village, if only to find out how it should be pronounced. It wasn't shown on my map but further research revealed it to be in the country lanes to the north-west of the capital and, if I was up for a real adventure, a minor road in that same direction would also bring me close to a dot on the map marked as Schrassig. Go to jail, do not pass Go, do not collect £200.

For someone who spent so much time in detention during his schooldays, it may surprise a few of my old teachers to learn that I never made it to prison. Not even as a visitor. Perhaps this was why the idea of getting into Luxembourg's premier penitentiary suddenly struck me as such a great wheeze – what better way to find out if there really were any proper criminals in Toytown? And so, not without a certain trepidation, I headed off along more empty roads, through more neat fields, all the while wondering if I really was going to see this through.

In marked contrast to its ugly name Schrassig turned out to be a quaint village with houses big and posh even by lofty local standards. I drove up and down its well-manicured main street and trawled the tiny lanes leading off at right-angles but this seemed like the last place in the world to find the country's number 1 (or even only) nick. Then I remembered the story of the tourists who caught the train to Yorkshire to visit the famous Leeds Castle, only to find out that it's actually in the heart of the Kent countryside. Had I made a similar error?

There was nothing else for it. For the first time in my life I approached a pedestrian to ask the best way to get to prison. My French was *merde* and I'd expected either a howl of laughter or a look of bemusement but instead received clear, concise and entirely comprehensible instructions to return a couple of kms to the crossroads, turn right and head up to the top of the hill.

And indeed there it was, all alone on a sort of plateau, an unmistakeable series of grim, rectangular brown buildings surrounded by watchtowers and the highest wire fence you ever did see. In the foreground an immense car park with a lot of vehicles, for Luxembourg, and a security office alongside a barrier. I found a parking space, turned off the motor and sat quietly. What the hell was I doing here? The metal gate was 100 metres away, either I walked up to it or I simply turned on my engine and drove away. Man or mouse?

My hands moved mousily towards the keys, hovered in mid-air, then snatched open the door. Followed by a deep breath and a long walk towards the barrier, no doubt filmed on CCTV. What was I going to say? Maybe I would just duck under it and make a run for the building, see if the bloke in the watchtower was really on his toes!

'Bonjour monsieur'. A lady, close-cropped hair and probably a black belt in karate, had opened a sliding window and lowered her head to peer at me through the small space.

"Je suis anglais" I offered somewhat tamely, as though my being English would explain the stupidity of what was to follow. Which translated roughly as I thought I might just pop in and say hello to my fellow countrymen incarcerated within.

The response was measured and authoritative and, to my surprise, gave the impression that holidaymakers in Luxembourg quite frequently dropped by for a chat. There was an official procedure for visiting "inconnus" (unacquainted people), she explained courteously, which would involve my making a formal application at "le tribunal" in the capital city. I attached a beaming smile to my merci beaucoup, learned that this was home to 700 prisoners, and then asked conversationally if she knew whether any Brits were amongst that number. "We have everything in here" came the answer with a half smile, the inference unambiguously that the Grand Duchy was very much the core of the gangster universe.

The visit felt more success than failure, a 1-1 draw away from home when a drubbing had seemed much more likely. There was no question of my pursuing the red tape option, life in Luxembourg was far too hectic to get bogged down in such officialdom, but at least I'd proved that even Toytown did have its more sinister side. I made it back to the car just before the snow started to come down and set off with an air of contentment in the hope of finding myself a nice little bird.

In relation to Luxembourg the capital, the rural villages of Schrassig and Nospelt sit at twenty past and ten to the hour respectively. I was all set for a non-stop journey across the heart of the metropolis and progressing nicely towards the outskirts when an important landmark loomed into view and forced me to brake with a vengeance. The Black Stuff was just opening for the day and it was my good fortune that the landlady was supervising delivery of barrels of the very same from the huge truck parked out front. Here was my chance to carry out more research, an unexpected opportunity to solve a mystery that had puzzled me long into the previous night.

The website of the Luxembourg Irish Club had advertised a comedy show for the following evening, promising visitors a true Gaelic welcome but declining to include any address for the club or even hinting at the venue. Didn't this constitute a flaw in the marketing strategy?

She laughed in a lovely Irish way, told me that it was just a "virtual" club with no premises of its own, and dug out a local magazine confirming that Patrick Moynihan, an Irish Iranian from Middlesbrough (I kid you not), would be performing at Scott's at 9pm the next day. Then followed her life story, more laughter, directions of how to find said bar, and without so much as a pint of the Black Stuff, I was once again on my way to Nospelt. Why can't everybody in the world be Irish?

Traversing the city was none too painful and I let my sense of direction decide which road to follow once out the other side. In hindsight it wasn't the smartest move as my reluctant – and long overdue – perusal of the map later showed I had been driving much farther south than intended. In fact, I was on the verge of slipping out of the country altogether and crossing the border into France.

All part of the adventure, at least there was a small road heading north to get me back on track, I just needed to follow the CR110 through the villages of Clemency and Grass. What better places for a jailbird to make for! First I had to get myself to the town of Linger (surely not the home of the bra?) where I thought of buying an orange so on arrival I could submit a peel for Clemency. Enough of this nonsense! Time to put me out to Grass.

I crossed the N4, the road I should have taken from the city, and buzzed along the lanes through the pristine countryside around Septfontaines. An unchanging world of green except for the small villages that popped up every few miles, generally just a cluster of garishly painted houses and, more often than not – rather incongruously it seemed to me – a Chinese restaurant. I followed the white signs to the village of Nospelt.

No surprise that the streets were deathly quiet but an unmissable erection in the village centre signalled that preparations were well under way for the big event. I drove past the marquee that would visit once a year and then followed a loop around what was an otherwise unremarkable cluster of houses. The only single point of interest was the word "Musée" above the door of a small building.

Having considered the alternatives on offer I parked up and wandered over, only to find a sign explaining that it was a small pottery museum, closed to the public except in the months of July and August. And Easter Monday of course. I was cursing ever so mildly and stooping to peer inside for a glimpse of the forbidden fruit when a voice from behind broke the silence.

The lady sweeping her step had spotted a car entering the village, one with its driver sitting on the passenger side. She couldn't speak English so apologised in German for the museum being closed and for the fact that she didn't have a key to let me in. Mme (Frau?) Lehnert then offered a historical presentation instead, explaining how many professional potters had once lived in Nospelt, pronounced Noss-pelt, but that these days very little material was produced, and even then it was purely as a hobby. Her son Alain was one of these amateurs and yes, he had already built up a stock of Peckvillchen for the upcoming extravaganza. At which point the charming lady invited me into her garage/ Alain's workshop, produced a large cardboard box of the little hand-crafted beauties and, for the princely sum of E 13, I was invited to take home any of the birds that took my fancy.

And so I departed Nospelt with a sense of fulfilment, smug in the knowledge that henceforth I could use the word in public without fear of embarrassment. The trip to the countryside had been enjoyable but I knew in my heart I couldn't lark about like this forever, it was time to get on and prepare for a new pace of life. The next day would see me taking up residence in the capital and so, to facilitate this mental readjustment, I decided to call in there on the way back to the Moselle.

It took no time at all to get sucked into a puzzling one way system and coaxed over a bridge with a vast gorge below. A unique landmark, a sort of half way line across the city is how it seemed to me, so I parked up by the station and headed back towards it on foot. Dazzled by the intensity and diversity of colour, movement, sound and language I could have been a Martian emerging from his spaceship. It was ...well, it was like being in an international city, bustling and stuff. Really nothing at all like Chesterfield.

Standing on the edge of that huge ravine it became clear to me that this seldom talked-of city was something in a league of its own. In every direction, vertically and horizontally, majestic buildings and architectural creations of all ages, shapes and sizes jostled for space with rocks and trees and all manner of natural phenomena. A three dimensional feast for the eyes that had been nurtured and developed over a period of at least a thousand years.

Adjacent to the bridge a steep cobbled street led me down the side of the cliff to a pretty village sitting in the floor of the valley, slap bang in the heart of the capital. The tidy rows of neat terraced houses and smart boutiques form the community known as Grund and to complete the picture two small rivers, the Petrusse and Alzette converge at its centre. What more could one possibly ask for? Toytown had come up trumps once again and by way of icing on the cake there were even two village pubs: one by the name of Oscar Wilde's and the other Scott's Bar, temporary home of the Luxembourg Irish club.

As Grund was the ground floor, so to speak, I could have taken an elevator up the side of the cliff to the town proper (yes, there really is a lift!) but chose instead to zigzag back up through the terraced gardens to reach street level. A serious climb but an effort that was more than well rewarded. The 360 degree panorama looked like a joining together of thousands of jigsaw pieces taken from different boxes, a scene so diverse and dramatic it bordered on the unbelievable. Steep ravines, rivers, city walls, turrets, spires, viaducts, trees (so many trees), parks, cobbled streets, mansions...and across towards the east side – amidst the flags of Europe – a separate and so very different world of modern, glass office towers. What an incredible, quirky sort of place and how pleased was I all of a sudden at the prospect of coming back for more.

* * * * *

Safely back in the Moselle I called in for a snifter at the Poll-Fabaires Caves at Wormeldange and, later, even closer to home, at their Wellenstein branch. Daniel wasn't on duty that day but in any event all wine tasting had to be done in a dismal, depressing room with an unpleasant chemical smell that reminded me of a crematorium. (But of course, where else would you go to drink Crémant? I'd finally found the true meaning of la Crem de la Crem.)

Five sample wines were delivered in tiny glasses on a spiral rack but the gloomy atmosphere and the fact that I had to pay for them anyway created no sense of obligation to purchase any stock. Did they intentionally create such a weary ambience to avoid excessive jollity or was this just purely a lack of insight on their part? As I spent more time in the country I realised the answer was probably the latter: in terms of warmth and cosiness a Luxembourgish bar is up there with something you might expect at your local dog track.

The two ladies at Wellenstein took an altogether more friendly and personal approach. I deliberately avoided another austere tasting room and instead stood chatting at their work counter swilling all sorts of lovely fizz that they willingly dished out. They were great fun, one of them Luxembourgish who talked openly about the very conservative and serious nature of her countrymen (country persons?), the other a German lady, amongst the many who commute across the border every day to secure a higher wage. Their informal policy had a much more pleasing effect and I came away with as much wine as I could carry.

* * * * *

Luxembourg's capital, as with all interesting European cities, boasts an imposing square as its central point. The vast array of P signs had helped me in to an underground car park within spitting distance of it (not that spitting would ever be tolerated in Luxembourg) and my next encounter with daylight was walking up the steps into the grandeur of the Place Guillaume II. I glanced at the map and made for the far corner, crossed in front of the classy, glassy Tourist Information Centre, then wandered down a stony passageway with a gourmet seafood delicatessen at its entrance. This was Europe at its very finest, and of course its very richest.

The Hotel Francais, my new home booked on the internet, was on La Place d'Armes, a smaller but no less charming square diagonally adjacent to Guillaume. It too brought a sense of space and splendour that rapidly dissolved as I moved indoors. The hotel reception area was small and cramped, the lift the size of a shoe box, the nondescript bedroom only marginally bigger. A world away from my bright, airy, and homely gaff on the Moselle, this the price of life in a city and every reason to get back onto those polished streets forthwith.

I walked for the next day and a half, and the more I paced, the more I marvelled at what has to be one of the world's best-kept secrets. A unique city defined by the remnants of high walls that for so long protected it, built around and within two steep winding valleys almost at right angles to one another. A geographical conundrum, a weaving together of the old and the new, all encased within a one-way ring road that disappears in and out of a series of tunnels. Whether it was more confusing by road or on foot I had yet to decide.

My favourite spot without question was the pathway known as Le Chemin de la Corniche, perched high above the Alzette valley and looking down over the rooftops of Grund. Up here I knew exactly where I was and when the calf muscles started to tighten I could sit on the polished benches, pretend to be old, and just soak up those fantastic views.

Luxembourg

It was up here that I came across the Museum of the History of Luxembourg, a five storey building cut into the side of the cliff with entrances at different levels. An absolute cracker: calm, spacious and almost empty (March has many advantages) and exactly what was needed to seek out answers to the many questions forming in my head. The glass lift was large enough to park a truck, the tea and cakes in the jolly cafeteria would alone have been worthy of the visit, and how cleverly the history of Luxembourg was presented.

It all started in AD 963 with a gent named Count Sigefroi of the Ardennes who built a castle on The Bock, the promontory above the Alzette just around the corner from where I was standing. A small town evolved around it, the fortress was constantly strengthened but this only served to convince Europe's most rich and powerful that here was a prize worth nabbing. For several hundred years The House of Luxembourg managed to hang on under great men of the era such as John The Blind (visually impaired, not soft furnishings) but unfortunately the dynasty was shattered soon after his reign.

One of the first of the foreigners to take over was the Duke of Burgundy, who became known in history (though not in Luxembourg, I suspect) as Philip The Good. The Burgundians ruled in the 15th century, the Spanish in the 16th, Austrians 18th, Dutch and Germans 19th and the French a couple of times in between. Throughout all this turmoil the city's fortifications were developed and then destroyed and Luxembourg's plight was further deepened in the two world wars of the last century when the Germans marched over the river and occupied for four years each time. Wow, some story, too much to take in really, but at least it made sense of all those big walls outside.

Walls that comprise up to twenty four forts as well as a network of concealed corridors and chambers that run for a total of fifteen miles. This secret world of caves and tunnels, improbably cut into the side of the cliffs, are known as the casemates, and they provided shelter for soldiers and horses while the deep dungeons served as kitchens, workshops and prisons. In the world wars they were again brought into play as air raid shelters and today, another hundred years on, these strange subterranean passages are protected as a UNESCO World Heritage Site for the tourists of the world to enjoy.

Though I can't say I enjoyed it. Once inside it looked just like...well, caves and tunnels and rather than providing shelter the blasts of icy wind felt more extreme than the constant temperatures at street level. All of which contributed to my inspection being of a cursory nature and I can't add a great deal on the cultural front other than to say I was happy to return to my shoebox, get the blood flowing again and plan for an evening of comedy down at Scott's.

* * * * *

Most of Luxembourg's wealthy population works in an office and an unmistakeable feature of the city's skyline is the towering expanse of glass on its north-eastern outskirts. This city-within-a-city was a couple of miles away to my left as I stood on the Corniche soaking up the views for the very last time and I decided that it would be worth a quick detour on my way north later that morning. My other project was to find the Kirchberg Plateau, a name that I'd seen on road signs all week and had rather tickled my fancy. Surely the city of Luxembourg couldn't possibly offer roaming antelope or herds of wildebeest to add to its seemingly endless list of surprises?

My credit card bore the brunt of the parking charges (paying with real money would have made me too angry) and in no time at all I was following signs for the Plateau and crossing The Red Bridge in the direction of Germany. The skyscraper city was now upon me and like everything else in the country it looked more like an enormous gleaming model than a series of buildings where real work is carried out. Which, on reflection, is perhaps not so far from the truth. This is the home of the Commission of the EC, the General Secretariat of the European Parliament and a swathe of other grandiose departments that few of us understand but silently fork out billions to keep afloat. Luxembourg was, remember, one of the six founder members of the EU back in 1957 and today, along with Brussels and

Strasbourg, still figures as one of its key centres of administration. Where would we be without those guys, eh?

My first and only disappointment in this cute little country was the discovery that this vertical world *was* in fact the much drooled-over Kirchberg Plateau. Entirely devoid of wildlife, not even so much as a Thomson's gazelle, my dream turned out to be nothing more than a fancy name for a business park with a staggering number of flags and roundabouts. A subliminal message perhaps that it was the right time to leave, to head back into the greenery and where better to make for than eastern Luxembourg, known to all as Little Switzerland.

* * * * *

The pretty region of rolling hills, golf courses, babbling brooks and forest trails was undeservedly empty and what a lovely place this would be in the summer sunshine. But in fact it felt positively winter and once again the snow was starting to swirl around. I decided to keep moving. Tomorrow would be Good Friday, day of the big football match in Diekirch, so I followed the signpost towards that town and then found myself driving along the banks of the Sure river. It was swollen from the winter rains and had started to flood in places but the solitary building on a large sweeping bend seemed to have escaped any damage. It was a hotel (an empty one judging by the car park) with a fabulous location, the mountains behind and a castle almost directly overhead. A room for two nights would not be a problem.

It was a stroke of luck that my visit to the country was to coincide with the top-of-the-table clash between Diekirch Young Boys and Colmarberg AS. I'd already decided that, as an Englishman, it would pay to take an interest in Luxembourgish football given that our national side was heading towards the same world ranking as theirs. Whereas our great rivals in 1966 were the Germans, who's to say that a hundred years later, in 2066 – when every Englishman aged 6-60 is either clinically obese, an alcoholic or too concerned about the environment to play football – that Luxembourg won't be seen as the arch enemy? At least it will be easy to get tickets for the Fourway Shield matches (the biannual battle against our other major adversaries, Liechtenstein and San Marino) and how we'll be able to taunt the Luxos about the 9-0 thumpings we gave them back in 1960 and 1982.

Dinner was superb, the appearance of several other clients warmed the place up and out of the dark sky the snow came down in diagonal lines under the lights. For the first time these were serious, enormous flakes and plenty of them. I even went outside to watch them coming down and it was no surprise that eight hours later the world was one very deep fluffy white carpet. This really was picture postcard material, the castle up on the mountain looked sublime but, on a more sombre note, the tussle for top spot in Division 1 would most definitely be postponed.

And so, whether I liked it or not, today would be a castle day. I swept the six inch layer of snow off the silhouette that had to be my car, drove slowly alongside the flowing river, and then up the winding road to a lay-by at the top of the mountain. Oh how smug did I feel to have a chunky pair of walking boots in the back of the car? There was absolutely no sign of life but on top of a snowy mountain in Luxembourg on Good Friday morning that should have come as no big surprise.

Ever so gingerly I walked up the steep track to the castle entrance, no sign of footprints in the snow I noticed, but to my astonishment came upon an entrance booth and a lady stamping her feet against the bitter cold. (Had she arrived by parachute?). She received me with a level of warmth and enthusiasm that indicated I would likely be her only client of the day and thus pleasantries were traded for several minutes before the Euros, a brochure and a set of headphones changed hands.

Bourscheid, I was soon to learn, is one of twenty plus castles dotted on hilltops around the country. As with Sigefroi's, it was first built over a thousand years ago on a site that had formerly been a wooden defence structure, possibly used by the Carolingians or the Merovingians. At which point you have every right to wonder whether I'm making these names up but no, these were the ruling dynasties of the seventh and eight centuries.

For the next five hundred years the castle was strengthened and extended and then in the five hundred that followed it was badly neglected and left to dilapidate. Thankfully, in 1972 the Luxembourg State acquired it and set about a restoration programme befitting what had already been declared a national historic monument.

That's as much information as I'm going to give you otherwise you'll be as numb as I was listening to the headphones describing every room within the crumbling interior. The big outer walls and the black conical turrets were the most impressive to me and the expansive views from the watchtower over the snow-covered Sure valley was what really made the whole thing worthwhile. I stood up at the top of the spiral staircase until the faint but chilling breeze started to freeze my face and then carefully clambered back down to the gateway and the warmth of the solitary car.

The bright sunshine turned everything back to a rich green over the next twenty four hours. Perfect driving conditions for the ride through more country lanes to the north-east, the town of Vianden, and my first exposure to Luxembourgish tourism. The streets were heaving, cafés and restaurants packed to the gunwales, vehicles lined the pavements and crammed into overflowing car parks. It all seemed so ...weird. But it was easy to see why they were there. Vianden sits in a valley with a pretty river flowing through, it has its own medieval castle set in the forest and its charming main street, winding down the hill to the water's edge, is everything a country village is supposed to be. It was more by good luck than good management that I'd saved the best till last.

And all that now remained of TLC 2 was the journey west through more sleepy villages and the now familiar picturesque landscape of the southern Ardennes. The rain and snow had gone for another year, the sunshine was at last warm and penetrating and my final treat was the delightful symmetry of arriving back in Bastogne at exactly the same time I'd first stumbled in there just one week earlier. Yes, a week older and a week wiser, one Sunday afternoon to the next and what a great privilege it had been to spend seven whole days exploring the wonders of Toytown.

Tajikistan/Kyrgyzstan

It was very confusing to an eight year old boy why the team in red had CCCP written across the front of their shirts. Things got even worse when my Dad explained that it stood for the USSR, and by way of further clarification, that this was another way of saying Russia. So I just sat quietly and watched the match, didn't pry any further, and decided to leave the matter well alone for at least a couple of decades.

It was only when the Soviet Union collapsed in 1991 that I got my head round the fact that the bit called Russia had only, in size terms, been three quarters of it. The rest was made up of a motley alliance of fourteen republics that had also been savouring the delights of communism for the best (or worst) part of 70 years, though I wouldn't for the life of me have been able to tell you what they were called. Let alone that five of them were about to become Ten-Letter Countries...

The Turkish Airlines captain announced that we were approaching Dushanbe, capital of Tajikistan. Comforting words, the first time I can recall hearing anybody say these strange names out loud. I'd left home at 07.30 Wednesday morning, four hours ahead of my flight to Istanbul, a diagonal journey across Europe that would take a further four hours. The transit time in Turkey had also been four hours, and now this onward connection, due east across the Black and the Caspian Seas, had – again – taken almost exactly four hours. A delightful piece of symmetry that brought more than a spark of pleasure into my nerdy world, and that was even before the next bulletin from the front of the plane. "Ladies and gentlemen, please adjust your watches. The local time is exactly 03.30." We were four hours ahead of the UK.

I found myself spelling Tajikistan out on my fingertips for the umpteenth time. There was no turning back of course but imagine getting dumped into

63

such a strange place in the middle of the night only to find that another vowel had slipped in unnoticed. Tiredness also demanded obsessive checking of passport whereabouts (it hadn't moved since the previous session of zipping and unzipping) and yet another nervous perusal of the Letter of Invitation from Goulya, my internet lady. Then just one final bit of faffing before the door finally opened and we shuffled down the steps into the warm night, the waiting bus and the visa office of the terminal building.

Don't ask me why but I hadn't expected the room to be packed. It was long, narrow and airless with the door at one end and chairs lining the walls, uncomfortably similar to a carriage on the London Underground. A man at a desk in the middle and another at the far end were evidently there to issue visas but the procedure went unexplained, the only communication coming from Far End Man who jumped up every five minutes and yelled "Sit Down!" to the exhausted, bemused folk jostling around with documents in hand. The fact that all the seats were occupied seemed to have passed him by.

Dawn was breaking over Dushanbe by the time my passport had been stamped. The tree- lined avenues were still and silent, it was already at least 25 degrees centigrade and destined to increase by two degrees an hour until well after noon. The aptly named Hotel Mercury was at the far end of town, neatly tucked away in a quiet little corner and as soon as the a/c had been zapped for immediate action and the alarm clock set for five hours hence, so was I.

* * * * *

If I'm honest I'm not sure I'd ever heard of Tajikistan. Even the term Central Asia was a blurry concept, an unknown territory somewhere east of Turkey but not quite as far as China. It was a part of the globe I'd always overlooked (quite literally), a rugged landmass that had only ever vaguely captured my attention from 30,000 feet between large gin and tonics or a break in the in-flight movies. Being a Manchester lad, the only Stans I'd ever come across were Bowles and Ogden.

Central Asia comprises five countries, all Stans, and all bar one with ten letters to their names. My idea was to start with the small and mountainous nations of Tajikistan and Kyrgyzstan in the western extension of the Himalayas, head northwards to the mostly flat, and eye-poppingly enormous, Kazakhstan and then loop back down to Uzbekistan at the centre of the group. Poor old Turkmenistan – a rare 12-er – was destined to be the odd man out though of course the rules of the game would not necessarily prohibit me from going there. In fact it was tempting to include her: perhaps I could keep heading west through the desert to the shores of the Caspian and sail over to Azerbaijan, the only Caucasian TLC?

I studied the page of the atlas ever more closely and the important rectangle with Russia to the north, Iran and Afghanistan to the south, Europe to the west and China to the east. For a region we rarely hear about Central Asia was not only very....er... central but evidently very large and I realised that to attempt four countries in one hit was already a mighty big ask. To contemplate more (to include a non-TLC at that) would be an act of sheer madness so the Caspian would have to wait, the original plan would be adhered to. All the necessary visas could be obtained in London ahead of departure except that of Tajikistan, hence the obvious starting point – in a long narrow room in Dushanbe airport.

* * * * *

Dushanbe is dominated by a 4 km boulevard known as Rudaki. It runs north to south through the city feeding countless small streets on either side and if photographed from the air would resemble the spinal column of a fish. My hotel was in the far north and thus, like it or not, my first day (in fact, any day) would be spent walking south along Rudaki.

It was early afternoon and the sun at its highest but the tall rows of trees along the roadside were enough to protect the Manchester legs against the vicious heat. There was little traffic and only a few people here and there, most sitting on plastic chairs, enjoying the shade, or just squatting toilet-style on their heels in the way that Asian folk do so readily. For a capital city the silence was almost deafening. The green and white trolley bus just occasionally rattled along the wide, empty thoroughfare and taxis sat quietly in neat rows, probably idle for most of the day, I couldn't help think. This was one calm, orderly, sort of place.

Graceful, elegant trees seemed to fill the city and were considerably taller than most of the buildings, which in themselves threw up a few surprises. Some were painted in pastel blues and pinks adding a quite unexpected charm and taking the edge off the grey, rectangular monstrosities that we have all come to expect as the Soviet norm. The tidy parks looked well cared-for and the sight and sound of the many fountains was a pleasing bonus. Day 1, happy as Larry. (Larry Foley, undefeated Australian boxer, 1847-1917).

I was hungry, found myself looking inside the small shops for something to munch on and ultimately sought help from a smiley lady by rubbing my empty stomach and mimicking a chimpanzee's picnic. She got my drift, indicated something across the road and down a side street, and five minutes later I was sitting at a table reading my first Central Asian menu. All fine and dandy except that foreign people use a different alphabet from which they create words that we don't understand.

The waitress stepped forward to take my order.

"English?" I muttered hopefully.

'Russki' she responded unambiguously.

"Aaagh, right. Russki", I acknowledged, wondering what the hell might happen next.

'Soup?' she offered, to my great relief. The same word in Russki, I later learned.

'Salat?' Ditto. Count me in on both.

'Shashlik?' Sounded familiar. Go for it.

The skewers of lamb were superb, the salad an inoffensive mix of chopped tomatoes and cucumbers and the soup turned out to be a tasty bowl of meat, potato and veg. Sure, it had a disappointingly large oil slick on the surface, but all in all it was a satisfying and filling 20 Somani (£3) lunch. Restored and refreshed, I headed back to the wide pavements to walk it all off.

In theory the street names were in Russian but attempts to find points of interest at addresses quoted in my guidebook proved impossible. There were very few signs at all in any script and it didn't take long before I'd managed to get lost in a maze of residential streets. Most were quiet and generally unremarkable so it came as a surprise when I spotted a large gathering of men assembled outside a house. They were all smartly dressed, the older ones noticeably wearing more Islamic style clothing and sporting small, black, embroidered hats. What could this be?

They spotted the lone foreigner peering down their street and in what was clearly an act of friendship beckoned me forward to join the group. Oh blimey O'Riley! Feeling more than a tad self-conscious I had no choice but to head towards them and after a few tentative handshakes found myself ushered into a large courtyard where maybe a hundred men sat at long, ornately decorated tables. A feast was about to be served. Plates of nuts and fruits and wrapped sweets had been laid out ahead of the banquet and whether I liked it or not I was to take a seat as the guest of honour. So much for a stroll after lunch.

Had it not been for Naz the event would have remained a puzzle to this day. It was my good fortune that the youngest member of the party was sitting on the same table and that, unlike all the other guests, (or anybody else I'd met so far), he spoke excellent English. Thanks to the five years he'd spent in Rusholme, Manchester (famous for a mile of curry houses and – for 80 beautiful years – within heart-pumping distance of the Maine Road floodlights) Naz was able to explain that this was a wedding celebration for all the people that wouldn't be able to attend the main event. A long-standing Tajik tradition where all the men would gather for a prayer and a meal and then, as soon as the eating was done, would stand up and return from whence they came.

He also explained that this was a Tajik family and that everybody was speaking the local language. Not surprising in Tajikistan, you might think, but this is a country where one in three of the 7m population hail from a different ethnic group. To complicate matters further their own language is a form of Farsi, as spoken in Iran, and completely different from the derivations of Turkish used in all other areas of Central Asia. Hence Russian, spoken by all, serves as a common language across the country and indeed throughout most of the region.

Prayers were said as the assembled sat quietly with palms open in front of chests, then came the "amen" and hands drawn down the face in a rinsing motion. The Islamic faith had evidently survived the years of Soviet-enforced atheism and, noticeably, unlike all the shops I had seen that day, not a drop of vodka was there in sight. Enormous platters of coloured rice arrived – known to us as pilau and the Russian-speaking world as plov – and upon each was a large bone from which the diners quickly started tearing chunks of meat with their bare hands. A proper free-for-all ensued, a hundred men simultaneously piling in to the nearest available food mountain though nothing so common for the VIP for whom an exclusive platter had been delivered. "But, I've just had....." I started to mumble foolishly, realising there was nothing else for it than to grab a handful of rice, rip off a lump of lamb and start munching.

Fifteen minutes later, following a slice of water melon, a cup of tea and another prayer with hand movements, we all stood up to leave. It was all over, just as Naz had predicted, and if I hadn't managed to snap a few quick photos I'd still be wondering to this day whether in fact the whole thing had just been a very weird dream.

* * * * *

Dushanbe turned out to be a pleasant city and a couple of days proved just right to get a feel for the country and to adapt to the substantial advances in time and temperature. This was the starting point for what promised to be a formidable adventure and I felt mentally and physically in good shape for the journey into the unknown.

Goulya had come highly recommended as a private tour operator and my extensive e-mail correspondence with her had been encouraging. She'd sorted my Letter of Invitation, a wacky bit of bureaucracy to permit the granting of the visa at the airport, and in return for a fistful of dollars would arrange my transportation and accommodation across the country and northwards into Kyrgyzstan. My apologies now if this all sounds rather Page & Moy but research into Tajikistan had revealed this to be a country with few roads, even fewer hotels and an abundant supply of very large mountains. The only way across them was by jeep, the only place to sleep was in private houses.

Jeep and driver turned up at the appointed hour, together with Goulya's associate who came along to shake my hand and trouser a large wad of notes. That was always the deal: honesty, trust and a hearty slice of good fortune was all I could hope for from here on in. Dimitri was the man with whom I was to share the rest of my days in the country and if he turned out to be a BO-ridden, smelly-fag smoking, alcoholic with a penchant for loud and nasty music then I would have no choice but to take it on the chin… or up the nose or… whatever.

The vehicle was clean and tidy, as was the driver, so the first minute spent in the passenger seat was one of considerable relief. Minute two was slightly less encouraging on registering the absence of a safety belt, ditto minute three as the seat shuttled back and forth in response to each application of the brakes. It didn't take too long to calculate that if the jeep were to come to a sharp stop the windscreen and I would be joining forces and heading rather more quickly somewhere in the direction of China.

But I needn't have worried. The first of the mountain roads announced loud and clear that we would never be going fast enough to warrant any serious braking. The winding track was peppered with deep potholes that Dimitri would either have us swerve around or simply bounce into, crunch through and wobble back out of. The surface was an awful mess, close to impassable in places and we were scheduled for two full days of rocking and lurching like rag dolls just to get to Khorog. And that would only be the starting point of the real challenge – to get across the Pamir Mountains.

Tajikistan is tucked away in the south-east corner of Central Asia, in size terms less than 4% of the whole region. It's shaped like a bow tie (Dushanbe on the left triangle, Khorog on the right) and though it's only just a little larger than England I'd been warned that distances would count for very little. My journey would be across 800 miles of the world's toughest terrain, to the most remote outpost of the old Soviet Union, a mountainous void known, somewhat dauntingly, as The Roof of the World.

This first section was tough enough, which is probably why we had the mountains to ourselves save a handful of trucks bearing Chinese plates. Progress seemed painfully slow though the landscape through which we tossed and bounced painted an ever changing picture: bleak and grey as a disused quarry one minute, the next lush and green as the Yorkshire Dales. Civilisation of any sort soon seemed a very distant memory so it was against all expectation when we parked up alongside a stationary vehicle and Dimitri calmly announced that we were calling into a café for lunch.

Tea was served under the tree on the tapchan, one of those wonderful wooden super-king-size bed frames I'd first seen when on 4-letter duty in Iran. Covered in rugs and cushions they serve as both chair and table, so you learn to keep your feet off and try not to sit in the middle. This time the tea was green and served, as it always would be, from a tall pot into wide cups with no handles. Two bowls of piping hot soup soon followed: a familiar mix of potato and vegetable, lump of dodgy meat, oil slick on top. And then a dunker's dream, a plate stacked high with freshly baked bread, oval and naan-y, still warm from the oven. (Or was it just the heat of the sun?)

Dimitri and I sat quietly enjoying the shade and the relative cool. We dunked and slurped, competed with the flies to tear lumps off the bread and chatted about his life and the changes from Soviet times. My new friend and driver, it turned out, was Armenian. He'd always lived in Tajikistan but, as was becoming clearer to me, nationality and country of residence would hold two very different meanings in this part of the world. His ancestors were from Armenia, his parents were born in Russia, he and his kids were born in Dushanbe. But they were all Armenian and always would be.

So what did he think of living in the free world, away from the clutches of the centrally planned state? Just how good was it to have shrugged off the miseries of communism? A key turning point in his life, surely? Dimitri's troubled face was an answer in itself; I'd gone in search of enthusiasm where clearly there was none. As far as he was concerned Tajikistan was no better, in fact probably worse than before, now a sinister dictatorship pretending to be a democracy, a struggling state with little infrastructure and no jobs. He would leave if he could, if it wasn't for his wife. A gloomy, pessimistic portrayal indeed and I couldn't help notice how he glanced nervously around after uttering these words, like a bird feeding in the garden unsure of what might lurk in the bushes.

The afternoon shift in the passenger seat was destined to be a long one so I profited from a unique opportunity to learn some Russian. "Spasiba" and "piva" – thank you and beer – proved none too complex so I was on something of a roll for my inaugural encounter with the Cyrillic alphabet, neatly laid out at the back of the book. Rather like learning Arabic numbers I figured: six Russian letters are the same as ours and also pronounced the same (A,E,K,M,O,T), five are written the same but sound like something else (B=V, H=N, P=R, C=S, Y=U)...and the other 21 are written upside down, or back to front, or have in some way been tinkered with. More than an afternoon's work I concluded, but it was an encouraging start, particularly if we were to find ourselves in need of an MOT.

We were winding ever higher but the sun was still viciously hot as we climbed above 3000 metres. The melting snows meant water was in plentiful supply and on more than one occasion Dimitri parked the jeep in a shallow river to give the engine a good soaking just as John Wayne used to do with his horse. The Sagirdasht Pass at 3252m was the highest point of the day, geographically and emotionally, and it was at the very end of that afternoon, some 10 hours and 240kms after setting off, that we finally dropped down into Kalaikhum.

All I could make out of this village in the half light was a random scattering of houses, a raging river cutting through its middle and a towering expanse of darkness behind. Dimitri parked up with the confidence of a man who knew where he was and I stepped out on to terra firma with a sense of excitement, a feeling that the adventure had kicked off and was going rather well. The volume of water and the raw power of the River Panj was deafening, daunting to the point of being a little scary, as was the sheer mountain face beyond that marked the boundary with Afghanistan.

We were to be guests in a family home on the bank of the river and the room allocated to me was almost adjacent to the water's edge. It was delightful in its simplicity. Ornate rugs covered the entire floor and two of the walls; the solitary piece of furniture was a dresser at one end upon which numerous quilts and pillows were stacked. As soon as my host retreated I sprawled out on the luxurious carpet, arms and legs akimbo, a starfish in the darkness. Eyes closed, lying quite still, the sound of the rampaging river was as good as any massage though, alas, the brain had retained the sensation of a moving vehicle and the heat in the room was almost suffocating.

The tapchan in the courtyard offered the only escape. There I sat quietly, drank tea, admired the silhouette of the surrounding Afghan mountains and listened to the water in all its glory. The sky was clear, the stars shone brightly and a slight movement in the air had just taken the edge off the searing heat. If there was any good reason to bounce around in a jeep for an entire day, this was most definitely it.

Dinner of soup and bread and salad was a resounding success thanks mainly to the addition of a bowl of exquisite home made yoghurt. I returned to the room a contented man but the heat was still overpowering and would remain so throughout the night. Sleeping was patchy at best, dawn seemed to take forever and the clanking of breakfast pots and pans competing against the flow of the river came as welcome relief.

I surfaced to a plate of rice with hot melted butter poured all over it, hardly the ideal prep for ten hours of bobbing and weaving in the motor but I gave it my best shot and told myself it could have been a whole lot worse. (Isn't there somewhere people eat sheep's eyeballs?). The catering was remarkable, given the basic facilities, and the hospitality extremely humbling from people whose lives were clearly a struggle in survival. What other region in the world sees temperatures rise to plus 40C in summer and drop to minus 40C a few months later? I can't think of anywhere.

If the kitchen was primitive, the two outhouses that served as bathroom and toilet were definitely not for the faint-hearted. A hose and a bunch of dodgy wires hanging from a rusty tank did combine to produce a gentle flow of warm water so in a sense the washing amenities were light years ahead of the sewerage department. The smallest room was a tiny, narrow shed with a Christmas tree-shaped hole cut into the floor, one that had evidently proved a challenging target even for some of the locals. It was with considerable reluctance that I undressed and lowered to a squat, my shoulders almost touching the walls and forehead pressed against the door to minimise any risk of a messy rearward tumble. Thoughts of the unpleasantness that lay behind and beneath proved a strong incentive to keep weight forward though it did mean that my left knee brushed up against the open plastic bin, which on this particular sunny morn was full to overflowing with well used toilet paper..... Time to move on perhaps.

The road south hugs the left bank of the Panj, a fearsome 100m-wide river dividing the two countries all the way to Khorog and far beyond. This is harsh terrain, brown/grey, rugged, absolutely brutal. We travelled roughly a quarter of the 1300km border, again there were no vehicles and no sign of life except for a handful of Tajik soldiers patrolling the river, trying to stem the endless flow of heroin from the world's biggest supplier. Or pocketing huge sums of money for not trying too hard. Not a place you would want your car to break down, and as though the geography wasn't intimidating enough, there were frequent signs warning of unexploded landmines, a legacy of the civil war of 1992 (a year after independence) when the various clans had battled for control. 60,000 lives were lost in that conflict but it probably didn't even get a mention in the Daily Mirror.

After a cool, windy night (this time in a sort of guest house without guests) and my first proper sleep in a week we headed for downtown Khorog to attend to the morning's business. Dimitri parked up in the main street where I sat and watched the world go by for half an hour while he took my passport to the police station for registration, another hangover from the days of communist control. The pedestrians were a clean and tidy looking bunch. The men all wore crisp pressed shirts and smart trousers, I noticed, and there was very little on show to suggest a devout Islamic following. Facial features were definitely more Middle Eastern than Asian and to my great surprise there was even a scattering of blonde and redheaded folk amongst the curious mix.

The second stop was my pre-arranged meeting with a gentleman (I presumed) by the name of Farruksho Fraidonov. Thanks to the internet I had come to hear of the University of Central Asia based in Khorog and figured that a visit there would offer another slant on life in Tajikistan.

Well, I can now confirm that Farruksho is a man, his English is flawless and he is responsible for raising the profile of what is perhaps the most unusual university in the world. The story goes that in the 1990s the Aga Khan pledged a significant sum of money to develop a centre of learning aimed at supporting the people of the mountains. This would not only serve to educate the local folk but draw in students from far and wide who would study all aspects of rural life and ultimately help to sustain it. Hence this campus at the foot of the Pamir range and two similar sites in small mountain cities of Kyrgyzstan and Kazakhstan. The additional goal would be to ensure that all students become competent in English, the language of the world, Russian, the language of the region and Tajik, the language of the country. The real locals, by the way, also speak Pamiri!

Farruksho explained that since independence the state schools have used Tajik as the principal language and as a consequence many younger people have a poor grasp of Russian. Despite the many challenges he seemed generally optimistic about his country, though acknowledged that the transition to a free market economy was too difficult for many people to cope with. A lifetime of state control, an expectation of guaranteed employment and a dependence on subsidies had instilled a mentality that could not be changed overnight. What made it harder, the Soviets had never developed their republics as self-sufficient units, merely as single cogs in a

74

very large machine. This single cog of Tajikistan was now in total isolation. It was mid-morning by the time we hit the road. Not just any old road but the infamous Pamir Highway which, according to a sign that even I could follow, would carry us eastwards, upwards and then northwards for 728 kms as far as Osh in Kyrgyzstan. It was a bleak start, a climb through what looked for all the world like a very large mine, and as for the term "highway"...... Badly Pot-Holed Dirt Track doesn't have the same ring to it, admittedly, so I can see why that very large Department of Bullshit and Propaganda in Moscow would have been eager to conjure up a rather different image. Not that the Soviets allowed anybody to use their highway.

They had built this road across the mountains in the early 1930s to create a link with their poorest and most remote little republic. But it could all have been a very different story. The latter half of the 19th century had seen the huge Russian armies moving south, taking over Central Asia bit by bit, and edging ever closer to Afghanistan, the Indian Sub-Continent and the mighty British Empire. This didn't go unnoticed by the suits in Whitehall who nervously despatched men to the region to spy on the enemy and attempt to establish a foothold in places that were still up for grabs. This strategic posturing between Britain and Russia was known as The Great Game and the last such bloodless battle was right here in the snowy no-man's-land of the Pamirs. Unfortunately for all concerned, and by way of a foretaste of our performances in the Beautiful Game, we got through the qualifying stages but didn't come home with the trophy.

We climbed from stony bleakness into a kaleidoscope of magnificent greens, pinks and purples, silhouettes that played tricks with the eyes by constantly changing colour according to proximity. After crossing the Ko-Tezek Pass at 4272m the empty road seemed to straighten out, the land was now almost flat for half a mile on either side but beyond the plateau snowy peaks dominated in all directions. Where did the Pamirs finish and the other mountain ranges start? Just to the north-east we were looking at China and the Tien Shan range, immediately south-east was the Karakorum of Pakistan (and eventually the Himalayas), and right behind us, the Hindu

Kush of northern Afghanistan. Yes, it really did feel like standing on the roof of the world.

The ground here was barely more than gravel with tufts of grass the only vegetation able to survive the desperate conditions. It was so bleak I felt compelled to get out, feel the cool air and soak up the solitude. This was the largest car park in the world, a wilderness that freezes for most of the year and in truth there was very little to look at in the foreground other than a line of telegraph poles. So far I'd seen just a few eagles and the occasional herd of yaks (a sort of large hairy cow) and so what a moment of great excitement when I heard a shrill whistling sound and caught sight of a couple of marmots (a sort of large hairy squirrel) scampering across the outback. I'm not sure what made me do it but I too felt compelled to go for a scamper and so, with camera in hand, I gave chase to one of the little buggers.

Not only do marmots run very fast but when they don't want to play any more, or they need a six month nap, they disappear into a hole in the ground. I bent down and peered into the angled opening that my marmot of choice had obviously prepared in advance but he was not going to be wooed by the sound of heavy breathing or gentle words of encouragement in a language that he didn't understand. I guess in the land of the snow leopard these furry little fellas are pretty handy when it comes to playing hide and seek so it was game over for me, back to the jeep and a rare smirk from one bemused driver.

Dimitri had promised a delicious fish lunch just beyond the village of Alichur. That any form of human settlement existed in these parts seemed so utterly improbable I couldn't even start to imagine how or where we might expect a mid-afternoon feast. This was a naked wilderness with a scattering of several small lakes, who could possibly live out here?

The answer was to be found in Alichur itself in the form of a ragged encampment of Kyrgyz nomads. Some lived in yurts, large circular tents made from animal skin, others in small rectangular portakabin-style houses. It looked a sad and desperate place even in the middle of August, one of the few months of the year the temperature rises above freezing. We carried on a few more kilometres to where a single yurt appeared at the roadside, a community of four people with a small cabin nearby and a telephone-box shaped outhouse for the powdering of the nose. "Lunch", announced my driver.

Mr and Mrs Yurtdweller had bright clothes, gold teeth, sloping eyes, high cheekbones and two excited children who looked very much the same. They all posed enthusiastically for pictures in front of their home and as always found great amusement in seeing themselves in miniature on the digital screen. Then they ushered us in to the cabin where tea was served ahead of a large plateful of something I didn't immediately recognise. It turned out to be a heap of dried fish which admittedly was slightly better on the pallet than on the eye, though its categorisation as "delicious" somewhat open to question.

I was eager to get back into the fresh air, to walk around the yurt (it would have seemed rude to wander in) and to steal a look at the strange world of these formidable people. Can you imagine spending every day of your life in a tent with your two children, stuck in a field with no sanitation and no running water? And here of all places, the remotest, most brutal corner of the Earth where temperatures routinely drop to 50 degrees below zero? Would you get up and go out for a pee in the middle of the night?

We continued on to Murgab, the main community of the eastern Pamirs and home to a few thousand hardy folk. In contrast to the glorious mountain scenery the town was an ugly hotchpotch of new (or part finished) buildings randomly thrown up amidst the rubble of others that had been abandoned or were simply falling down. The word "planning" had obviously never made it into the local vocabulary.

I grabbed a fleece and stood outside the decaying house that was my home for the night. The sun had dipped from sight, there was already a chill in the air and the only sign of life came from a pair of scrawny dogs scavenging amidst the debris. The semi light offered only the silhouettes of ramshackle edifices and the poles and wires and cables that drooped and dangled in their thousands to link them together. The streets themselves were the spaces left in between, rough tracks with piles of loose bricks and all manner of household waste. Darkness was most definitely the best thing for it. It was thoroughly depressing, a veritable "what the fuck am I doing here?" moment and how pleased was I to suddenly recall that Murgab was an hour ahead of Dushanbe, that clocks would move forward and that I would be spending one hour less in this dreary god-forsaken town.

The memory of Murgab was not entirely a negative one. The soup that night was particularly good and followed by a sort of pizza, a highly unexpected departure from the norm. Our hostess was a charming lady in her thirties who spoke very good English and seemed far too cultured to be living in a falling down house in a town from a spaghetti western. I found myself feeling terribly sorry for her and disgusted with myself for being so grumpy: she'd be there for life, I only had to do twelve hours.

In the end, it might even have been thirteen. We soon climbed a thousand metres to hit the highest point of the journey, the Ak-Baital Pass at 4655m, where the large barbed wire fence running parallel to our right indicated that we were almost within touching distance of China. This the western-most point of the world's most populous country, the Xinjiang province, closer to Saudi than it is to Shanghai and home to 10 million Muslims who would prefer not to be part of China at all. But that's another story. To have reached here felt like a double achievement, a magic moment aboard the traveller's roller coaster and as I got out of the jeep and stood proudly on the top of the world, something quite unexpected happened. It started to snow.

Only three days earlier, in the homestay at the riverside, the stifling heat had kept me awake for most of the night. That all seemed such a long time ago now as we pushed on further north to reach Kara Kul, a surprisingly large and attractive lake with a cluster of basic houses forming a community at one end. Our original plan had been to spend the last night here but even in the early afternoon it was too cold for any sort of relaxation and Dimitri was more than happy to keep on going. We would head for the border then the Kyrgyz town of Sary Tash, and possibly, if time and energy would allow, try to make it all the way to Osh.

The snow had stopped swirling by the time we reached the small border post at the top of the hill but the air was icy cold and blowing a gale. We parked the jeep behind a group of motorcyclists from Poland (how come we had never seen them before?) and went to meet the customs and immigration men who were well wrapped up for the Arctic conditions and sitting casually on the front step by the doorway of their office. They laughed and joked and invited us in for tea (hospitality seldom found at Harwich or Heathrow) and posed for pictures in front of their windswept mountain shed. Conversation was limited but they tried hard, stamped my passport with the minimum of fuss, thanked me for visiting Tajikistan and expressed good wishes for a pleasant onward journey. A nice touch and a lasting impression. One Stan down, three to go.

KYRGYZSTAN

We had to cross another mountain pass and motor a further 20 kms to reach the Kyrgyz border post so a rare half hour was spent in Nomansland. The passports were stamped without a problem but the Customs man made a point of keeping us waiting and eventually ambled out a with a sniffer dog straining at the leash, a stick with a hook on the end and a collection of tools with which to carry out his examinations.

The luggage, once hauled out on to the tarmac, seemed to satisfy the eager hound, so the two-legged beast (noticeably less frisky and agile) ordered the boot to be emptied of all other contents in readiness to do a bit of sniffing of his own. Dimitri stared contemptuously as the stick prized away the panelling and then I watched his lip curl in disgust as the guy unapologetically bashed a hole with hammer and screwdriver into the metalwork of his cherished vehicle. It was only then that a horrible thought entered my mind. Supposing my driver *was* part of a drug-running syndicate and the belly of the jeep *was* packed with heroin. Would I be charged as an accomplice and locked away in a Kyrgyz jail for the next forty years? It just didn't bear thinking about. Who would put my bins out every Thursday night?

The vehicle was clean from a narcotic standpoint but oily enough to blacken the customs officer from head to toe and offer Dimitri a smidgen of revenge. The whole process of dismantling and rebuilding the jeep had taken the best part of two hours, a tedious exercise that has to be repeated day after day, week in week out – not just here but all over the world. And what does it all accomplish? Nothing more than an artificially high price for drugs making the business so lucrative that it grows with every passing day.

I suggested a late lunch in Sary Tash, which first time round I'd mistaken for Scary Tash, as worn by the ladies of Portugal. My colleague managed only a short grunt by way of a response and backed it up with an unenthusiastic nod; the border shenanigans had left him in no mood for conversation. It didn't take us long to get to that first main town but as we slowed down to survey its ramshackle streets, two men in military uniform gestured for us to pull over to the side. Dimitri winced, stopped the jeep and leapt out. A loud argument shortly ensued.

Given that my Russian had not advanced beyond "piva" and "spasiba" I had no idea what was going on, even when the noisier of the soldiers opened the passenger door to speak to me in English. He was shaking with anger, he was drunk as a skunk and he wanted to know where we were heading. It was a frightening and bewildering scenario and it got very much worse when I told him that Osh was our destination. He ran round to where the other two were standing and with bared teeth and the glassy eyes of a madman released a flood of abuse at the Tajik (the only word I could pick out) followed by a wild kick aimed at his thigh. It turned out that he was trying to get his mate a lift towards Osh, but Dimitri, not wanting to have anything to do with them, had said that we weren't going that way. Thanks to my unwittingly spilling the beans there was no way out of the situation other than to make space on the back seat for the younger, quieter drunk and his enormous rifle.

One very silent and sulky driver steered us Oshwards as I tried to make conversation over my left shoulder with the unwanted guest. The stench of the vodka and the size of the gun by his leg had persuaded me that we would be doing nothing to irk this chap – I was ready to be the most compliant hostage he'd ever taken and was grateful for his few words of English. His utterings didn't make a lot of sense but he smiled the smile of a dangerous drunk and I couldn't work out whether he was friend or foe. He mumbled something about drugs and Americans and then slid his hand into an inside pocket.... and pulled out a pistol.

I looked him in the eye to gauge whether his plan was to kill us there and then or follow the far more tidy and practical route of blasting our brains out on the edge of a steep ravine. My hands sweated, bowels threatened to open and heart pounded so loudly that it must surely have echoed through the valley. The blood that would escape in all directions from a bullet at close quarters was pumping at a phenomenal speed. Then a few surprise words from the hi-jacker: "Do you have children?"

I told him no, to which he looked puzzled, and on my returning the question he pointed the gun towards me, put it on top of the luggage, took out his phone and with a glowing vodka smile, showed me the pictures of his loved ones. How they were very, very, very beautiful children, I assured him.

Five minutes later he was fast asleep. After my declining his offer to get out and do some shooting his drunken ramblings revealed that the USA was sponsoring his unit to try to stem the flow of drugs through the country and that he and his fellow officers spent night and day beavering away along this notorious smugglers' route. He was grateful to Uncle Sam, and no wonder: a nice little earner for the lads, uniforms and guns dished out to bully people at will and a plentiful supply of vodka to wile away the hours in the sunshine. I looked back over my shoulder to see the unfired pistol sitting atop my bag and the soldier slumped in the corner, head lolling, mouth open, fetid alcohol breath filling the car. It seemed I wasn't destined to die just yet but still it took another ten or fifteen minutes of calm before my fists unclenched and the tension slowly started to ooze away. Welcome to Kyrgyzstan.

Two hours later we dropped the drunkard at his barracks and two hours after that, at 9 o'clock in the evening, we arrived on the outskirts of Osh. Dimitri had had the cheek to chastise me – the customer! – for the latest ugly incident and when asked how he felt I should have responded to

81

the situation he merely added: "Kyrgyz. Bad nationality." It was a dreadful, silent end to what had been a good trip and, for the most part, a pleasant relationship. Was I really going to hand over the very generous tip, a wad of Somani set aside in the pocket of my bag?

I weighed up the pros and cons. He had been driving for twelve hours, had his car abused by officials and taken a verbal and physical assault at the hands of the military. Prior to this he had done his job in a professional manner but he had been as rude as hell to me for the last six hours and on occasion had told a few porkies to steer things his own way. So when we reached the centre of Osh he found a taxi to take me to the guest house I'd booked (albeit for the following night) and we parted, awkwardly, in the dark on the pavement. I gave him a hug, two thirds of the money and, perhaps with a little embarrassment, he smiled for the first and only time that day.

* * * * *

The TES guest house was a single storey building with five bedrooms that led out onto a lawned garden. There was a communal kitchen with a TV and a computer and the homely little establishment felt more like a well run youth hostel in a European village than a hotel in Central Asia. A cheery, friendly sort of place to be ill.

I knew it would only be a matter of time before a battalion of bacteria went on the march and it was a curious assortment of ailments that kept me confined to barracks for most of the next three days. Perhaps even a form of delayed mountain sickness, I considered, in my eagerness not to go down with anything too run-of-the-mill. It was a frustrating waste of time and my main regret was having to turn down the invitation of a beer with room neighbours Ben and Irene, an English/Norwegian couple driving the long way round on the London to Mongolia rally. I'm sure they would have had plenty of interesting tales to tell.

There wasn't a whole lot to do in Osh anyway though walking round the sprawling market made a pleasant change from sitting on the toilet (at

82

least it had been a sit-down facility). The people were more interesting than the produce in that their features were noticeably more Asian: high cheekbones, narrow eyes and ruddy faces that smacked of poor diet and too much vodka. Many men wore small black hats similar to those in Dushanbe but the local speciality was obviously a large, white felt number with black embroidery, like a tall and rather more absurd version of that found in the Austrian Tyrol.

Standing outside the museum, way up on top of the hill, the view gave a sense of a green and symmetrical city at the end of the pink, dry corridor of the Fergana Valley. Osh is the second largest metropolis in Kyrgyzstan, home to 500,000 people, but the land in the distance was the long slender finger of Uzbekistan that pokes out into her neighbour's western border. Uzbeks make up the larger part of the city's population, a sore point amongst many of the ethnic Kyrgyz and one that – in June 2010 – resulted in grotesque acts of violence and thousands of people fleeing to safety across the border.

The temperature was a comfortable twenty something now, at last a happy medium between the punishing heat and the icy winds, perfect conditions for the wedding party in the middle of which I was standing. I met the same crowd again down in the city where their fleet of 30 gleaming BMWs (dirt poor country fighting for survival?) took over a square to drive around a statue of Lenin, still an iconic figure 20 years after the communist collapse. This unmistakeable cortege seemed to pop up all over the place and it was later explained to me that according to local tradition the happy couple should have photos taken at all of the city's major landmarks. So they weren't following me around after all.

* * * * *

As we discovered in eastern Luxembourg every country with a slightly hilly region refers to its prized possession as Little Switzerland. But why stop at that, why doesn't somebody go one better and take the so-far unclaimed nickname

83

of Little Kyrgysztan? This country is five times larger, home to 88 mountain ranges and has as many as forty peaks above 6000 metres. The highest, Pobeda Peak, is over 7400m. Compare this to Mont Blanc, the best the Alps can offer at 4800m and you have Mike Tyson taking on Ronnie Corbett.

Not surprisingly the flight from Osh in the south to Bishkek in the north crossed over mountains for most of the way. It took just an hour in a rickety old plane but the contrast between the cities of departure and arrival couldn't have been greater had I been strapped into a rocket for a week. Gone were the fancy hats and the traditional costumes and the ever-present smell of shashlik cooking at the roadside. This was a land of jeans and mini-skirts, I-pods and mobiles, Coca-Cola and pizza.

The trees that lined the wide boulevards gave a pleasing impression initially but once the surface had been scratched it eroded rather quickly. Most of the buildings were grey and very Soviet; the important ones noticeably bigger, uglier, and surrounded by acres of unnecessary concrete. The many parks looked sad and neglected, the grass overgrown and the fountains long since waterless. Garbage gathered everywhere and the hours of darkness gave the unlit streets a mildly sinister edge.

On the plus side it was refreshing to have more variety, to meet people who could speak English, to have a bundle of dirty clothes returned as a clean, gift-wrapped package. I used the time to set up plans for a journey into rural Kyrgyzstan and arranged with a local tour operator for a guide to take me trekking across the mountains four days hence. We agreed that the expedition would start out from Karakol, a town at the far end of the country's largest lake in the north-east corner, and that on returning from it (positive thinking) I would be driven over the border to Almaty, the commercial hub of Kazakhstan.

The Silk Road Lodge in Bishkek was a peculiar hotel but the staff were extremely helpful. I outlined the itinerary and they arranged for a driver to take me to the lake and beyond with a two day-stopover en-route in the "alpine village" of Kochkor. The manager even called ahead to speak to the folk at the Community Based Tourism (CBT) office there who would make arrangements for me to stay with a family and take in a visit to a nearby jailoo. Which you now have to guess is either a) a prison b) a toilet c) a form of igloo or d) none of the above.

The pretty picture-postcard image of Kochkor, so vividly created by the otherwise excellent Lonely Planet authors, was not merely shattered upon my arrival but obliterated into a billion tiny, worthless fragments. The car crawled slowly along the main street and I peered through the window feeling like a charity worker turning up in the wake of a disaster. The road was wide and empty, silent and ugly. It was a world of junk and rubble where things that used to be were no more.

The beauty of the green, snow-capped mountains in all directions had the effect of accentuating the plight of the sad, dreary village. It was a culture shock I really hadn't expected and it was only the enthusiasm of the lovely CBT lady that stifled the fast-emerging thoughts of an escape bid. She had fixed it that tomorrow I would be collected at 9am and taken off to a jailoo and today, right now, I would go to the homestay where my hostess awaited.

She was tiny, quite elderly and utterly charming. There are people whose grace and gentleness is such that the absence of a common language is no barrier at all and this lady was most definitely amongst that number. Her pleasant demeanour lifted my spirits, convinced me to make the most of a short visit, and I felt substantially less miserable for an afternoon walk and a pre-dinner nap. The house was impeccably clean and, in keeping with local tradition, the room was decorated with large brightly-patterned rugs across the floor and two of the walls. A pile of quilts and mattresses was stacked in the corner, next to a large wooden dresser that housed old photos and a full series of encyclopaedias behind a glass door. A single, extremely dim light, dangled from the ceiling, soon to be supported by my torch to allow the option of reading. Without doubt I would be warm and comfortable for the night but by day, despite my new found optimism, I couldn't help but reflect that a typical Central Asian house was rather less cosy than a morgue.

The driver arrived at 9am as agreed. He offered neither a smile nor the faintest glimmer of warmth, and as with a number of people I'd encountered, looked puzzled by my attempts at friendliness. I'm old, I've had a shit life and I've got nothing at all to be cheerful about was very much his message. He pointed to the door, led me grumpily to the ancient Lada, bounced us along the potholed sidestreets and silently steered us out of town.

An hour later we were climbing high on a mountain track into a world that seemed too wild and remote to support any form of human life. I couldn't imagine what we were going to find at the top, all I knew is that we were on our way to a jailoo. Another half hour passed and when it seemed we would be winding up the hillside for ever Mr Miseryguts cut the engine and invited me to disembark.

It had taken almost two hours but the view alone was worth every second. Miles and miles of bright green fields, wild flowers, a storybook landscape scattered with the contrasting colours and shapes of the many animals that grazed in the sunshine. My eyes eventually sorted them into groups of horses, sheep and cows and then followed the thin grey line, the track we'd ascended, as far down as the tiny specks that made up the villages in the distance. The only sign of human life was a yurt adjacent to a sky blue trailer with the word WELCOME incongruously painted on a piece of wood above its door.

Bobby, an unusual name for a Kyrgyz herder I couldn't help think, introduced himself, his wife, their three grown up sons and the single grandchild. This was it, the jailoo, and lest you plumped for answers a) b) or c) it's a high pasture where country folk set up camp in the summer to offer their animals a new place to feed. I smiled and shook hands with every human I could see, ascertained that Kyrgyz was their only language (not even Russian, though they did understand my *spasiba)* and I quickly came to the conclusion that we wouldn't be doing a whole lot of talking. Then I looked out at the views again, gestured my immense satisfaction at their location of summer camp and started to wonder what else a jailoo visit could possibly entail.

As though reading my mind Bobby pointed me into the trailer for tea and bread with cream and blueberry jam, all of which was extremely pleasant, and a cup of kumys, which was extremely repulsive. I'd read about this national drink, fermented mare's milk, but at no point had I imagined that this innocent-looking stuff would be quite so disgusting. The closest comparison I can offer would be a mix of white emulsion and turpentine, a toxic, fume-laden cocktail you might find in a jam jar in your shed playing host to a stiff and rusty old paint brush.

The CBT lady had suggested I explore the pastures on horseback and she had evidently conveyed to my jailoo host, by way of an ancient and highly secret mode of mountain communication (probably mobile phone), that I was willing to give it a go. Somewhat reticently, I should add, given that my equine experience to that point had been restricted to a school pony-trekking outing, and that said pony had despatched me back to Mummy with fractured arm in plaster. Anyway, it was too late for loss of bottle, the nags were being prepared for action.

In the deaf and dumb world to which I was fast growing accustomed there was no way of explaining my lack of horsemanship or the burning desire to return intact, preferably within the hour or, better still, twenty minutes. All I could do was put on a smile, feign bravery, climb into the saddle and exchange waves with my old mucker Bobby as his son, my new guide, led the way up the mountain.

The horse walked very slowly and stooped down for a nibble whenever he felt the urge. The sun was warm now, the scenery absolutely glorious and everything in that majestic garden was as rosy as could be. More plodding, more stopping, often more stopping than plodding. And so the first hour passed by.

There was no indication after two hours of indifferent progress that a return to base was imminent. My left leg was cooking to an embarrassingly bright pink below the shorts and I was starting to get hungry, dare I say even a teeny bit bored. It was time to add just a little spice, to start taking the bull by the horns, or the horsey equivalent. So I gave Neddy a sharp whip across the buttocks – known in Kyrgyzstan as a Max Moseley – whilst making loud clicking noises and viciously jabbing his soft underbelly with as much power as my heels could muster. It was time to teach that lazy nag just who was bossing the show.

Whip, click, heels and away we went into a world of utter pandemonium. A rag doll atop a rampaging beast, all I recall for certain was that every three seconds my little peach of a bottom was hurled skywards only to come crashing down onto the crazy animal with the force of an angry ocean lashing the rocks. With every stride I gritted my teeth, let out a pointless curse and tried to prepare for the next violent assault on my coccyx. OW!..ya bastard… OW! ya bastard…OW! ya bastard….A man in a wheelchair pushed down a steep, never-ending flight of steps.

But it did end. In fact, the horse probably kept up the trot for only thirty seconds by which time the balance of power had been well and truly restored. From that point on he ambled and munched and stopped to drink water whenever he felt like and for another three hours we gently toured the mountains. Only once in that time did we part company; he was tied up and rested while I paddled and collected water from one of the many crystal clear mountain streams.

By the time we returned to Bobby & Co my buttocks and patience were both in shreds, I was badly dehydrated and the legs had turned a frightening shade of maroon. Not dissimilar in fact to the colour of the beetroot soup Mrs Bobby had prepared for my homecoming. Once again I found myself sitting in the dining shed for a family slurp, making conversation with sign language and gazing out through the door at the breathtaking valley below. The sociable Bobby seemed happy and playful and even managed to get a half smile out of Mr Miseryguts, perhaps on account of their having spent the afternoon preparing the "day out to a jailoo" invoice that was soon to come my way.

* * * * *

There was more pleasure in leaving Kochkor than there had been in arriving and I was in good spirits for the morning drive to Karakol. The evening before I'd rewarded myself with a Baltika beer and a plate of spicy Chinese noodles (*laghman*) in the local "restaurant", a now familiar sort of eatery with bare walls, a tiled floor, and a bright fluorescent light. This followed by a walk to the back of the town, best remembered for the sad old man with vodka legs and the discovery of the derelict open-air stadium. In fading light, with the cold evening air biting into my face, I'd stood for a long time on top of its outer wall and admired the silver roof of the mosque in the distance where it poked out through the trees at the foot of the mountains. Few sporting venues could compete for such a dramatic setting so what a sombre experience it was to see the abandoned terraces, the broken windows of the changing rooms, the weeds and wild flowers growing round the goal posts. Yet another poignant reminder that life after communism is sometimes more hopeless than communism itself.

We followed the road to the north of the vast lake, an attractive coastline massacred by holiday villages created for wealthy Russians. Some of the buildings were old, some were new, but it didn't make much difference either way. Ancient or modern, ugliness is ugliness and this, alas, very much a Soviet speciality. Fat people with white bodies waddled around through the rubble, tacky shops dangled buckets and spades and all manner of inflatable objects. It reminded me of going to North Wales as a kid.

Lake Issyk-Kol is an impressive 180 kms long and the second largest saline lake in the world (after the Caspian Sea, which isn't a sea at all). The deep blue of the still water contrasted beautifully with the surrounding snow-capped peaks and it was a relief to see that the shoreline towards its eastern end had been far less damaged. Here the elegant trees and golden fields gave rise to much greater optimism and as we coasted into the town of Karakol, now close to the country's eastern border with China, I felt much more positive about the days ahead.

If all went as arranged I would be collected from Jamilya's B+B the following morning and led into the mountains for a 200 km trek. Only now had the magnitude of this undertaking really sunk in. Just because I had a pair of bashed up boots and a flimsy sleeping bag did it really mean I was fully prepared for an expedition on this scale? And what about my dodgy ankle from years of football abuse? As the thought went through my head we passed another stadium, decaying but not yet disused, and my mind was once again in the present as we pulled up at the door of Jamilya's. I checked in, drank tea, ate sweets as an act of politeness, then went for a walk.

Karakol is a town of over 60,000 people and it immediately struck me as another shabby, disappointing offering. It felt grim and impoverished and had that border town feel, delivering an unspoken message that this was a place one should not hang around for any longer than was absolutely necessary. The main street provided little more excitement than a line of currency exchange offices, all advertising identical rates to swap Kyrgyz Soum for Euro, US Dollars, Russian Roubles or Kazhak Tenge, and my gut feeling was to get back indoors without further ado. The sight and sound of a dog being crushed beneath a car was the last thing I needed.

The optimism was ebbing but a couple of unusual points of interest popped up to save the day. Both were places of worship. A remarkable wooden cathedral with five yellow onion-shaped domes had made a comeback after years of enforced closure under the years of anti-religious Soviet rule and an old mosque, built like a Chinese temple, stood out amongst the drab and dusty streets to the west of town. But my biggest thrill of all was finding an internet café with lightning fast computers and a smart, modern little hotel just around the corner where I reserved a room for five days hence.

* * * * *

Jamilya had broken with local tradition and embellished the four upstairs bedrooms with beds. It was impossible not to observe from the landing that each of the separate quarters had a distinctive and brightly coloured theme and I was lucky enough to be allocated the unforgettable purple. Meanwhile, down in the lounge, it was very much business as usual: table & dresser, tea & sweets, nuts & raisins, photos & encyclopaedias.

A pretty young lady, name of Marina, arrived as agreed after breakfast.

Her smile and impressive command of English offered the best possible introduction and, whilst she wasn't exactly the guide I'd visualised, it was a happy old camper that clambered aboard the minibus. She was my "social guide, to do the cooking and the translation", she explained without so much as a nudge nudge wink wink, and the blokes inside the bus turned out to be our mountain guide and three porters. All of which filled me with a rather overwhelming sense of privilege. It had never occurred to me that a whole team of people would need to be assembled to get the white man over the mountain.

It was 11am by the time we started walking, a gentle sloping path alongside one of the many white water rivers. An idyllic setting but, for the first time since arriving in the country, the sky was looking uncertain and it was no surprise when the rain appeared just as we stopped for tea and packed lunches. The weather got steadily worse by mid-afternoon and the prospect of traipsing through the mountains for five days wearing a light jacket and a pair of shorts was diminishing in its appeal by the minute. A situation made worse when my left foot slipped off a stepping stone and dunked me up to the knee in an icy stream, and worse still when I did the same ten minutes later with the other leg. Bent double, with my head cowered into the oncoming wind, I was just going through the process of thinking how miserable life can be when you're cold and wet when the rain finally stopped... and the hail began.

My hands had turned blue, all fingers paralysed in a half-grip position, and my teeth had started chattering uncontrollably. I was standing in a field, in a hailstorm, wet from the waist up, soaked from the waist down. The only bit of good news was that three of the lads were putting the tents up, an indication that there would be no more walking for the day. At least a chance to change into dry clothes, take shelter, maybe even stop trembling.

The missing porter appeared in the distance, his bright jacket standing out against the black sky, and I noticed as he drew closer to the rest of the party that he didn't look ever so happy either. He yelled something to Marina through the noise of the weather and she explained to me, the smile now gone, that he had fallen in to one of the rivers. He was drenched from head to toe, as indeed was all the stuff that he'd been carrying; the poor guy must have felt more miserable than I did. And only then did the penny drop…within his dripping wet 30 kilo pack was my precious little bag of dry clothes.

But they weren't *dry* clothes, were they boys and girls? They were the wettest fucking clothes you could possibly imagine, a sodden lead-weight package handed over with a mumbled apology and dumped unceremoniously into the corner of the tent. I'd managed to get the boots and socks and shorts off and could think of nothing else to do other than sit there trembling on the lumpy groundsheet, a sorry huddled figure clad only in wet walking jacket and, if you must know, extremely damp underpants. The only slither of good news was that my sleeping bag had been elsewhere and thus had been spared.

The team worked hard to try to cheer me up. A calor gas heater was introduced to the tent, followed by tea, hot soup and, later, plastic bottles filled with boiling water. My blue hands returned to a sort of crimson as I lay there in the 3-seasons sleeping bag, reflecting that this was obviously the season it hadn't been designed for. The bottles proved an essential tool but the pleasure of their warmth was replaced by the fear of their possibly melting, or simply leaking on to my bare flesh and scalding my legs beyond repair. Just what on earth was I doing here?

By 3am it was freezing cold, and once again, so was I. My back hurt from the bone hard ground and everything else ached with the tension of trying to keep warm. There had been far more hours of lying awake than sleeping, ample opportunity to reflect on camping as a leisure pursuit, and more specifically, to question whether there had ever been a point in my life when I'd actually enjoyed it. Most certainly four more nights of this did not seem like a good idea, in fact it seemed the craziest, most depressing prospect known to man. At least I was the only paying guest, I was the boss, and if I decided we weren't schlepping across the mountains with a bag of dripping laundry, my entire wardrobe for the next four days, that was entirely my prerogative. By 3.30 am, if not before, my mind was made up. Enough was enough.

When darkness lifted I poked into the spongy mess of clothes to see if there was anything at all that might be redeemable. To my surprise there were a few garments in the "extremely damp" category, as distinct from "piss wet through", so I took the more promising little bundle in hand as I unzipped the canvas wall and scrambled out into the soggy field. It was a relief to stand up, to regain the freedom of movement and to be able to put up a challenge against the elements after more than twelve hours of feeble capitulation.

The cows took a break from their dawn munch to watch the strange man in sandals spreading his clothes out on the rocks. Little did they know that he would be putting them all back in his wet bag a couple of hours later and buggering off to a nice warm hotel to reconsider his immediate future as a Central Asian explorer. Then they stared in unison as the weird human walked up the side of the mountain, breathing air loudly into his lungs and flapping his arms like a flightless bird.

The sun came up over the highest of the peaks and announced to the valley that a new day had begun. It mattered not to the cows that wandered around regardless of the hour or to the white bubbling river that flowed around the clock... but it made all the difference in the world to me. The sight and the sound of raw nature reminded me why I was there in the first place and what had prompted me to embark on this journey without really thinking what might be involved. I should have known it would be tough at times, maybe most of the time, nature always is, but it only serves to make the rewards that much sweeter when finally they arrive. And by the time the rest of the team had emerged to share the new day, I already knew that we wouldn't be turning back.

* * * * *

The sun shone for the next four days. We walked through meadows and valleys and followed pathways through the pine forests. We traversed boulders and scrambled over piles of loose scree to reach mountain passes almost 4000 metres above sea level and we climbed up to alpine lakes as green as the waters off the islands of Fiji. We saw cows and horses grazing amongst the wild flowers, cashing in on the final days of summer, and at night we camped alongside rivers that moved at the speed of a train. We feasted on hot soup and pasta and all sorts of other tasty treats and my smiling team of servants brought tea and biscuits to my tent as the meals were being prepared. Day one was soon a distant memory. Camping wasn't so bad after all.

The thirty hours of walking to cross the Valley of Flowers, the Teleti Pass and then the Ala Kol Pass brought numerous opportunities to chat to Marina and learn more about her country. She was 24, born in Bishkek and carried a Kyrgyz passport but her nationality, as with all but one of the lads, was Russian. She'd lived in Kyrgyzstan all her life but her ancestors were from Russia and, as with many people in the country, she couldn't speak the local tongue. It hadn't been an obstacle, she assured me, newspapers and TV channels were available in both languages and it was easy to get by. She did concede that there was a move in some quarters towards Kyrgyzstan becoming less "Russian" in its ways but even the folk that were beating the nationalist drum had spent most of their lives under Soviet rule and were often unable to speak Kyrgyz themselves. All a bit odd you might think – but then how many residents of Cardiff speak Welsh?

On the final day the minibus collected us according to plan and I was duly delivered to the door of the Hotel Amir, tucked away on one of Kochkor's more pleasant leafy streets. It was the best thirty quid's worth of hotel I've ever known. Smart, stylish, the breakfast even offered a touch of sophistication, three adjectives that don't come out of the bag very often where Kyrgyzstan is concerned. The shower and the laundry service performed the required miracles and my last day in the country offered nothing but pleasure. A Russian restaurant round the corner did the business and even had a menu in English to tempt you into such delights as "cornstarch in jelly with vinegar sauce". It all left me with a happier memory of the town, although the stinking, rotting corpse of the dead dog from the week before was a stark reminder of its many problems.

Marina and the driver returned the next morning for the last leg of our journey together. The deal was that we would head in a north-easterly direction to the Kazakh border, cross the Karkara Valley and from there motor west to Almaty, all of which would be a full day's drive. They would then continue home to Bishkek on the fast road that links the two cities.

In no time at all we'd left Karakol behind and re-entered a world of wide valleys where entire families work the land, when it isn't frozen, and ruddy-faced men gallop around on their horses. I'd read somewhere that these distinctive people originated in Mongolia, which would explain their physical features and a passion for travelling around on horseback. With the sun shining there could be no finer riding country than these wide, lush meadows at the foot of the Tien Shan mountains and had I not been spoiled throughout the week with some of the world's most beautiful scenery it might have been tempting to find somewhere to stay there. But I felt it was the right time to move on and as always there was that tingle of excitement and apprehension when we reached the isolated border post and the wooden barrier blocking the road.

Marina got out, took the passports into the office and returned several minutes later muttering the very word that I didn't want to hear. Problem. She relayed the story. We were still on the Kyrgyz side and the gentleman inside the brick hut was not satisfied with the entry stamp I'd been given on arrival. Yes, the visa had been date-stamped and initialled but why wasn't there a second stamp on the adjacent page? To my way of thinking it was a ruse that had dollars written all over it but I resolved to keep calm and headed into the office with a contrived smile.

The uniformed official pointed at my visa and Marina translated what had already been said. So what did he expect me to do? Return to the Tajik border hundreds of miles away and request another stamp? I elected not to make that suggestion even as a joke for fear that he might deem it the best solution. Instead he went for the stalemate stare, then the resigned shrug of the shoulders. It could easily have meant "it's your problem mate, you'll have to work it out", the ploy they so enjoy and one that only a wallet can resolve. I returned the silent gesture, we smiled at each other, and there was a long nervous pause. Then another shrug, the arm raised and the rubber stamp thumped onto the page. I was released without charge from Kyrgyzstan.

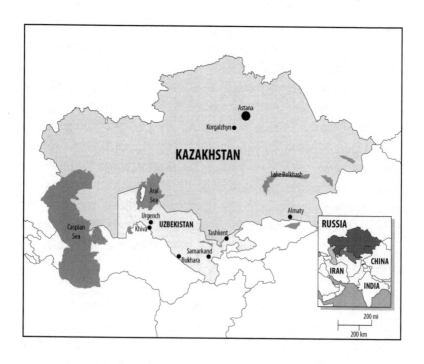

Kazakhstan and Uzbekistan

Kazakhstan is one of the largest countries you will ever read about. It covers more than a million square miles, spans two continents and is the biggest landlocked nation on the planet. It dwarfs all ten-letter rivals and not even a four-letter country can get remotely close. I could go on, so I think I will. Try adding together the areas of UK, France and Germany, Holland and Belgium, Spain and Portugal, Italy and Greece and Poland and Austria and Switzerland. I did, as you might have guessed, and found that not only would all twelve fit comfortably inside Kazakhstan but, to my great satisfaction, there would still be enough room to chuck in Albania.

The five hour drive to Almaty from the remote Kyrgyzstan border post took us across a spectacular moonscape and through a series of rural communities, best remembered for their roadside stalls with rich and colourful displays of fresh fruit and vegetables. It was just getting dark as we hit the outskirts of the city but even through the fading light I could see that this was going to be a very different experience from either of the previous Stans. This place had the feeling of money, the sense that in Monopoly terms I'd thrown a couple of double sixes and fast forwarded from the Old Kent Road to something more in line with Piccadilly or Leicester Square.

It was the end of the road with my friendly twosome from Bishkek, they had done me proud, and as we said our farewells on the streets of what seemed such a magnificent city centre I felt a nagging stab of guilt, even a sense of sadness for them: having travelled all day they had to drive for another five hours through the darkness, back to the very much poorer cousin that was their native Kyrgyzstan. I hoped that they didn't feel the same.

The map from the guidebook steered me up and across the grid of streets towards the famous landmark of the Hotel Kazakhstan. In a city where accommodation is reputedly more expensive than London this one was indicated as good value for money and seemed a logical place to choose as a base. The 26 storey tower was impossible to miss, not just because of its sheer size but the enormity of the digits that glowed on the side of the building. 2030. I checked it off against my watch, satisfied myself that it was indeed exactly half past eight, and stepped into the lobby with credit card in hand.

* * * * *

Mr Nursultan Nazarbaev is the only president the country has ever had. Whether this is due entirely to his popularity – in 2005 he was voted in for a further seven years – or the fact that mysterious things happen to those who challenge him is open to question, but on the face of it Kazakhstan has done rather well under his stewardship (repressive though it may be). I lay there on my overpriced bed and enjoyed reading about the recent history, particularly grateful for the luxury of not needing to use a torch.

This is a country with vast resources and huge ambition and the unshakeable President has set out a series of clear objectives for the next two decades. The book made interesting reading, some of which I'll tell you about later, and went on to explain that because the year 2030 has been set as the goal, this date appears as a reminder in public places throughout the country. Sure enough, as I found out the next morning, it is always half past eight on the walls of the Hotel Kazakhstan.

The humongous hotel building resembled an airport terminal and the mega breakfast buffet pulled in an army of business suits alongside my "T-shirts and trainers" comrades. The food was plentiful but grim and I'm sorry to report that my attempt at light social intercourse with the restaurant staff triggered little more than the disdainful glare one might expect of a pit bull. For a brief moment I'd almost forgotten that in this part of the world smiling is the exclusive domain of the mentally retarded but at least today the grumpiness amused me, nothing could dampen my excitement. The sun was shining and a new city there for the taking.

The pavements of Almaty were impeccably clean, the parks well tended, the lawns and flowers sprinkled and nurtured. The people looked smart, the cars looked smart, the buses looked smart. In all directions there were trees and more trees and just to the south, towering above the city, the rugged mountains bearing the last (or was it the first?) snows of the year. The geography reminded me of Teheran, another city with affluent suburbs climbing up the hillside and a cable car to shuttle tourists up to the higher peaks. It all felt, well... civilised, pleasant, a thoroughly decent place to live.

Almaty is tucked away in the far south-eastern corner and is easily the largest city in the gargantuan oval of Kazakhstan. So it came as a surprise to many when the President announced that with effect from 1997 it would no longer serve as the country's capital. Following Brazil's example of the 1960s (in itself, a dangerous tactic) a small town thousands of miles from anywhere was nominated to fly the flag and an obscene amount of money was poured in to create a sort of politician's Disneyland. Astana, way up in the northern Steppe, wouldn't know what had hit it.

By all accounts this move didn't go down well with the folk who were obliged to relocate and as I wandered through Almaty's elegant parks, and past a seemingly endless supply of chic bars and restaurants, it wasn't difficult to understand why. This was a proud city surrounded by mountains to ski in the winter and lakes to picnic in the (albeit, very much shorter) summer. Why would anybody want to be transferred half way to Siberia?

I enjoyed the city's greenness by day and the variety of its restaurants in the evenings. And having read that the nightclub scene was amongst the best in the world, with Deep-Tech (?) and Tribal (?) and American House (?) on offer through till 6 and 7 in the mornings, a small part of me was actually tempted to go along and find out what all the fuss was about. They probably wouldn't play Rod Stewart or Simon and Garfunkel or any other of my favourites but what the hell, you only live once.

Weighing against this nascent spirit of nocturnal adventure was the fact that, under normal circumstances, I would happily opt for the solace of a dentist's chair in favour of the noise and claustrophobia of a night club. And then there would be the inevitable jet-laggy disorientation for the rest of the week as a consequence of being out of bed all night. How would I keep awake that late anyway? Unless…well, I suppose I could get up early and pop along before breakfast, or perhaps even get room service to deliver some cereals in the hours of darkness. But just what sort of cool dude would do that?

I'd even got as far as checking the map for the hippest clubs and calculating proximity to the hotel when I came across the paragraph on "face control". This was all new stuff to me, the process by which the doormen of the must-be-seen-in establishments ensure that only the young, the rich and the beautiful are granted admission. It was the final straw. Foregoing a shedload of money and sleep for a night of ear-pounding misery was one thing but no way was I running the risk of humiliation at the hands of a bald thug with muscles in his snot: "Sorry mate, you're too old and too bloody ugly. And by the way, you've got Corn Flakes stuck to your chin."

* * * * *

It was time to make a new plan, Stan, and the Kondor Travel Company seemed willing to help. The lady there was ever so bubbly, possibly to the point of being barking mad, a theory that gained weight when at one point she actually burst out laughing. It turned out she'd spent time in Europe, learned to speak fluent German and, on this dazzling performance, had evidently picked up peculiar foreign traits such as joviality. Her name was Zhupar and she sorted my flight up to Astana, made a call to fix me up with a family in a village for a few days and booked an onward ticket to Tashkent in Uzbekistan.

The hard work done for the day, I walked through Paniflov Park and found a seat (green, nicely painted, no graffiti) in the sunshine to admire the immense Russian Orthodox cathedral at close quarters. Now functioning again as a place of worship this stunning piece of architecture, predominantly peach in colour and made entirely of wood, had been used as a museum and concert hall throughout the years of Soviet-enforced atheism. The colours were breathtaking: a multi-domed roof with a pattern of green and red diamond shapes, gold minarets pointing up to the bluest of skies and all surrounded by a blanket of dahlias and marigolds in full bloom to add the finishing touch. An idyllic picture: oh yes, give me a park bench instead of a night club any day of the week.

The next building I was to visit could not have been more different. The Arasan Baths is also a domed edifice but it's a depressingly grey, ugly mass of concrete with tiny slits that serve as windows. My initial thought was that the place had been abandoned, it somehow seemed too gruesome to be operational as any kind of public facility, let alone a venue dedicated to health and relaxation. Yet there had to be something going on because a small group of vendors had gathered at the entrance to offer bunches of birch twigs bound together like tennis rackets. I was keeping to a safe distance, watching and wondering, when a very large Kazakh couple stepped into view, bought two bunches, then headed up the steps and through a swinging door. I didn't want to do it, but I'd brought my towel specially and I knew there was no turning back.

The inside, let's call it an entrance hall, was marginally grimmer than the prison-like exterior. Though I didn't know what I was paying for, I handed over the notes requested in sign language by the charm-free lady at the desk and walked through a door to which she had vaguely pointed. It led to a changing room, or rather a sort of warehouse with concrete floors, bashed up lockers and lots of naked men.

I tried to blend quickly and as soon as my pants were down there was a man in white T-shirt and trousers standing behind me. He was pointing, offering something and indicating a price and after several minutes of nervous confusion it became evident that he was a masseur running through his menu of treatments. In for a penny, in for a pound, I agreed to upper body only, but flashed him two fives with my hands to indicate I needed ten minutes to wander.

The adjacent room was tiled in a shiny brown colour that brought back memories of toilets in railway stations when I was a kid. Who can forget that overpowering smell of urine, the 1d slot machine for the right to sit down, the crude poems on the walls and those strange diagrams with phone numbers of girls who promised all manner of entertainment? (Not a bad pennysworth, in hindsight.) This place didn't smell of wee but as I walked by the concave shower cubicles I couldn't help thinking it was a venue more suited to torture and execution than any form of leisure pursuit.

A wooden door, thick and heavy, opened into an incredibly hot room, a wooden box with dark brown walls, dark brown benches and an array of human bodies of all shapes and sizes. Men sat in rows in complete silence, birch twigs in hand, all completely naked except for those that had dressed for the occasion in ...white felt hats! What on earth was going on? I chose a space to ensure full view of the headgear, placed my towel on the searing hot seat and after only a matter of seconds the remarkable show began.

It was one of the be-hatted, a huge man with a sagging belly and an extraordinarily small penis who stood up and unashamedly started thrashing himself with his miniature broomstick. He was sweating profusely and clearly having the time of his life as he exhaled loudly with each blow of the branches upon his back and buttocks. Others stood up and joined in, some trading swipes with their friends, as I just sat there, a quiet self-conscious Brit contemplating what a strange world we live in.

Outside in the corridor my man was waiting, as those with the promise of dollars can always be relied upon to do. He gestured to a slab in the corner and indicated that I should lie face down such that my genitals occupy the same spot as the twenty thousand scrotums that went before. Then he set about throwing buckets of warm water over me as though washing his car, a not unpleasant experience and a sharp contrast to the activities that were soon to follow.

I think the most memorable manoeuvre was the digging of his elbows into my back, the third cycle of which provoked the release of a grotesque, tortured scream that could only have come from me. Whether he always did three, or just carried on till his clients could take no more, is something I will always wonder. It didn't get any better when he climbed up and went for a walk along my spine and, though I didn't exactly take it like a man, the teeth clenching and controlled breathing replaced what could easily have degenerated into a total mental breakdown. The instruction to sit up and face the lunatic led me to believe that things might get better but the simultaneous jabbing of his fingers deep into my ears soon put paid to that one. It seemed the objective was to try to get his fingertips to meet at a halfway point inside my skull and when that didn't work he simply took my ears in his hands and screwed them up tightly like bits of scrap paper destined for the waste bin. Then six more buckets to slosh me down before he muttered the only word of English he knew. "Finish".

He probably thought, bless him, that my big smile was a measure of how much I'd enjoyed his company. It had certainly been an experience – and one that won't be forgotten – but my back hurt like hell and as I hobbled towards the circular swimming pool, bracing myself for some icy misery, I couldn't help thinking that the little chap might have caused some permanent damage. Why hadn't I just gone to the museum like normal tourists do?

* * * * *

I did make it to the state museum and there were a handful of normal tourists. They were all European visitors and presumably as narked and perplexed as I was to find that the Kazakh authorities had declined to translate the labelled exhibits into any other language. Was it too much to ask, just half a day's work that would serve one of their key attractions for the next fifty years? Customer service Soviet-style, the "why lend a hand when it's so much easier to give someone the finger" approach, later to be trialled and perfected in the UK by British Telecom.

The one section that was offered in English detailed the mind-boggling depth of the country's natural resources. The Tengiz Oilfield in the west was discovered in 1979 and quite a discovery it was: a lake of oil with a 50 mile circumference, thought capable of turning out between six and nine billion barrels of beautiful black gold. Added to this Kazakhstan boasts phenomenal reserves of gas and almost every chemical element that appears on the Periodic Table can be found somewhere in the country. All of which means loadsa money, but in whose pockets is it going to end up?

The museum was not the most exciting but my final evening in Almaty was uplifting in every sense. The Kok-Tobe cable car hoisted me up the mountain just in time for the setting of the sun and a glass of Baltika on the café terrace at the peak. As the orange ball prepared to dip I picked out the now-familiar landmarks amidst the urban sprawl and the ubiquitous cranes pushing the city limits in three directions. The oil money was floating in the breeze, the architects enjoying a feeding frenzy not seen since plastic surgeons arrived in Hollywood. Out with the ugly grey slabs of Soviet concrete, in with the tall, elegant towers of glass. As many as space would allow.

It was a stylish finale to a stylish city and the right time to move on. Tomorrow would be a different adventure, an early flight north to the new capital and a drive into the countryside to stay with an unknown family. A strange thing to do really, I concluded as I lay there on the bed, bags packed once again and passport in hand ready for safe stowage. Not forgetting the little slip of paper from the immigration police, the one that read in perfect English: "All visitors must register within 5 days. Failure to do so is punishable by law".

Oh shit. Shit. Shitty shit shit.

* * * * *

It was 7am Sunday morning when I poked my head into the offices of the Immigration Police at Almaty airport. The hotel bod had told me it would do no good, I would have to go to a special department in Astana known as OVIR and, to make it worse, Monday was a holiday. Public offices would most definitely be closed, my late registration would be even later, the punishment would likely be more severe. Thanks for that mate.

He was right of course, the regular uniform blokes at the airport understood my problem but waved me away with the word "Astana" and pointed to the calendar two days hence. At least they didn't tear up my boarding card, slap on the handcuffs and take me off for a lesson in what happens to folk who mess with their deadlines.

There were very few passengers aboard and how a whole row to oneself makes flying feel that much more luxurious, doesn't it? I studied the map in the in-flight magazine, a temptation I can never resist, and plotted the route across the miles of empty land. Kazakhstan has few cities of any note, is almost entirely flat save for its eastern borders with China and Kyrgyzstan yet, quite incredibly, its entire population is little more than 15 million people. Less than that of Holland, a country one sixty-fifth its size.

The most distinctive geographical features are the areas covered by water, most significantly the Caspian Sea in the south-west, the largest lake in the world, and the Aral Sea, which used to be the fourth largest until the catastrophe we will discuss in the catastrophe paragraph below. We had just flown over Lake Kapshagay, only 70 miles north of Almaty and about to be marketed as Kaz Vegas (!!) with a raft of new casinos, golf courses, even a racecourse, and an eight lane highway under construction to ferry the punters in. And my destination for the day was the village of Korgalzhyn and the wetland region around Lake Tenghiz, just a tiny puddle on the map compared to the banana-shaped Lake Balkhash that we were shortly about to cross. I'd never heard of this one either, and suspect I'm not alone, but shouldn't we know about a lake that is almost twice the size of East Anglia?

It was the vastness and the emptiness of Kazakhstan that had once given rise to all sorts of Soviet ideas. This was the jewel in their crown, a playground rich with possibilities and far enough away from prying eyes to permit as much jiggery-pokery as they would see fit. In the 1950s they decided that these "Virgin Lands" would be ideal for cotton production so an irrigation system was created by diverting water from the rivers that fed the lake known as the Aral Sea. Not only did the system fail but over the next forty years the lake, that in the 1960s measured 400 x 280 kms, lost most of its water and shrivelled into two separate puddles. The fishing industry all but died and with it 60,000 jobs. The climate changed, it became dry and dusty and caused massive health problems for the local population. The wildlife, once so abundant, was almost eradicated. This project was one of the bigger communist-led disasters though not the biggest of all.

In the north-east of the country, close to the city of Semey, the Soviets carried out a programme of nuclear weapons testing over a forty year period. The people of the region were never officially told about it, let alone offered any advice or protection; they just knew that another test was being carried out every time the ground started to shake. It was only with the passing of years that the horrific consequences could start to be measured: half a million people dead or dying from cancer, grotesque genetic mutations, radiation-induced diseases on a terrifying scale. The protests that eventually came brought an almost immediate end to the project once Kazakhstan gained independence (1991) but for too many people, a number that will never be truly known, it was already far too late.

* * * * *

It was almost noon and a surprisingly pleasant 25 degrees when the plane taxied up to the blue dome of Astana airport. There was little activity in the passenger terminal on that Sunday lunchtime, thus my name was easy to spot amongst the small group of waiting people in the immaculately presented arrivals hall. The chap holding the piece of paper lowered it from chest height, shook me by the hand, and announced his name as Valihan.

Together we walked out to his car but as his English was zero, so the conversation was zero, and it all felt rather weird. Just who was he? A driver? My host? A bloke from a travel company? The silence was almost embarrassing but there was nothing else for it but to sit there and wait to see what might happen next.

The land was so flat and empty that the tall buildings of the city rose up in the distance like pyramids in the desert. The highway was wide and smooth as velvet and, as Valihan indicated with the word "Police" (one that everybody seems to know), the few cars it carried were monitored by speed cameras all the way into the southern fringes. The road was eerily silent and it took us only fifteen minutes to reach the centre, leaving time enough for a short tour of the capital city.

There was indeed a pyramid shaped building, and an enormous gold cylindrical one, and a peculiar blue-domed one, and one with fake icicles hanging from it, and one shaped like a Chinese pagoda... and this was just the start. We toured what is known as the Government Zone and my chauffeur pointed out the President's Palace and the sci-fi creations of the parliament buildings. Not a single person was there in sight, not one vehicle in the vast expanse of car parks. The only movement I could detect was a gentle flapping of the flags, distinctive pale blue with a yellow sun at the centre; hard to believe that this was the engine room of the world's ninth largest country. And what a peculiar, yet intriguing place: Las Vegas crossed with Dubai, with a small helping of Milton Keynes on the side.

Valihan looked pleased with my enthusiasm for his city (if it was his city?) and was now ready to get down to his core task of transporting me to Korgalzhyn. A dot on the map, a village that I'd tracked down on the internet, 140 kms from Astana and pretty much in the middle of nowhere. Its attraction, if you'll forgive the exaggeration, was its proximity to a protected wetland region that was, by all accounts, home to a fascinating array of birdlife. There were families in the community willing to put you up and show you the sights and, well...I thought I'd give it a whirl.

The road headed out in a south-westerly direction, a dead straight line across the Steppe. I remembered the term from schooldays and later checked its definition as a grassland plain too dry to support vegetation but not dry enough to constitute desert. And this was it, a green expanse of almost nothing as far as the eye could see. A few cows, the very occasional cluster of trees, a never-ending line of telegraph poles. The driver had nothing to do but rest his foot on the gas pedal and his hands on the wheel, breaking the tedium with a cigarette every fifteen minutes and a respectful raising of his palms to his face each time we passed a cemetery.

I'd almost forgotten that the Kazakhs are predominantly, at least in theory, an Islamic people. Nothing I'd seen thus far had indicated this but with almost half of the tiny population originating from outside the country anyway – mostly workers sent from Soviet Russia – the indifference to religion should not have been surprising. Up here in the north we were now close to the Russian border whereas the bigger concentration of true Kazakhs, and perhaps more devout Muslims, would be found in the south.

It took only an hour and a half to reach the family home on the edge of the village. I was greeted with warmth and without embarrassing formality by a man, a woman and what I guessed to be their teenage kids – but sadly the words of welcome were offered in a language of which I knew diddly squat. The smiling lady invited me to drop my bag off in a conventional-looking bedroom then led the way into the lounge where other guests were gathered. A scenario that for the hard-of-speaking-or-understanding-a-sodding-word had nightmare written all over it, until a lady came across to shake my hand and speak to me, in German! This was a result beyond my wildest dreams and whilst I am only a rusty intermediate, compared to Russki I was on home turf.

The house belongs to Marat and his wife. They have a son and a daughter. Marat has two brothers. She is married to one of them (points to grinning man). They live in Astana where she is a professor of German at the university. Valihan is Marat's other brother. No mention is made of a Mrs Valihan. Wow, how sehr gut it felt to rejoin the talking classes, to engage with people albeit through an interpreter. And also to explain, seek advice and request translation (make hay vile ze sun sheins) about my possibly being in deep shit with the authorities for being an unregistered alien on the run.

Life moved up another notch when a large lady with a mop of blonde hair walked into the room. "Hi – I'm Jessica, I'm from Portland, Oregon and I live close by here in Korgalzhyn. How ya doin'?" I hope my staring didn't seem rude. This was a remote village not so very far from Outer Mongolia and in the last five minutes I'd fast forwarded from a frustrated mute to an excited little boy on Santa's knee. "I'm doin' fantastic Jess. Bloody fantastic."

She'd been placed by the Peace Corps to help with the development of the National Park and had lived in this very house in the months following her arrival the previous year. This was a lovely family and great fun to be with, she assured me, I couldn't wish for better hosts. And with that, right on cue, Marat ushered us all to sit down at the lunch table and with the cheekiest of smirks, insisted that we make a start on what would be the first of his many bottles.

The dish of fresh pasta placed in the centre of the table was twice the size of a dustbin lid. This was Besbarmak, the national dish, covered with chunks of mutton (or often horsemeat) and on this occasion, by way of a series of toasts, washed down with several large shots of vodka. Marat, the jovial host, was in his element as Master of Ceremonies, ensuring that the men's glasses were drained quickly – especially mine – and replenished when he felt the moment was right. He was not only the head of the family but, according to Jessica, the much respected "character" of the village, and from his personality it was easy to see why. It was he who had set up my visit with the agency in Almaty, guaranteeing that an interpreter would be available for my tour of the lakes. Only now did Jessica discover, as Marat's grin widened further, that she had been nominated for the job.

The house was larger than others I'd seen and, true to the norm, would most kindly be described as functional rather than cosy. One of the few in the village with internal plumbing but on this day, as many other days, the water wasn't working and would have to be collected from a well in the street. After the high-tech, fast-growing cities of Almaty and Astana I was shocked to learn that public services here had all but collapsed, jobs in the countryside were almost non-existent, and since the end of the Soviet era, there was no money from the state to put things right. Even the small hospital couldn't afford heating in the winter and had to send patients home at night.

And in this part of the world, winter really does mean winter. At least six months a year of temperatures well below zero, often to minus 40C, and winds from Siberia blowing across the plains to make it feel substantially colder. If it's *possible* to feel colder than 40 below. Jessica tried to describe how hard the dark winter months are for the local people: burning coal to keep warm, surviving on a diet of potatoes and occasionally meat (if you have money) but no vegetables or salad or greens of any sort. She also touched on the misery of going outside in the night to use the toilet or, as she confessed with a smile, making alternative arrangements. And to think that these poor folk live on the same line of latitude as London, where one day of snow is a crisis and even the foxes live on M+S food from the dustbins.

The plan for the next day was an early morning trip to the lakes, back for lunch, then for me to borrow a bicycle and go cycling on my own. We all agreed on the times but after several more beers and a few shots of vodka Marat reversed the schedule, announcing with that cheeky grin that getting up early on a Monday would be a bad start to his week. Jessica then had a long discussion with him in Russian, after which she explained that it was time for me to remove all my clothing. Marat was ready to take me to his *banya*.

Across his back yard, beyond the parked cars, stood what looked for all the world like a garden shed. Perhaps the size of a single garage, and heated by an Aga-style stove in the wall, it was divided by walls into three separate sections: a changing area (a bench, three hooks), a washing area (hosepipe, barrel of water, shampoo) and a sauna (two benches, large bowl of boiling water). Marat and I got naked, passed directly through the wet zone into the heat of room number 3, sat down and closed the door. Then he popped out and returned with a grin and a bottle of beer, not at all out of character except that he poured most of it onto the white hot slab of concrete boiling the water in the corner.

First came the hiss, then the boozy fumes and then an intense heat that surely man was not designed to tolerate. A wave of torture that started with the scalding of the scalp and which slowly, steadily moved south, attacking the face and penetrating the earlobes as though they'd been nailed to the wall. I did all I could to contain the gasp, sensing from Marat's face that this was Kazakhstan v England, if only a friendly. He checked I was OK, offered me a swig of beer which I declined, then poured some more into the corner.

We sat through the whole process again, head bowed (at least mine was) and teeth clenched as the cloud of heat struck another vicious blow. The evil hissing, then silence. Hang in there lad, just hang in there. Pools of sweat formed, trickled and dripped on to the bench below. This is good for you, I repeated silently over and over, wondering how it could possibly be true. I turned towards Marat, who was no longer grinning, and to my relief he pointed to the door. It was time for shampoo and the simple pleasure of being washed down with buckets of warm water.

* * * * *

I woke up to a new day feeling pleasantly refreshed, an evening of beer and pickles, soup and vodka, obviously having done the trick. Everything about this homestay was turning out to be a remarkable experience and I lay in my bed thinking about Marat and his *banya* and the way his friends and family had come round to take turns in using it once the word was out that it was stoked up and ready to go. The more time I spent in this country, the more it was becoming obvious why the sauna and vodka played such a critical part in the lives of the people.

There were two bicycles, one with a flat tyre and another with a small frame and tiny wheels like those used by commuters who don't mind being laughed at. It didn't have any brakes or gears either but then why would you need them for cycling on terrain that is flat and empty for several thousand miles in all directions?! So I got on the strange little contraption, cycled through the village, took a look at the silver-domed mosque, and headed out into the fields.

The road that I followed soon offered a smaller track off to the right and a signpost to somewhere or something written in Cyrillic that was 5 kms away. Ideal. The sky was clear and the weather perfect and what better way to start the week than cycle across the Steppe in the summer sunshine. This was wide open space on a scale few people ever get to experience and the sheer vastness of it was more than adequate compensation for the fact that the landscape offered no variation. At least so I thought. But I was wrong.

After what seemed rather more than five kilometres a group of buildings appeared in the distance adjacent to a thin blue line that could only be a lake. Fifteen minutes more pedalling revealed that the community was no more, the houses had been abandoned and the agricultural machinery left to rust. The only sign of life, but a picture that would grace any calendar, was a group of twenty or so horses standing quietly at the shallow end of the lake. I pedalled towards them with great excitement and had almost reached the water's edge when it dawned on me that there were no brakes and only the most spectacular manoeuvre was going to keep me dry.

I stood by the lake, soaked in the silence and captured the scene on the camera. The sun was getting hotter, my water bottle almost empty and I knew the supply was less than adequate for the ride back. Still, if all went to plan I'd be sitting at Marat's lunch table within the hour. And how could that simple plan go awry, unless I suffered cardiac arrest or one of the tyres around those unconvincing little wheels had a puncture? At which point the power of suggestion encouraged me to look suspiciously towards the bike, and more specifically, to focus on what had become a rubber pancake beneath the rear wheel.

The good news is that my ticker held out for the long, thirsty walk home. Marat gave me a "Don't worry, mate" shrug when I showed him the knackered, deflated tyre, blissfully unaware that his knackered, deflated client had just had to leg it across Central Asia in the midday sun. I wanted to explain why I was late, tell him where this occurred, but instead we sat quietly at the table, munched on bread and soup and waited for Jessica. At least my consumption of ten consecutive glasses of water amused the rest of the family, who knew nothing of the bicycle story and had presumably only ever seen drinking on this scale performed with vodka.

For reasons that I will never know, Jessica didn't turn up. Marat seemed unfazed by this, even pleased at the prospect of a lads' day out, so as soon as his mate came round with the 4x4 I squeezed into the back seat with son and brother and the five of us set off across the plains. Windows down, breeze in the face, bottle of beer passed from hand to hand, this hinted at a bird-watching outing with a difference.

We were heading towards the Korgalzhyn Nature Reserve, a UNESCO-protected wetland area the size of Luxembourg. A massive delta comprising thirteen shallow lakes, of which Tengiz is far and away the largest, though as it turned out we found everything we wanted to see around the smaller lakes Sholak, Isei and the delightfully-named Sultankeldy. We'd been hurtling along rough tracks for about an hour – exhilarating, dusty and more than a little frightening – when a wall of reeds away to our left announced that water was nigh. A short bounce across the fields took us a little closer and the five part-time ornithologists clambered out to stand in the sunshine and take turns to peer through Marat's binoculars.

The view was that of lake, field or nothing at all, depending on neck tilt and one's mastery of what should have been a straightforward piece of equipment. Well, at least I held them the right way round. There was not a whole lot else to report, in truth, until several minutes later when Valihan spotted movement in the sky some distance away and announced this to be a pelican in flight. We all took turns to (pretend to) watch it through the bincs and then Marat made an announcement which led to a flurry of activity. I looked on, somewhat confused, as the hatchback of the vehicle was raised and a number of plastic bags retrieved from under the seats.

Thanks to the dexterity of a well-practised team the rear shelf was speedily transformed into a makeshift bar, snacks of bread and pickles were presented as a finger buffet and the top was unscrewed from the inevitable bottle of vodka. "A toast – Pelican!" declared Marat contentedly, once all the glasses had been filled to the top. He looked over at me with a smile and a wink, followed by a quick nod to make sure I paid my respects in full. "Here's to the pelican!" I confirmed in English. And with that, I raised my right hand and braced myself for the first drop of the day.

We moved from lake to lake, spied an impressive flock of flamingos and drank a toast to acknowledge any species of bird seen in flight. At Sultankeldy we even had the good fortune to meet the park warden who kindly invited us into the lodge to take vodka at his table and enjoy the photographs of the many impressive species of birds that, in the best interests of my liver, I hoped we would never see. And indeed we didn't, the journey home yielding a single eagle and even that had to go untoasted with the last of the vodka already supped.

It had been a long and eventful day. Dehydrated from cycling, bird-watching and another trip to the banya, my only thoughts at the dinner table were of an early bed. Yet I still did exactly as any other fully paid up member of the Fat Greedy Bastards Association would do: I agreed to a second enormous helping of pasta and one last beer, for tactical reasons I convinced myself, to try to keep the hard stuff off the agenda. Just ten more minutes to hang in there. I could sense my eyelids were starting to fold when suddenly Marat jumped up, left the table and returned five minutes later sporting a smart shirt, a pressed pair of trousers and a dangerous grin. "David! Picnic!"

At which point baffled David further crumples his already crumpled face.

'Picnic?'

"Picnic."

'Picnic?'

"Picnic". Only this time he points at his posh clothes, my room, his watch, the door. He wants me to get dressed up for a fucking picnic.

Instinct tempted me to point to my rear end and gesture a kiss but

114

instead I drew his attention to my bloated belly and the empty plates. But I was the footballer protesting an awarded penalty, he the ref pointing unwaveringly to the spot. Nothing was going to reverse his decision, so I meekly departed, doused my face in cold water and dressed up in my best Kazakhstan Picnic gear.

Marat's wife had also donned her finery and the three of us drove to a house at the other end of the village. It had turned cold, it was very dark, and not for the first time, I found myself wondering what might happen next. There were perhaps a dozen smartly-dressed people inside who shook my hand and nodded politely and it didn't take long to work out that I was one of fifteen guests at a dinner party. Probably a celebration, I figured, but as there wasn't a word of English or any other European language despite the wide range of ages, all I could do was sit and watch.

And eat. Again. It was that familiar dish, the dustbin lid, only this time the Master Of Ceremonies stood up at the table as we all watched him tear chunks of meat from the animal carcasses and scatter it by the fistful over the mountain of pasta. The jug of mares' milk was passed round, that fumey brew I'd dabbled with in the pastures of Kyrgyzstan, and the picnic got under way. Every person at the table took it in turns to make a speech – five minutes of something quite earnest judging from the assembled expressions – and I sat there very quietly pretending to eat, pretending to drink and pretending to listen. And dreaming of the moment that my head might hit that pillow. Please can we go home Dad.

* * * * *

Thankful that the picnic had been an alcohol-free event, I crawled out of bed an hour before the sun came up and drank tea in the kitchen with Valihan, the very much quieter brother. The farewells had been completed the night before, Marat the genial host accepting his payment with some embarrassment and imploring me to return the following year, even writing down the number to ensure I'd understood. A gentleman, a diamond geezer, and head of a thoroughly nice family. He will never be forgotten.

Two days in Astana would hopefully be enough to sort out my tardy registration and enjoy the peculiar sights. It had been agreed on day one via the vanishing Jessica that Valihan would take me to the appropriate police department and then, assuming they didn't load me on to a train for a salt mine in Siberia, drop me off at a hotel booked by the nutty (but so far, dependable) lady in Almaty.

The cops were surprisingly well organised with a board at the entrance allocating numbered desks according to nationality, and the solo Brit was registered on the spot without punishment and with the minimum of drama. The valiant Valihan then not only insisted on tracking down my hotel but indicated with the aid of pen and paper that he would be in Astana two days hence and available to transport me to the airport. What could I say? I knew he had little work – "arbeit mini", as he told me several times – so if he was going to be in town anyway, at least it would offer me an excuse to put a few quid in the pocket of one very likeable man.

Having agreed the details of our next rendezvous we shook hands in the lobby and then he was gone. I was alone, completely alone, as I have been in hotels around the world for as long as I can remember. But for some reason, just then, it felt strangely discomfiting. In the last few days I had become a silent member of a happy family, laughed and joked and mimicked as an alternative to language, drunk endless beers and vodkas and raised a toast to pelicans, even stood in a shed bollock naked throwing buckets of water at a man I barely(!) knew. New places are always interesting but it's the people that make the world go round.

August turned to September, the cool wind arrived from the north and Astana's short summer was over for another year. Shirt became sweater and sweater became jacket in the two days that I walked the city, the chilly breeze cutting into the face and serving notice that nine months of bitterly cold weather was just around the corner. Fortunately for me a miniature version of the capital, indeed the whole country, has been constructed as a tourist attraction just south of the river so I was able to look at the model replicas of all the weird and wonderful buildings without having to schlep to the respective zones in the outlying suburbs. This was an interesting "tour through Kazakhstan", an outdoor feature roughly the size of a football pitch with impressive displays of the geography, industry and architecture throughout each one of the seventeen regions. It was a couple of hours well spent.

Lunch in a tidy little Russian eatery warmed me through – potato and barley soup with gherkins and sour cream – and there were plenty of NHTEPHET cafés in which to take shelter and catch up with e-mail. In truth I had little appetite for pounding the streets of a modern city so my main objective that afternoon was no more ambitious than selecting a traditional Kazakh restaurant for my last evening in the country.

The venue earmarked for a pre-dinner drink was rather less conventional. Plucked from a guidebook it went under the name of the Premier League Bar and was supposedly run by an avid Chelsea supporter who'd strayed rather further than usual from the King's Road. I found it on the map in the far north of the city, right across the other side from where I was housed, but the temptation was just too much when I discovered it was directly opposite a well-known city landmark – The Arsenal Theatre!

The taxi driver knew The Arsenal even though it was a long way out, almost hidden in a side street in what looked like a seedy part of town. I paid my dues, waved him off then walked over to the bar. Now, hindsight is a wonderful thing and with the benefit of it I would definitely have retained the services of my chauffeur pending verification that said boozer hadn't closed down some months, or even years earlier. So when the locked, rusty door failed to budge I had no option but to embark on yet another unscheduled stroll vaguely back in the direction of the city centre. It didn't feel like a good thing to be doing and I wasn't at all sure how to respond when an unmarked vehicle drew up alongside, wound down the window and gestured towards the passenger seat.

Kazakh taxis are mostly unofficial and accepting a ride from a stranger seemed the lesser of two evils. He dropped me in the main street at a place

I recognised and it was whilst walking the few blocks to my restaurant of choice that I realised I was hungry enough to eat a horse. So when I was shown to the table, that's exactly what I decided to order. A horse kebab – and also my usual lamb version just as a back up.

Horse meat has long been a delicacy of the region and, whatever we think about it, this isn't going to change. It was my last chance to try it and whilst I thought I never would, the prospect of missing out seemed worse than giving it a go. It was actually very tasty, not greatly different from beef but a little stronger in flavour, and of course I wolfed it down with most of the lamb shashlik to follow. I know, you probably think I'm a cruel, callous person but come on, a fiver on a horse never did anybody any harm.

Valihan apologised for being slightly late, indicating with a backward pointing finger and a surprising piece of vocabulary that yesterday had been his birthday. The smile and the drinking action confirmed it had been celebrated in predictable style with Marat and so, after all, he'd driven for two hours from Korgalzhyn to help me with the fifteen minute journey to catch my flight. There was so much I wanted to say to him, to ask him, to thank him for, but it would never be possible. All I could do in that airport car park was give him a big hug, a warm handshake and the few dollars that he so very much deserved. This kind, honest man seemed genuinely saddened by my leaving and when I turned round at the entrance of the terminal building he was still standing at the door of his car, waving enthusiastically and doing his best to put on a smile. What would he do now? I wondered.

UZBEKISTAN

Tashkent airport looked tired and the toilets were closed so I lugged my disappointed bladder over to currency exchange for the acquisition of a startling 266,000 Sum. The shabby notes came in the form of three rubber-banded bundles, each the size of a wardrobe, together with a smile from the

118

young chap who had already slotted my two crisp one hundred dollar bills under the clip in his drawer. Ten minutes later it was a scruffy taxi driver with very few teeth that was doing all the smiling. Even chuckling he was, as he helped himself to twenty 1000 sum notes in return for the short ride in his ancient little motor. Good-bye fancy, oil-rich Astana. Hello cotton-picking Uzbekistan.

The lady at reception welcomed me warmly and explained in astonishingly fluent English that the taxi price from the airport should have been 3,000. Tourists always got fleeced, she conceded apologetically, some shelling out as much 10,000. No surprise then that her chin dropped and eyes widened on hearing I had just doubled the previous record. She was ever so pleasant, as was the cosy family hotel and – from what I could see – its quiet, leafy residential street. All three were worthy of a smile, of thinking positive thoughts, and of banishing the constantly repeated headline running across the bottom of my screen: "Alphabet Traveller Taken For a Ride in Seven Fold Rip Off".

The country-lane feel of the sidestreets defied the fact that this was Central Asia's most populous city and one which – less than twenty years earlier – had been the fourth largest in the entire Soviet Union. According to my beloved stats there were a couple of million people out there and so I earmarked a few days in the capital to get out amongst them and see what they were up to. It turned out to be time very well spent.

* * * * *

Tashkent is a civilised sort of place, a sprawling capital with wide roads, numerous parks and gigantic roundabouts... but no tangible centre. I couldn't instantly bring myself to love it or loathe it but a couple of hours striding alongside a featureless carriageway, traversable only via an underpass, confirmed that it definitely wasn't one for a casual wander. This city definitely required a shortlist of places to aim for, by taxi, and preferably in some sort of logical geographical sequence. And thus, with nerdish enthusiasm and military planning, I set about the task of drawing one up.

The Chorsu Bazaar was everything a market should be and it made for an encouraging start. Almost a town in its own right, this series of wacky, ancient buildings is organised according to its dazzling range of products: herbs and spices in one building, clothing in the next, a pick'n'mix sweet selection in the massive enclosed emporium at the far end (no wonder they have such dodgy teeth)....The vendors were playful, eager to shake hands and willing to engage in any form of banter to sell you a lump of horsemeat sausage (flogging a dead horse?), or a kilo of nuts, or a pair of silk pyjamas. Or simply just to say hello to a foreign face. It was so uplifting to mix with cheerful people that I didn't want to leave Chorsu so I bought a pot of tea, sat at a wobbly table in the sunshine, and with the glorious spectacle of the Friday mosque away to my left, soaked it all in as slowly as I could.

My guidebook also used the opportunity to soak in the tea that I'd spilled all over the table but I could still read the map well enough to pick out my lunch venue in the far north of the city. The Central Asian Plov Centre had been described as a canteen dedicated to the regional variations of the national dish, but how many ways could there be to stir bits of lamb and vegetables into a cauldron of fried rice? I was intrigued, particularly by the story that the drinking of the oil from the bottom of the pan had been doing the trick long before Viagra had ever been dreamt of.

It turned out to be a cavernous restaurant in the shadow of the city's TV tower. Much smarter than I had imagined: long rows of tables, white linen and outrageous chandeliers beneath which groups of middle-class people chattered away. I felt like a gate crasher at a conference.

The waitress arrived, menu-less and English-less, but rather than exploit my plov-naivete she was kind enough to announce in Russian what she thought a deaf and dumb person from the other side of the world might enjoy. And she was right, the standard fare with a mix of lamb, nuts and raisins went down a treat but I opted for a pot of tea rather than the oil from the bottom of the cauldron.

I was starting to like Uzbekistan. The food so far was good, the people were friendly, the vibes were positive. The distinctive sky-blue/white/green of the national flag seemed to fly everywhere as though announcing to the world that this was a proud and confident nation. To drive through Tashkent felt like a journey through history, though I have to admit it was history that I'd long forgotten or, more likely, never even known. There seemed to be no end of memorials and squares paying tribute to great men through the centuries: the battles fought by Timur, the national hero since the 14th century, right up to Yuri Gagarin and the Soviet cosmonauts who led the way into space in the early 1960s. And then there were the heroes and victims of the earthquake.

To many of us, the year 1966, just the sound of those very words, immediately conjures up images of a jubilant Bobby Moore holding aloft the Jules Rimet Trophy and a toothless Nobby Stiles dancing around the old Wembley Stadium. Not so for the poor folk of Tashkent. Three months earlier, on April 26th, a massive earthquake had struck right in the heart of their city, destroying houses and leaving well over a quarter of a million people without shelter. Incredibly few actually lost their lives according to the Soviets, thanks to the unseasonably hot weather that day (people who were sleeping outside in their backyards survived) and the unspoken certainty that fatal catastrophes could never happen under a communist regime.

The epicentre of that earthquake is now marked by The Monument of Courage: a sturdy, powerful statue of a man and a woman, erected as a gesture of thanks to comrades who came (or were sent) from all over the Soviet Union to help rebuild the city. And sitting just alongside it, rather more poignant I thought, a black granite block like an enormous Oxo cube with a diagonal crack bisecting its face. Stone City, the literal and very apt translation of the word Tashkent.

The story goes that many who came to lend a hand ended up settling in the city and never returned home. Uzbekistan's population of today, the largest in Central Asia at around 25 million, is indeed a veritable mixture of nationalities, though I must confess that most of them look pretty much the same to the untrained Mancunian eye. But one ethnic minority that was very noticeable, and a big surprise to me, was the sizeable Korean community. What on earth were these guys doing in faraway Tashkent?

I asked the question and unearthed some interesting answers. It all started apparently in 1937 when Joseph Stalin created a policy known as "systematic population transfer". He had come across these strange-looking people in the Russian Far East and didn't quite know what to make of them, so rather than have them pose a threat, he sent 170,000 ethnic Koreans to what is now known as Uzbekistan. Many of them, or at least their offspring, eventually prospered and today run successful businesses, attracting substantial investment from their homeland. One such gent has even had the foresight to build a golf course.

I couldn't resist the temptation. Oh, I know, it's not the sort of thing an alphabet traveller should be doing but it had seemed ages since I'd played a round of golf, and the sun was shining, and well....I hope you don't mind a break from culture and stuff. It took half an hour in a cab to the Lakeside Golf Club and to neatly illustrate the injustices of the world the fare of US$ 4 was also the price of a single golf ball in the pro shop. (Hence few Uzbeki cabbies knock off early to play nine holes). I enquired at the desk as to the possibility of finding a playing partner and it was agreed that the best tactic would be to wait in the restaurant to see if anybody appeared. Not surprisingly, somebody did – a waitress – and in keeping with the menu, and all the other diners, she was Korean. So I ordered up a plateful of garlic breath noodles in rampant heartburn sauce and let the chopsticks do the rest.

Word of my arrival had reached the ears of a Mr S.D. Nam. En-route from Seoul to Paris to purchase machinery for his country's hospitals, he had engineered a three-day detour into Tashkent to play 72 holes of golf and would be only too pleased to give me a wupping. I wasn't quite sure how to address somebody called S.D. Nam but he was a very nice bloke, was indeed far more competent than I with club in hand (ie. he could hit the ball beyond the ladies tee) and extremely interesting company when we returned to the 19th to sink a few cold ones. We talked about grown up things like volatility of world currencies and more importantly the prohibitive costs of playing golf in Korea. And that was when he went on to explain, with voice lowered and eyes firmly focused on the men around the bar, how agents attracted his fellow countrymen to Uzbekistan with a package that included as much golf, women, sunshine and beer as they could handle. Poor Mr Nam looked embarrassed and quite disgusted, I just hope that my pained expression and repeated tut-tutting was equally convincing.

* * * * *

Uzbekistan sits right in the middle of Central Asia, sharing borders with five other Stans. Not one of these neighbours has a coastline, which means, along with mighty (13-letter) Liechtenstein, it is one of only two countries in the world to be classified as "double landlocked". It's a quizmaster's dream and there is still more excitement to come. Because if you were to draw a line on the map from Istanbul to Beijing, two cities 7000 kms apart and almost on the same line of latitude, the half way point would be slap bang in the centre of Uzbekistan.

So what? Another pile of useless Jenkins trivia, I hear you say. And there you would be wrong. For it is this epic journey from The Far East to the Mediterranean Sea that established itself as the world's most important trading route for over a thousand years. It later came to be known as The Silk Road along which China traded its fabrics, porcelain, tea, spices, rhubarb and lots of other goodies in return for commodities from the west: gold and silver, jade, glass, horses... and of course, the all-important rhino horn for those not willing to lick out the dregs of the plov pan.

Right at the heart of the cosmopolitan action, with goods, services and animals of their own to offer, were the thriving markets of Tashkent, Bukhara and Samarkand. Great business for Uzbekistan but the Silk Road meant far more than just the movement of cargo. It brought education, new ideas from distant lands, the spread of religions from all directions and a merging of artistic and musical styles. With the arrival of Islam and subsequent wealth to Central Asia came the most splendid works of architecture: magnificent, often outrageous buildings that would repeatedly be destroyed and rebuilt at the whim of whoever was ruling the roost at the time.

So it is no surprise that Uzbekistan, unlike the rest of the region, has a thriving international tourist industry. It is rich in history, delightfully inexpensive and the climate either side of the summer heat makes it relatively easy to travel around. It feels safe and stable to backpackers and tour groups alike (despite its lowly rankings in the World Peace Index). Compared to the small, mountainous, and sadly down-at-heel nations of Tajikistan and Kyrgyzstan to the east, the wallet-busting monster of Kazakhstan to the north and the political and religious extremism of Turkmenistan and Afghanistan down below this is a country with everything potentially in its favour. It also benefits from a road network that functions well and, to my great excitement, a rail service that extends the full 1400km width from east to west.

The train I opted for left Tashkent as the sun was going down. It was the old-fashioned type with a corridor running alongside the compartments and a door that slid back and forth when the vendors came around with their hot dogs, beer and vodka. It felt like a proper adventure and such a romantic way to travel: the privacy of my own berth for 16 hours, an unlimited supply of tea from the urn at the end of the corridor and – a very civilised touch I thought – fresh, polywrapped bed linen and towel courtesy of Uzbekistan Railways.

My cabin mate was a local guy though he wasn't an Uzbek. (I was finally starting to get the hang of this.) Marat explained in very good English that he was a Tatar, yet another ethnic group with its own language, and that he would normally speak Russian in everyday life. Clearly a very well-educated young bloke, he was able to offer some insight into a wide range of topics. I was surprised to hear, for example, that Uzbekistan would not grant visas to visitors from Islamic countries outside the region for fear that their own moderate approach to the religion might be destabilised. The conversation then moved on to the Andijon Massacre, an ugly event that was reported around the world but not in Uzbekistan itself.

124

The story goes that on May 13th, 2005 a group of Islamic fundamentalists in the western city of Andijon stormed the local prison and set free some of the inmates, following which thousands of people poured out onto the streets to vent their frustration at high levels of poverty and unemployment. They assembled en masse in the main square but as this action was deemed to be a protest against the state President Karimov sent in the troops and ordered them to open fire. Many innocent civilians were killed, it is thought well in excess of a thousand, yet the government refused to allow an independent investigation to be held.

* * * * *

I woke up in the middle of a desert. There was something very exciting, almost magical, about boarding a train in a city of two million people and having breakfast twelve hours later chugging through an unchanging landscape of sand and scrub. The Kyzylkum Desert, a new one to most of us I suspect, is almost the size of Poland, and I found to my surprise that its emptiness and sheer simplicity kept me well entertained for the rest of the morning.

We arrived in Urgench ahead of schedule and stepped down into the searing heat. I was two thirds of the way across the country, by far the most westerly point of the entire Central Asian adventure and little more than 400 kms from the shores of the Caspian Sea. Crazy as it sounds, it was time to turn round and head back towards Tashkent. Only this time it would be by road, a little more slowly, and taking in the cities of Khiva, Bukhara and Samarkand.

Khiva isn't so much a city, or even, for that matter, a town. It's a tourist spectacle like no other, a feast of historic buildings tightly grouped within a rectangle, protected by a high fortress-style wall. The large gates at each points of the compass today merely serve to usher in visitors and collect the entrance (and camera) fees but the history books tell us that this part of Central Asia, the Uzbekistan of today, wasn't always such a happy place.

The Arab conquest brought Islam to the region in the 7th century and the religion flourished for the next five or six hundred years. Bukhara in particular became a centre of learning but in contrast to the spiritual influence from the south and the west came death and destruction from the north and the east. Things went seriously pear-shaped in 1218 when a trade delegation from Mongolia was deemed enough of a threat for a local governor to instruct that they be executed. Bad decision, mate. Their chief and the leader of the Mongols was a chap named Jenghiz Kahn, something of a hard nut, and upon hearing news of this aggression he personally assembled an army of 200,000 men and led them on horseback in the direction of Central Asia.

Rape, looting and death became the name of the game under Jenghiz Khan's brutal and fast-expanding empire. Thankfully, it didn't last too long. He died nine years later and at the end of the following century the locals came up with a hard man of their own. Timur (aka Tamerlane), from Samarkand, was not only a military genius but a cultured, educated man and a lover of art. His armies slaughtered millions of innocent people from Turkey to India throughout thirty five years of bloodshed but in Uzbekistan, I couldn't help notice, those minor indiscretions have been carefully put to one side. Timur is their greatest hero of all time.

I walked through Khiva's west gate into a world of mosques, medressas (schools of Islamic training), minarets and mausoleums. A labyrinth of alleyways linking buildings of all shapes and sizes, mostly built for the purpose of worship, study or death but sometimes created merely as a symbol of power, ego or eccentricity. Many had been destroyed and rebuilt – often more than once – throughout a period of seven hundred years, though some, it transpired, were relative newcomers. As I would later find out, some "historic buildings" in Uzbekistan are not historic at all, but in fact new buildings where historic ones used to be!

The history might sometimes be blurred or confusing but let nothing detract from the mind-blowing beauty of this Islamic architecture. The ornate decoration of the mosques and palaces, the graceful domes, towering minarets, all with the predominance of pale blue bringing the soul closer to the heavens, was intense, utterly magnificent and, frankly, overwhelming in its detail. I wandered around in something of a daze, kept moving in and out from the baking afternoon heat to the cool interiors of the buildings and I tried everything I could think of to capture the scene on camera. But even from the top of one of the many towers it was impossible to do justice to the overall picture, so I stood there alone for as long as the sun would permit, breathed in the silence, scanned the walls and the turrets and the rooftops of Khiva and had to trust that my memory would carry me through.

* * * * *

Bukhara is five times the size of Khiva and as such, a proper city. It too has a string of architectural gems, albeit more spread out, but my appetite for palaces and fortresses and the ubiquitous medressas had already been well and truly sated. So I spent time in the bazaar, admiring the displays of ceramics, listening to musicians playing unusual instruments and purchasing one of their CDs in what can only be described as a moment of sheer recklessness. And then, perhaps by way of a punishment for my indulgence, I was taken to prison.

It's a bit gruesome really but I wanted to have a look at the "bug-pit", an underground trench below one of the cells where a couple of fellow Brits had once been held. It was 1839 when Colonel Stoddart, an emissary of the Governor-General of India, upset the local emir by turning up without any gifts, a crime deemed worthy of being forced to reside down below with burrowing rodents and lots of other creepy-crawlies. Captain Conolly arrived a couple of years later to rescue his old mate but by then the emir was in an even worse mood and CC also found himself lowered into the black hole. Only a letter from Queen Victoria could save the day but alas it never arrived; Stoddart and Conolly were retrieved from the pit, forced to dig their own graves, and then beheaded.

I enjoyed the journeys as much as the towns and cities themselves. The landscape was mainly flat and the scenery unspectacular but there is still always much to see through the window of a bus. Unusual sights such as bottles of petrol for sale at the roadside brought over the border from oil-rich Turkmenistan, that enormous 12-letter country away to my right. On the opposite side there were clear remains of caravanserai in the desert, an intriguing name for what used to be overnight encampments, the Silk Road equivalent of the motorway service station. This is where the men and their camels would have stopped to take rest, re-charge their batteries and prepare for another day of plodding across the sand.

The bus headed east to where the land was less arid and the furry white cotton plants were in full bloom. This being September, the teams of pickers were out in the fields, each one plucking up to 150 kilos a day with their backs bent double and their bottoms in the air. The production of wheat and cotton from the 75,000 or so farms is what drives the Uzbeki economy – the cotton seed also produces oil for cooking – and it is these crops that give the country the edge over their smaller, more mountainous neighbours who have neither the land nor the hours of sunshine to compete. The lower altitude also means that the winter weather is usually less brutal, though that year it had dropped to – 35C and those households that hadn't left taps running had had to wait until spring for their water pipes to thaw.

I camped overnight in a yurt to the north of Nurata, now closer to the border with Kazakhstan. It was something of a contrived tourist gimmick but a welcome break from urban life and a chance to swim in the crystal clear waters of Lake Aidarkul, a 250 km body of water that only appeared in 1969 as a consequence of the Soviets bodging a dam project on a Kazakh river.

And on, at last, to the mysterious-sounding Samarkand, that evocative name I'd often heard but could never have placed on the map. An important crossroads in the Middle Ages when the Silk Road was it its pomp, it is probably the most famous city of Central Asia and indeed reputed to be the oldest. Today it is home to nearly half a million people, many of them students, and it was upon the impressive tree-lined University Boulevard that the bus deposited me into the heart of the action.

In contrast to the random nature of Tashkent, the central square of Samarkand, known as The Registan, leaves you in no doubt at all that you've arrived. Vast, high walls of blue mosaic stare at each other across an open space like boxers on opposite sides of the ring, three medressas and a mosque in all. They are amongst the most magnificent buildings you will ever see, rectangular in shape yet given added form by graceful archways, polished blue domes and – the finishing touch on top of the mosque – the gold crescent of Islam pointing up to the sky. Leaning minarets stand left and right like wonky factory chimneys either side of the medressas but these too are decorated as precious works of art and preserved as such.

Even to a burnt-out and travel-weary punter the stunning Registan serves up a cocktail with a helluva kick, a pick-you-up to lift the spirits and get you through the rest of the day. Or in my case, the week. I like mosques and medressas, sometimes even minarets and occasionally a museum but a line has to be drawn and no sooner had I made a vow to avoid anything beginning with M for at least ten years than some bright spark came along with the suggestion of my going to see a mausoleum. A "must see" apparently – that M word again. I wasn't sure. This could be the one that pushed me over the edge.

There were in fact two mausoleums: a relatively modest one for Timur with his sons and grandsons and the other, commissioned by the man himself for his wives, friends and (female) family. The latter was unquestionably one of the highlights of Central Asia. It might seem an odd tourist attraction but this row of polished, ornately tiled buildings is certainly no ordinary burial site. The rows of tombs combine to create a fairytale village of breathtaking beauty, each one effectively a palace, an individual work of art with fantastic colour and intricate decoration, much of which has only recently been restored. This spectacle was without question the icing on the cake, and yes, I have to admit, A Must See.

* * * * *

It was nearly time to go home. The half day journey back to Tashkent went almost unnoticed, though I do recall that the signpost for Dushanbe, a few hours drive to the south, brought a modest smile of satisfaction. My circuit had been completed. The final kebab was nigh.

Back in the big city, and how big it felt, the last day could not go to waste. So I walked through an old part of Tashkent that could have been central Iran, along narrow streets and alleyways – many leading to nowhere and forcing me to retrace – and past high walls and metal gates that obscured the houses beyond. There was no movement, no traffic, a seemingly abandoned world on account of the midday heat, completely silent until the eerie call to prayer emerged from an unseen mosque. The crackly intervention made me jump and forced my attention to a loudspeaker strapped to a wall and beneath it an open door. I poked my head inside and saw a small room like a prison cell, its sole occupant a man, stooping, deep lines etched into a face that had seen many years of life. He was dressed in white robes and baking bread in an ancient oven that far outdated the man himself; in fact it seemed nothing had changed in this part of the world for several thousand years.

A turn of the corner revealed a different generation, an army of schoolchildren flooding onto the streets. The boys were dressed impeccably in shirts and ties, I even saw one little fellow wearing a suit with a waistcoat, and it was noticeable that a good number of the girls had elected to wear the headscarf. It was a happy scene and the lads in particular were keen to show off, lark around, and offer crazy poses for my final pictures.

Well, almost final. I decreed that the last supper should not be a kebab after all so treated myself to a restaurant by the name of Caravan, a quaint little place with an interesting water feature and a band that played live music. It was a stylish way to bow out and would add to my list of cherished memories of the city... yet it was the building across the street that had first captured my attention. Reminiscent of 1970s Belfast there was a mural bearing the faces of men that I recognised, famous characters from recent history, and though it wasn't a pleasing sight, I just couldn't resist taking a picture of Frank Lampard, Didier Drogba and the rest of the jubilant team upon the walls of Ye Olde Chelsea Arms.

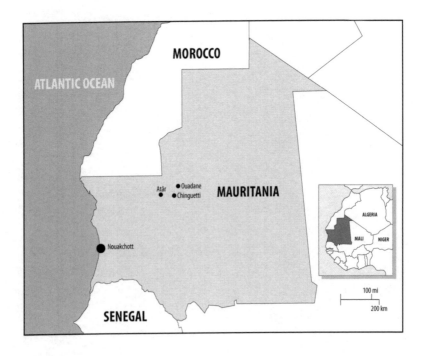

MAURITANIA

Some of us will never forget the harrowing experience of seeing our beloved Britain coming under attack from the skies. Those terrifying moments will be forever etched in our memories when all but the hardiest yeomen were forced to abandon their places of work, flee the streets, gather loved ones and take to their homes in a state of panic. There they huddled at the fireside and tuned in to wireless sets for news of a country gripped by fear, a once-proud nation plunged into chaos. Yes, everywhere there were stories of devastation on a massive scale; it seemed the entire infrastructure of our mighty kingdom had all but collapsed. Thank goodness we don't get three inches of snow *every* year.

I had always known that a journey to the Sahara Desert would present complex logistical challenges though the circumnavigation of the M25 had never been uppermost in that reckoning. The blizzard on that particular February afternoon delivered snowflakes the size and volume of which Hertfordshire had never seen before. Buses and trains across the South-East had to be cancelled, cars veered and careered drunkenly in all directions or simply packed up and refused to move. London had pretty much closed down with the exception of Gatwick airport. And if I was serious about catching the flight to Banjul, I had to get to the South Terminal before dawn.

Against all the odds, the Monarch flight departed on schedule. £120 for a taxi ride to West Sussex made a mockery of my having shopped around for a cheap flight to West Africa but at least I was airborne and only six hours away from the sunshine. I was heading for the tiny slither of land known as The Gambia, a former British enclave with the rolling waves of the Atlantic to the west and the much larger, ex-French colony of Senegal

133

wrapped around the other three sides. The plan, in so far as I had a plan, would be to enter that neighbour as quickly as possible, so to speak, then follow the coast in a northerly direction to reach the little-known, and hard-to-find-about, Islamic Republic of Mauritania.

For a country twice the size of Spain, Mauritania figures rarely in everyday conversation. Its only serious foray into world news, aside from a tame little military coup, was the sad occasion on Christmas Eve 2007 when a group of bandits slaughtered a family of French tourists picnicking in the desert. The following week the Lisbon-Dakar rally was cancelled as a result, despite the fact that the 600 (soon-to-be-very-pissed-off) car drivers and bike riders back in Portugal had already donned their gloves and were revving their engines for departure. It was to be the end of an era. The historic race had started in Paris back in 1978 but in the interest of safety the organisers decided that from 2009 the event should be staged somewhere without risk of violence or robbery. So they moved it to South America.

Despite its geographical enormity, Mauritania's population is little over 3 million. I was readying myself for emptiness, a visit to one of the sparsest lands on earth where an average square kilometre would be occupied by just three people and maybe a few camels. What a contrast to Bangladesh, at the opposite end of the scale, where incredibly the calculation produces a density ratio more than three hundred times greater. Both Muslim countries but the latter blessed with rather a lot more water.

With Morocco to the north and Senegal to the south, Mauritania is the bridge between the brown and the black people of a large and complex continent. History records that the Berbers and the Arabs of the Mediterranean – collectively known in English as the Moors (les Maures in French) – proved to be the more powerful of the two groups so it was their religion that gained momentum, spreading as far west as the Atlantic coast. When Mauritania was granted full independence from France in 1960 it wasted little time in declaring the country a strict Islamic state but thirty years on it softened its stance, joining Egypt and Jordan as the only Arab countries to officially recognise Israel.

I had some reservations about going to Mauritania, though not many. The British Foreign Office had declared it an unsafe place to visit and used its website to issue warnings of terrorist activity but then they had said the same of post-coup Fiji where the most serious threat to the well-being of a tourist would have come from the possibility of choking on an ice-cream. There are cynics out there who would say that the Brits wield their influence in devious ways and that it's highly unlikely they will write nice things about a Muslim country run by an unelected military government. I'll leave you to draw your own conclusions.

* * * * *

It was 28 degrees and 2pm on landing in Banjul, The Gambia being in the same time zone as UK and its climate at least 28 degrees more pleasing. With a chapter to write and ever eager to get off to a flier I filled the time void at the baggage carousel by dialling the phone number from my pocket to assess the chances of applying for a Mauritania visa that afternoon. Alas the answer was much as expected: we are a consulate, we only work twenty minutes a day and it's almost time to go home. Come and see us tomorrow.

I did, finding them easily, thanks to the driver from the cute Safari Garden Hotel who knew the place well. Two photos, two hours and two thousand dalasi would do the trick I was told, though "dalasi" with an African accent sounds scarily like "dollars" to the untrained ear. My miscomprehension amused the genial chap at the desk and once this was clarified I gleefully and unquestioningly handed over a large bundle of grubby Gambian notes, only later calculating that this was £60 for a visa that costs ten Euro when issued in Morocco.

At this point I normally embark on a visa rant but instead I'll tell you about the pleasant dinner I enjoyed with Geri, one of the hotel owners, and the two guests who had just driven from UK as part of the Plymouth-Banjul Challenge. We sat by the pool aside a wall of purple bougainvillea and my new friends outlined the history of this annual event. It had started out as a

135

tongue-in-cheek rival to the serious rally but the idea here was to auction the vehicles on arrival and donate the proceeds to local charities. It had been growing year on year but then came the threats from Europe's governments of Al Qaeda's menace in West Africa and so this year the number of participants had dropped to a third.

I got up next morning in the dark to catch the first northbound ferry across the wide mouth of the River Gambia. It was a plan that ultimately failed as my taxi was singled out at the police roadblock and we were subjected to an extra ten minutes of time-wasting by torchlight as a punishment for offering neither dalasi nor dollars. I boarded the second floating platform 45 minutes later, a pink face amidst hundreds of very black ones, feeling a little nervous but pleased to be part of this daily festival of noise and colour. A chaotic jostle: ladies clad in traditional dresses carrying parcels and products on their heads, a picture of elegance compared to most of the men with their creamy, bloodshot eyes, stained football shirts, track suit bottoms and woolly hats. A man in robes recited passages from the Koran, young boys sold drinks and biscuits and dolls and watches, a blind beggar worked the crowd and dodged the over-laden vehicles with a white stick in one hand and a microphone in the other, linked to a speaker that he'd somehow strapped to his chest. It was good to be back in Africa.

The crossing was relatively peaceful but as soon as we'd docked I was surrounded by men competing to carry my bag, a posse of barefooted children tugging at my arm and tray-bearing ladies offering peanuts and oranges. Every one of them was either bawling instructions or asking questions or repeating their mantra of a thousand times a day. My challenge was to be firm, polite and most of all, not to get distracted. The deal was a one km taxi ride to the border so I clambered into a rusty vehicle with an uncountable number of people, had my passport stamped by the authorities and re-entered the world of madness, this time in French-speaking Senegal, to secure a seat in a *sept-place* to Dakar.

This a Peugeot estate share taxi with one seat next to the driver and two rows of three seats behind. There will always be many of them parked up in the dust but in that lovely African way there exists no system of queuing or system of any sort to permit a just and orderly sequence of departure. The first to sell seven tickets, one for each of the seven places, is the first to leave so each driver engages a vendor to recruit passengers and collect the money. The competition is manic and the noise deafening; pushing, shoving, swearing and even fighting are par for the course. Amidst the chaos the prospective passenger clings on to his luggage for dear life despite the efforts of the vendor to snatch it from his grasp and load it on board his master's motor.

I went through a pointless selection process (just checking I wasn't missing out on a limo) then allowed myself to be manhandled into a car and wedged into the far corner of the rearmost seat. Only then did I start to mentally uncoil, the relief at escaping the mayhem overriding any sensations of claustrophobia, discomfort or the blinding heat. I don't even recall any undue concern about embarking on an all-day journey in a vehicle that was at least forty years old and looked as though it had been picked off the scrapheap and mistakenly dropped back in to service. The driver didn't look much better either.

The scenery was drab, a flat scrubland that changed little throughout the first five hours until the outskirts of Dakar introduced mountains of garbage, dirt poor villages and ultimately four lanes of dense traffic. The journey was hot, tiring and sadly unrewarding, vindicating the decision I'd made in Banjul to purchase a plane ticket to take me north from Dakar up to Nouakchott in Mauritania and another that would eventually return me south to The Gambia.

Dakar itself offers flashes of former colonial sophistication but the main street, Rue Pompidou, also serves as a gathering point for Senegal's less savoury individuals. They lurk and they linger, stalking and baiting their prey with a phoney smile and a sweaty handshake, desperate to pocket cash by fair(ish) means or foul. Europeans, few in number, are a favourite target. When the initial pleasantries don't work the tactic switches to confrontation, insults, accusations of racism and all manner of menacing behaviour. I have waited all my life to have someone rip my pants off but never in my wildest fantasies did I imagine this would come at the hands of a gang of Senegalese youths on a street corner in Dakar. It happened within five minutes of my leaving the hotel; within another five, more than a little shaken, I was back in the lobby showing the staff an English knee cap through my torn and tattered strides.

Though I'd lost nothing more than a pair of cotton trousers the incident hardly endeared me to the city. I tried to make the best of it but the constant intimidation, more intense than I can recall in any of the hundred or so countries I've visited over the years, forced me to take refuge indoors every few minutes. One such escape was to take the lift to the top floor of the Hotel Independance, an establishment so grubby it would make you want to weep but from the top, the 17th floor, the views of Dakar and its spectacular peninsular were the best in town. It gave me an idea for my final day in Senegal.

Dakar's airport sits 8 kms to the north of the city and close enough to the Atlantic coast to feel the spray off the ocean. Close by is La Pointe des Almadies, the most westerly point of the African mainland, an exclusive suburb claimed by millionaires' mansions, a range of hotels and a cliff top golf course. With my flight northwards scheduled for late the following afternoon, wouldn't a brief sniff of affluence be a pleasing contrast to this life of urban chaos and perpetual torment?

I believe the expression is a "no-brainer". Next morn I took a cab to Le Meridien, handed over my dusty, tatty bag for the concierge to add to the Louis Vuitton collection in his storeroom and went off to enjoy the seaside. I didn't play golf but four hours spent walking in a warm breeze to the sound of crashing waves was to put Senegal in a very different light and the tasty lunch that followed set me up for the rest of the day. The batteries were recharged, I was thinking positively and feeling as ready as I would ever be for the impending TLC challenge. Nothing was going to be allowed to spoil this afternoon of pleasure, not even the greedy, bad-tempered taxi driver who dropped me at the airport or the two watery-eyed thugs prowling outside the terminal in the hope of a farewell sting.

* * * * *

If you don't count the city of Luxembourg, which really would be cheating, Nouakchott is the only ten-letter capital of a ten-letter country. Probably the least famous city in the world, it looks uncannily like an anagram and I must confess to having contrived a lexical obscenity from it in a rare moment of childish behaviour.

It was a special Saturday afternoon back home, the opening week-end of the Six Nations rugby, a point probably lost on the twenty odd passengers with whom I shared the small, propellered plane. It was 2.25pm and at that very moment the players and spectators, the latter already handsomely Guinnessed, would be rendering their respective national anthems with passion and pride. And here I was in seat 6A, heading for the desert and making rude words out of Nouakchott.

Fifty minutes later and descending quickly, the scratched, oval window revealed a symmetrical landscape of white rectangular buildings, many with towers and speakers, and roads so long and straight they could have been drawn with a ruler. We landed at the small airport with something of a thump. It offered no challenge in terms of formalities, nor services in terms of a taxi or a bank, but a five dollar bill was enough get me a ride in an old car with a bloke who was hanging around. The hotel I'd booked on line turned out to be just around the corner.

The main thoroughfare and its sizeable roundabouts were smart enough but the other roads seemed to be little more than tracks of sand with piles of garbage at either side. Such was the street along which I was delivered to the door of L'Escale des Sables, an elegant-looking hostelry that seemed to belong in an entirely different world. Beyond the buzz of the security door its interior was more stylish and sophisticated than I could ever have imagined, adequate compensation I hoped for its remote and somewhat squalid setting.

The plan was to stay for two nights then head off into the desert. The best I could hope to achieve that first evening was to change some cash and find a place to eat, so all fell into place when my host, Mohammed, offered a lift into town. Daylight had all but gone when we pulled up at the kerb alongside three men (probably Mohammed, Mohammed, and Mohammed) entirely wrapped in robes and turbans, six eyes poking out of the semi-darkness. The crinkling of my three 100 Euro notes sparked much animated dialogue (in Hassaniya I was told, a version of Arabic) and thanks to my man's negotiations 110,000 rubber-banded Ougiya came in through the open window. As with most African banknotes they were presented in large bundles, worn to the point of disintegration and so utterly revolting to touch that any form of skin contact would be kept to an absolute minimum.

A few more blocks and I was dropped on a dismal, unlit street outside a pokey little café. I was grateful for my chauffeur's help but it seemed an odd recommendation for dinner and a weird place to leave me to my own devices. Why here? It felt like an industrial estate where all the businesses were closed or abandoned and only a burger trailer remained open for trade. Nonetheless there were lots of robed and turbanned people milling around in the darkness, none of whom, I observed with relief, paid me the slightest attention. I looked in all directions, trying to figure out what they deemed to be so millworthy and headed off through the sand to find the town centre.

A crossroads with traffic signals and a filling station brightened my hopes but they turned out to be the highlights of twenty minutes brisk pacing. Other people were also walking and plenty of cars filled the streets but in a strict Muslim country with no chance of a bevvy, where did people make for on a Saturday night? Or perhaps they weren't actually heading for anywhere, the drive and the walk in themselves providing the evening's entertainment? I found a small shop that was open and hugged its lights to illuminate the pages of my guide book.

Having broadly figured out my location I set off for the area on the map with the cluster of dots and numbers that indicated activity. But the plan went awry when I discovered my direction was the opposite of that intended, the penalty for knowing the road name and nothing more. Another thirty minutes of frustration followed with just the sound of car horns and the occasional belly-dance music floating through the darkness. Everywhere looked exactly the same hence my tether, not known for its lengthiness, was nearing its end. So I plucked the name of a restaurant from the book and, the last resort of any proud man, asked assistance of a local person. It would be just two turnings and three more blocks he assured me, ten more minutes of trudging through the sand.

And he was right. Ten minutes later, I was there. I was back at the very spot Mohammed had dropped me an hour before, outside the very caff that he, and my guidebook, had so enthusiastically recommended. This was it. This was Downtown Nouakchott. Unbefuckinlievable.

I refused as a matter of principle to enter the establishment and instead walked in the other direction to a sort of tea shop with a restaurant menu. The place was almost empty – 8.30 pm, Saturday – but the pizza was fine and the opportunity to take stock of my visit to Mauritania was one that I welcomed. Decisions had to be taken and, upon returning to the incongruous surroundings of my boutique hotel, the most important of those was announced to my host. I would be leaving Nouakchott immediately after breakfast.

* * * * *

It was still cold when I arrived at the "gare", a car park on the edge of the city staring out towards thousands of miles of desert. This was the departure point for the city of Atar, where passengers and their cargo would assemble throughout the morning to be loaded in groups of six into the waiting vehicles. I had just missed one so was offered the choice of the front passenger berth in the next one to leave, a stroke of good fortune except that the single seat commanded a double fare on the basis that it would usually have to be shared!

The ticket sellers were a friendly bunch, eager to chat and offer tea, and the hour of commotion as we waited for people to arrive and for the sun to rise higher in the sky was a warming experience in every sense. The threat of spending six hours sitting on somebody's knee, or vice-versa, had convinced me to part with the extra fiver and I left Nouakchott behind with cheerful waves, honest handshakes and numerous wishes of Bon Voyage. The smiles of genuine people no less poor than the folk of Senegal but evidently of a very different mindset.

The drive across the desert taught me much about deserts. It taught me that a sandy landscape can be as varied as a grassy one, that shades of pink can change as much as shades of green, that trees and bushes may thrive in abundance or be absent for miles on end, and that hills and even mountains are just as likely as pancake flatness. Here the colours ranged from a white floury powder to a dark grey concrete mix, often with a covering of green scrub thanks to the unusually heavy rains of the previous summer.

It was good news for the groups of camels that grazed at the roadside, delaying their annual exodus to the south of the country where water, and hence food, would always be in more regular supply. The time passed quickly and as we neared our destination a range of mountains unexpectedly dominated the picture; grey and flat-topped like Cape Town's famous Table Mountain and a sharp contrast to the miles of white sand and the deep green clusters of palm trees that gathered at the lower levels.

The fascinating journey was broken just once. We stopped at the only town of any note and took shade in a large tent bedecked with rugs and mattresses where tea was served by a very tall, handsome man. It was strong and black and extremely sweet (as was he, the lady passengers were no doubt thinking), served boiling hot in a small glass filled only half way but with an intriguing white foam on top. A crucially important feature of Mauritanian tea-drinking, I was soon to learn, an art form whereby the steaming brew is poured from a great height and returned several times to the pot to generate the requisite number of bubbles. We drank three glasses at five minute intervals, a pattern I would soon get used to, then returned to the bright sunlight and the very empty road.

Mauritania

Mauritania

All but one of the back seat passengers remained silent throughout thus conversation was a three way affair between myself, the driver (Mohammed) and a chatty young bloke behind my left shoulder. He was an engaging sort of chap who worked as an independent tour guide and he laughed heartily when I excitedly pointed out a lake in the distance through the shimmering heat haze. There was, of course, no lake. The dark blue shadow in the sand was a figment of my imagination, a mirage, that trick of science that comes about when two different temperatures collide head on. Je suis un plonqeur.

As the story unfolded it transpired that my back seat friend and Mohammed worked as a team and they were heading to Atar to make preparations for a group due in from Spain four days hence. Neither spoke English but they were proficient in Spanish, which I often understood better than their French, though in truth I spent a lot of time nodding and smiling because I couldn't follow either. The tour guide introduced himself as "Mean", a little shocking at first but far less sinister when written in French. "Min", as he later wrote on his e-mail address, was a contraction of his family name Lemine and so much more practical than using his first name. Which, you'll be surprised to learn, was Mohammed.

Atar was the town in which Min had grown up and still the home of his parents and siblings. He and Mohammed were heading there for lunch once they'd dropped off the Silent Three and it would be their great pleasure if I would accept an invitation to join them. They seemed very genuine people and given that my social calendar in Mauritania still had one or two blank spaces I was only to pleased to accept.

The house was on the outskirts, along a dusty track where children played amidst the garbage and scrawny donkeys wandered around with seemingly no purpose. From the featureless walls on either side of our 4x4 it wasn't easy to ascertain which of the buildings were occupied or what they actually were, until we pulled up outside the tall grey gate. It led into a courtyard and thence a large room with no furniture and very little daylight. It was mercifully cool; a large empty space with nothing more than rugs and

143

cushions on the floor and it could have been a scene from the 5th or the 15th century. Until Min stepped outside and returned with his laptop.

He was proud of his country and eager to show a video of its wonderful geography and the smiling tour groups that he'd led. The images were indeed fantastic and if his subtle plan was to sell his services to me then he'd done a first class job. I would anyway have needed to find a driver and a guide and so, as the enormous platter of food was placed on the ground before us, it was I that suggested we open negotiations.

The rice and fish and vegetables flavoured with chilli was nothing short of delicious and a spoon was provided as a courtesy to the delicate foreigner. I did feel a bit of a wimp as the boys dived in to the communal feast with their right hands and when in Rome I usually prefer to behave like a Roman (peep my horn, wave my arms around, sob hysterically etc.). But when in Mauritania I like to keep my hands nice and clean.

Min suggested an itinerary and a price that he assured me was much lower than his Spanish guests would be paying: 100 Euro a day to cover the cost of their time, fuel, transport, camping in the desert and preparation of food that we would buy along the way. It sounded pretty fair in the absence of any sort of sensible yardstick. We would start out the next morning and they would collect me from the small hotel in the main street of town.

* * * * *

The Sahara desert is larger than the whole of Australia and covers all or part of eleven different countries. Its central section, the wild expanses of southern Algeria and northern Chad, is surprisingly mountainous, but here in the West End the highland areas are far more the exception than the rule. Hence the attraction of the rolling dunes of the Adrar Plateau, one of Mauritania's thirteen regions of which Atar is the capital and Chinguetti the main tourist draw.

The Auberge Monod was handy for the town but depressing enough for one to question the rationale of trading the comfort of one's home for the facilities of a Dickensian jail. Its most distinguishing feature was the semi-permanent smell of sewage, a turbo-charged wave that would sweep through perhaps twice an hour giving the impression of a septic tank being emptied out into the wardrobe. A point I felt obliged to raise with the proprietor the next morning only to be reminded, and even given a demonstration, that I must always flush the toilet after using.

I walked around the town soon after the sun came up, profiting from the sight and sound of the streets slowly coming to life. In truth it wasn't a pretty picture, just a typical higgledy-piggledy desert town of mosques and market stalls with robed men, colourfully-dressed ladies and stray animals wandering around in the alleyways of sand and garbage. However the people were calm and extremely friendly and there's always something pleasurable about returning home with a hot fresh baguette wrapped in newspaper, even if it is to be consumed knee-deep in the fumes of human excrement.

The boys arrived ahead of schedule and we set off on the journey east for Chinguetti. A glance at the map had already revealed there was no proper road but still it seemed strangely shocking to be driving over mounds of virgin sand with nothing to offer an indication of distance or direction. Mohammed was evidently untroubled, he was in his element, the desert was his place of work and he seemed to enjoy it. We bounced at speed across the incredible and little-changing landscape – how did he know where to go? – and at one point he parked the jeep on the slope of a beautifully formed dune so we could all get out and play like children. We were the only people around for miles and miles and miles.

Or so I thought, until twenty minutes later, when we spotted a man walking through the sand. He was alone, except for a few camels, and to all intents and purposes he was my first ever desert nomad. It was an exciting and totally unexpected moment; I asked Mohammed to stop at a respectable distance and just had to go over and say Bonjour.

I must say the chap looked rather taken aback, indeed anxious, at the sight of a man from the north of England running clumsily through the sand towards him. Whether he was a particularly timid nomad I can't be sure but his handshake was lettuce limp and he seemed a trifle miffed at my turning up uninvited and disrupting his morning's work. Conversation didn't go well either, "Bonjour. Etes-vous une nomade?" prompting nothing more than a furrowed brow and the exposure of a row of teeth that had seen better days. A relief, then, for all concerned when Mohammed came over to offer some explanation (in Hassaniya) for my inane and embarrassing behaviour.

There are many strange ways to earn a living but surely few can compare to that of the life of a nomad (at the time of independence 90% of Mauritanians were nomadic, today less than a quarter of that figure). I thought about the Kyrgyz family huddled in their tent in the sub-zero wilderness of the Pamir Mountains and now this chap wandering about in the blinding heat of the desert, grazing his animals by day and retiring each evening to his canvas home once the sun goes down. And then what? For sure he will never experience the emotion and the pain of Strictly Come Dancing or Manchester City's inconsistent away form but then the threat of starvation if the rains fail to show is probably all the drama he needs.

Chinguetti is to Mauritania what Timbuktu is to Mali. Important for what it used to be rather than what it is today, this town flourished as long as 800 years ago as a centre of Islamic learning and a major hub along a trans-Sahara route travelled by thousands of men and their camels. This was back in the days long before a caravan was a holiday home on wheels and the story goes that as many as 30,000 camels once passed through Chinguetti in a single day.

I'd read this basic history and should have been prepared. But when we arrived there in the heat of the day and parked the jeep up in the old town, the sense of abandonment and dilapidation was at once overwhelming. The streets and alleyways were all but deserted (perhaps not surprising in the middle of a desert) with just the souvenir vendors to show from an alleged population of 4000 people. Despite this being the country's number 1 tourist attraction, I saw no tourists.

We wandered through the labyrinth of tall stone walls, those great

146

survivors. The old mosque stood proud as the focal point within one of the many empty compounds and we clambered up onto a rooftop to get a full view of its rectangular, almost castle-like tower. Only then, looking down from the top of the ancient city and the phenomenal sand dunes that surround it, did I start to appreciate the fullness of its charm and the extent of its vulnerability. Surely – one day – these huge waves of sand will completely take over.

The intensity of the heat and the silence of the desert added even greater impact to what was truly an extraordinary picture. Was it sad that almost everybody had left or merely an indication that man should not be meddling where Mother Nature is destined to rule? The tranquillity, and my thoughts, were finally broken by the voice of a lady who proved an unyielding determination to exchange her hand-made jewellery for the money in my pocket. I was soon to find that "Merci, Non" was not an answer to her satisfaction and, in the absence of any other visitors, she decided the best policy would be to stick around with me for the rest of the day. Unfortunately for the poor lady (non-)vendor I didn't hang around that long. Having originally planned to spend two days in the town the realisation very quickly dawned that two *hours* was probably more than sufficient to allocate to the admiration of a maze of ancient walls. "We could stretch it to three", I put it to the boys, thus allowing time for lunch and a visit to the library.

It was a silent library (as libraries used to be), located in a cave and protected by a tiny door with an ancient wooden lock. The room was blissfully cool and there was barely space enough to accommodate me, the owner and the several neat rows of files and folders that formed the basis of his presentation. The engaging gent gave a polished account of the lives of his forefathers from the great days of the desert adventurers and supported his tales with old manuscripts from the Middle East and places even as far away as Uzbekistan. Fascinating stuff, this was indeed the western extreme of the old Silk Road.

The restaurant, a room with three tables, was empty save for a few thousand flies and a lone *toubab*, the West African word for a white man. He was evidently known in the town, he dressed in a robe (*boubou*) and turban just like a local and his demeanour was unlike that of a tourist. Shortly after we entered he went upstairs to sit on the roof terrace and that's where I spotted him an hour later, legs crossed and eyes closed. Mohammed explained that the Frenchman would visit every year and almost always left alone to make the 700 mile overland journey, by camel, to Timbuktu. He would take a few possessions and carry salt to offer to the Tuaregs (the tribe that roams, and defends, the desert) in the hope that they would be less inclined to kill him. So far, Mohammed observed without humour, it seemed to have worked.

Bloody hell! And I thought I was being adventurous having a couple of servants to chauffeur me around the country in a four wheel drive. On which note I called a meeting to discuss a revised schedule to cater to the whims of this rather more pampered *toubab*. There was no good reason to stay much longer and the lads were happy to keep moving, to head forthwith for the oasis of Tanouchert, a few more hours further east across the dunes.

I recall there was lots more sand, a plentiful scattering of trees, scrub and prickly bushes. There was also a very large flock of sheep which, to the amusement of my buddies, I mistook for goats, a species that seemed rather more likely to inhabit the Sahara Desert. That was back in the days before I knew that a goat's tail goes up and a sheep's goes down.

We stopped on the top of a hill where the boys got out to talk to two men who were walking, to somewhere, with a donkey. As they all chatted away in that guttural Arabic dialect (few donkeys speak English) I too crawled out to stretch my legs, let the warm breeze ruffle my hair and take the opportunity to marvel at the landscape in all directions. An emotional experience to spend a few minutes cast adrift on an ocean of undulating sand – calm here, choppy there – nothing to interrupt the gargantuan views on any point of the compass. No variation in colour save the random scattering of bushes and a belt of dark green at the bottom of a valley towards which our vehicle was pointing. The desert was absolutely still despite the gentle movement of the air but there was no mistaking the potential for menace, just a snap of the fingers could turn a sleeping giant into a deadly monster.

My vision of an oasis had always been that of a small pond with a palm tree leaning over one side and a huddle of camels taking a slurp. Tanouchert didn't look anything like that. It was an established community of small houses and straw huts and open-fronted wooden constructions that were somewhere between the two. We parked up in front of one such shelter, dragged our bags inside and spent the next ten minutes rolling around on the carpeted floor like infants in a kindergarten.

I could see no people at all, nor a pond for that matter, just our pretty garden, lots of trees and a couple of bulky hose pipes that evidently served to irrigate the village. Mohammed set about the serious business of brewing up on his camping stove and explained that this was where we would drink tea and have dinner. We would move to the adjacent building to sleep. As he spoke he pointed with one hand to the identical structure next door and carefully poured tea back and forth between pot and glass with the other. The foam on top was very important, he confirmed. No mention was made of our host.

It was late afternoon and the light was less harsh, perfect time for a stroll around an oasis. I left the boys to the food prep, wandered out of our compound – was it a camp site? – and was surprised to find a network of established pathways. There were fences and allotments around the groups of huts and altogether rather more orderliness than one might have expected so far away from any other form of civilisation. I followed a trail through the trees, emerged with the sun at my back and started to clamber uphill through the powdery sand.

The wind picked up, cooling the beads of sweat on the side of my face and whistling just enough to stifle the sound of heavy breathing that dune-mounting induces in the grossly over-fed and under-exercised. The loose sand did little to assist in my ascent but the pain and hardship were to dissolve in a nanosecond upon reaching the nearest "summit", the one that I'd meekly set as a target. The moment I poked my head over the top a violent gust hit me full in the face but its impact alone made very little difference. It was the view before me that almost swept me off my feet.

The pyramids were perfectly symmetrical, the height of battleships yet contrived from sand the texture of flour. An astonishing feat of nature, the wind had drawn diagonal lines across a horizontal world with such precision that the edges of these huge pointed creations looked as crisp as freshly folded bed linen. Though the light was dimming fast I could see the weird and dramatic shapes for many miles into the distance; a secret planet, touched by neither man nor beast. I was utterly transfixed.

I followed one of the razor-like edges to its peak and sat for almost an hour to wallow in this science-fictional world. Gusts of wind were lifting the sand, moving the finest of sprays from left to right, yet the surface of my vast triangle remained unchanged (pure as the driven sand?) except for the set of ugly footprints that had recorded my every movement. My attention turned to the village below with its peculiar cluster of trees and out to the horizon where the sun was about to set over the otherwise empty landscape. It was then that I caught sight of something in the middle distance that was most unexpected. A man dressed in a white robe was standing bolt upright, quite alone, out there in the almost-dark desert. The sun was dipping behind him, he seemed to be looking at me.

It was only when he dropped to his knees and lowered his head to the ground that I realised he was praying. He was facing east in the direction of Mecca (and me, as it turned out), an everyday ritual in the Muslim world but one that seemed so much more graceful and poignant in the Sahara at sundown. It was getting cold now but thanks to this unforgettable experience I was glowing inside. Whatever else Mauritania had in store would simply be a bonus. This was as good as it could possibly get.

I headed back to camp a different person. The TLC project that on a bad day could seem so silly had again been rendered worthwhile and that mental tonic brought a physical boost. I felt stronger, more alert, my head as clear as the night sky. There had to be some truth after all in that old slogan many of us grew up with: "Dunes help you breathe more easily."

Two big smiles and a large pan of stew greeted my return. A thoroughly pleasing mix of meat and vegetables that tasted almost identical to my Mum's Lancashire Hot Pot, which I should tell you now she always makes with beef skirt instead of the traditional lamb (we lived in Cheshire, you see). Mohammed had plumped for a very acceptable third option and one I would be happy to endorse, though I don't suppose camel meat is that easy to come by in Chorley. We drank more tea sitting under the stars and talked about football, sport in general and a recent marathon a French bloke had organised in this part of the desert. A marathon! I thought back to the panting and wheezing of an hour earlier and wondered if it was the same nutter that spends his holidays riding solo to Timbuktu.

The subject moved inevitably to the frustration of national politics and the helplessness of a public so desperate to bring about change. A single party regime had ruled the country for its first 18 years but in 1978 had fallen to a military coup after a disastrous attempt by the French-elected leader to expand its borders into (what is now) the Western Sahara. That set the tone. Further military coups overturned the government in 1984 and 2005 and the people of Mauritania had to wait until 2007 to elect their President for the first time in the country's history. Mr Sidi Ould Cheikh Abdullah had pledged to curb the excessive influence and privilege of the military and once in power he set about his task with gusto. So you might guess what happened next. The generals stepped in a year later and booted him out.

Min and Mohammed, a brown man and a black man, also talked of the racial problems of the past. In the late eighties tens of thousands of people regarded by the government as too dark-skinned were bundled over the border into Senegal, especially the Haratin, the "Black Moors" considered to be of the lowest caste. Those that were allowed to stay continued to work as slaves and although the military government officially outlawed this in the 1980s (150 years after the rest of the world) slavery is said to be widespread in the north of the country even today.

As 9 o'clock approached the lads unfurled their sleeping bags and assured me with boyish excitement that the night would get very cold indeed in this particular oasis. Less joyous, however, was the man whose own sleeping back was rolled up in a cupboard twenty five miles north of London. I had nothing more to unfurl than a pair of lightweight trousers and a flimsy fleece and even the blanket that they kindly loaned to me seemed no more substantial than a large flowery sheet of toilet paper. So I spent the following nine hours underneath the aforementioned; teeth chattering, knees wrapped inside arms and everything tucked as tightly as possible under the chin. Why on earth would anybody want to be a foetus?

The journey eastwards continued after breakfast and how welcome was the boiling tea and warm bread after a cold, sleepless night and two more hours spent up on the dunes as the sun crept back into the sky. But I had no complaints, it had been worth trading a few hours' kip for another helping of the desert solitude. The moon and the stars had, quite literally, presented my pyramids in a different light and the wind that had whistled the night before had diminished to barely a whisper. Everything to follow the experience of the oasis was surely destined to be a disappointment.

But the ancient and, yet again, mostly abandoned town of Ouadane was anything but. Two towns in fact, the former one clinging on to a steep hillside, a skeleton of a once-important settlement built almost a thousand years earlier and today preserved by UNESCO as a World Heritage Site. We parked at its base and clambered up through the remains of the old buildings. For centuries these had been the homes of desert traders, many thousands of people ultimately forced out of business as ships and planes and 4x4s replaced the doughty but ever so slow camels as a means of moving goods between east and west.

The newer town on top of the plateau was the usual hotchpotch of tiny houses and even tinier grocery shops, several mosques, a school and a vast number of screaming children who were all very excited to see the *toubab* strolling along their sandy streets. I walked and they followed in ever increasing numbers, the cheeky ones demanding gifts and photos of the Pied Piper, the shyer and the more serious (generally the girls) observing with quiet curiosity.

We saw all there was to see of modern day Ouadane, which in truth was more about the panorama of surprisingly lush scenery below and beyond than anything spectacular within. Mohammed brought the jeep up to collect Min and myself and the three of us departed to much enthusiastic waving, stopping only to purchase baguettes from an arm that popped out of a hole in a wall. It reminded me of Thing from The Addams Family.

The setting for our lunch was in the shade of an overhanging rock adjacent to a large lake and surrounded by palm trees, a spectacle unlike any other I'd seen and a treat that the boys had kept up their sleeves for the picnic they were about to prepare. Mohammed brewed and poured the tea in the meticulous way an Irish landlord might take pride in presenting his pint of Guinness: always half a glass each (the tea, not the stout), always half an inch of foam on top, always three servings. Meanwhile Min carefully chopped his onions and tomatoes to serve with the bread and tuna as I beavered away selflessly taking photos.

It was viciously hot out of the shade and I tried to imagine what it must be like in the months of June, July and August. "The best time of year" the lads assured me, the "Guetna Season", when people from all over the country flock to the area to harvest the dates, enjoy a few drinks and throw parties for family and friends. Min pointed out the igloo-like houses that dotted the landscape, holiday homes of the city folk who would return here to spend every summer. The temperatures would be up in the 50s Celsius at that time of year but the air conditioning systems would keep them cool: piles of freshly plucked palm leaves soaked in water and stacked in the corner of the room. And the drinks in question? Camel or goat milk, depending on what sort of day you'd had.

The dirt road back towards Atar ran across the top of the plateau, stones and boulders for the most part taking the place of sand. It was dusty and rugged, as if we were traversing a large flat quarry, and the sandy valleys far below created the illusion of our being much higher than we really were. To my surprise we turned off the track onto a smaller and even bumpier one and ten minutes later we arrived at a cluster of huts with a makeshift sign introducing a camp. At its centre was a rectangular building inside which we found a few empty tables, a bar of sorts, and a smiley young lady who was clearly not from those parts.

It could have been a pub in the Australian outback except that there was no booze, no men with hats and dangling corks... and this particular sheila was French. Carole had driven from Europe with her boyfriend and as it was her first time abroad decided it would be fun to stay on in Africa. So she was travelling alone through the remotest place on earth when the owner of this desert camp, beguiled by her plucky spirit and jovial personality, invited her to unpack her bag and become the manager of his enterprise. "Why not?" she asked me rhetorically with the Frenchest of shrugs, as we went back outside to select my hut for the night.

Tikits are small and round, the size of a two-man tent (or man and lonely French woman, you're probably thinking) with walls of stone and pointed roofs of thatch. I crawled inside the nearest, took the left mattress for myself and designated the right one for my bag and its contents. We had become a married couple. I lay back, mildly amused at the thought, and focused my attention on the stylish patterned fabric that served as a ceiling and so cleverly transformed my bland little shed into a cosy home. This was the life, thought I, as the breeze drifted in through the arched opening that was my front door, perfect conditions for a pre-dinner snooze.

Carole's two members of staff (with whom she shared no common language) produced a magnificent, spicy vegetable stew that evening, as tasty a meal as I can ever recall. We passed the rest of the time exchanging stories in a muddle of French and English then I sat outside in the darkness to soak up the silence. The night was warm, beautifully warm, and it seemed every star in the universe had come out to twinkle over the desert. How I liked being in Mauritania.

* * * * *

The expression "picture postcard oasis" is seldom heard these days. Let me point you in the direction of Terjit, a tiny community weaved into a valley of densely packed palm trees, watered by a babbling brook and blessed with a natural shaded pool. Min and Mohammed had cutely saved the best till last and we all duly responded by paddling and splashing around in the stream as though it was the first we'd ever seen. This was quite believably an oasis like no other, mercifully cool and so visually delightful that it could have been purpose built as a tourist attraction. There was even a 1000 Ougiya charge for the privilege of entering the "site", a couple of quid very well spent.

The track from Terjit led us back to the main road, a T junction with Atar to the right and Nouakchott 450 kms in the other direction. The deal was that Mohammed would return me to the capital and so it was here at the roadside that my new friend Min and I hugged our good-byes. He had been true to his word and more besides and it seemed an unfitting ending to leave him in the middle of nowhere to hitch a lift back to his family. "Pas de probleme" he assured me with that toothy smile but it was still a sad and awkward moment when we shook hands and waved at each other for what, we both knew, would be the very last time.

The journey back to Nouakchott took five hours, a test of concentration for a one-to-one conversation in a language I'd barely used since school. It was often easier to just smile and nod but I learned much about life in the desert, the mafia gangs that steal camels and the small planes that mysteriously appear from across the Atlantic with drugs from South America. Mohammed talked knowledgeably about his country's resources: gold, copper, even water drilled from under the sand and bottled for human consumption.

But the biggest earner by far is iron ore, mined in the north-eastern region of Zouerat since the early 1960s and today responsible for half the country's export earnings. Such is its importance that a 675 km railway line was built to haul it to the coast upon a train considered to be the longest in the world. Its two hundred carriages are reputed to be a whopping three kilometres from end to end and each is regularly filled to capacity with the huge lumps of stone. And if you want to make a note of the annual tonnage the figure you are looking for is 16.6 billion.

It is possible to travel aboard The Iron Ore Express as a passenger if you're willing to spend a twelve hour night sitting on the floor. I must admit a small part of me was tempted. Unfortunately a large part of me argued that it would probably be very uncomfortable, I might be bored rigid, would have to spend time in two places I didn't want to be and I might get kidnapped and ultimately tortured by Algerian terrorists ducking over the border. So I decided to leave that one to "Mad Mick" Palin and the BBC crew.

Following more hugging and handshakes at the roadside yet another Mohammed disappeared out of my life and into the distance. I was back upon the familiar turf of L'Escale des Sables where the rooms seemed more luxurious than ever (to a desert veteran) though the welcome, despite my being the only guest again, was one of total indifference. No matter, I was in a clean, safe and quiet environment and in a good frame of mind to spend a couple of days getting to know the capital city.

* * * * *

It was late afternoon when the taxi dropped me into the heart of Nouakchott and the place that had seemed so unappealing by night, to my great disappointment, looked even less appealing by day. Not especially ugly, not especially dirty, not especially threatening. Not especially anything at all. I walked around for an hour or so up and down the hot, sandy streets but it was merely to convince myself of something that, deep down, I already knew. In the world rankings of "must-see cities" this was definitely at the bottom of the pile.

Lost for a better idea I went to the same café that I'd visited on the first evening and sat there alone. The joy of Mauritania was no more, my mates, and the thrill of the desert, gone forever. The prospect of another 36 hours in Nouakchott held no more appeal than spending a day and a night in a disused phone box. I tried to lift my spirits, to consider which unfortunate city might take penultimate spot in my new league table but couldn't come up with anywhere at all so remotely uninspiring. The sad truth was that the inclusion of Nouakchott in any sort of international listing would be like comparing the reserve team of your local pub with, say, Chelsea or Manchester United. (Or even Manchester City for that matter). And with that final depressing thought, I paid for my Coke and went home.

It was a very good thing that I didn't slit my wrists. The next day took me on a fascinating walk around the local neighbourhood where I watched the donkey carts deliver drums of fresh water to people's doors and chatted to shoe-menders and tool suppliers and all manner of folk trying to eke out a living in the nearby market. The place had a great buzz about it... and not just because of the billion flies that were feasting on the camel meat of the butchers' stalls.

And from there to the seaside, a twenty minute cab ride away. The Moors, being desert people, chose to build their capital a few kilometres inland in preference to the shores of the Atlantic and, even to this day, many country dwellers remain suspicious of the ocean. Some refuse to eat any form of seafood (an old school attitude?) and most of the local fishermen are Senegalese by birth. I was heading for the beach where the boats come in.

I expected it to be smelly and filthy, just shows how wrong you can be. The sea was crystal clear and the long beach impeccably clean despite the number of people and the hundreds of fishing vessels lined up on the sand. I walked back and forth to watch the daily ritual unfold. Every few minutes a brightly painted canoe would sail in to the shallow waters for the day's catch to be transferred onto a wooden cart and pulled up on to the beach by a donkey harnessed thereto. At which point the crew, usually six men, would climb out to drag their heavy wooden boats fifty metres ashore with a series of well-rehearsed zig-zag movements and a chorus of chants to ensure absolute co-ordination.

The only negative in an otherwise perfect day came in the form of a conversation with the Senegalese taxi driver to whom I'd outlined my onward travel plan. Speaking from his years of experience he promised me that the border crossing back to his homeland would be "tres dangereux", so dangereux in fact that his head wagged despairingly from side to side and he felt compelled to repeat the warning no less than four or five times. But dangereux or not, it was a journey I had to make the following day, Friday 13th.

I thought long and hard that night about my battle plan and set about it with purpose early next morning. The daypack was emptied, its contents stuffed into my main holdall and padlocked inside with everything else including money and one of two credit cards. It weighed a ton, not great for schlepping in the tropical heat but a formidable challenge for a snatch and run. A small amount of cash, together with my passport, went into a hard-to-access, hard-to-razor, zipped trouser pocket and the other credit card was secreted elsewhere. In the interest of self defence, one hand would be kept free at all times. This was it, my last day in Mauritania. It had all gone so well, please Allah, don't let it go tits-up now.

The three-hour drive to the border was predictable enough with six other passengers and one goat in the rear sections of the taxi, none of whom spoke or baa'd at any point. The last town on the Mauritanian side was Rosso and it was here that we all disembarked, claimed our luggage from the driver and, clutching on to it for dear life, dispersed into the loitering (mostly Senegalese) crowd. My game plan was to be calm but extremely assertive and to let the thugs know loudly and clearly that they were not to lay a hand on any part of my person or baggage. It felt a little cruel and perhaps a tad excessive but it worked like a dream, my ferocious bark persuaded them to back off and some, dare I say it, looked even more terrified than I was.

The River Senegal divides the border posts of the two countries and the short ferry ride across the water offered welcome respite ahead of the chaos that I knew lay in store. And indeed it came quickly. I was directed to join a triangle of people, some fifty in number, who were jostling for position in front of a shed that served as the immigration office. This the Senegalese system for welcoming visitors, a product of years of time and motion study whereby every arriving passenger simultaneously thrusts an outstretched arm towards the open hatch in the hope that a proffered passport will be snatched and stamped by the uniformed person on duty.

It wasn't working too well that day or perhaps I was just unlucky. The midday sun, the swirling flies and the deep sense of misery felt by all led to verbal abuse of the solitary official, which inevitably made a bad situation worse. His displeasure at having to face the baying mob (and no doubt at copying passport numbers in a ledger for a living) thrice resulted in a petulant downing of the pen and ultimately a throwing of arms in the air, a slamming of the door and a temporary abandonment of post.

Unlike many, I was lucky enough to be able to release a free arm to wipe sweat and insects from my face and to check down below that fellow jostlers weren't dipping my pockets. Lucky? To be back in Senegal? Who was I trying to kid? And then the penny dropped and a wave of satisfaction floated over me, putting the surrounding madness on hold. I was no longer in Mauritania, I'd been there, done it, loved it, met some great people and made it safely out of the country. It brought a smile as my passport was finally stamped and it emboldened me to take a deep breath and charge as fast as my bag would let me through the waiting crowd of vendors, beggars and thieves.

My escape from the melee was on a donkey and trap and the back seat of a fifty-year-old taxi that had to be pushed by the police each time we were stopped at checkpoints. Against all the odds, late that afternoon, I made it safely to the city of St Louis.

The Ten-Letter Countries

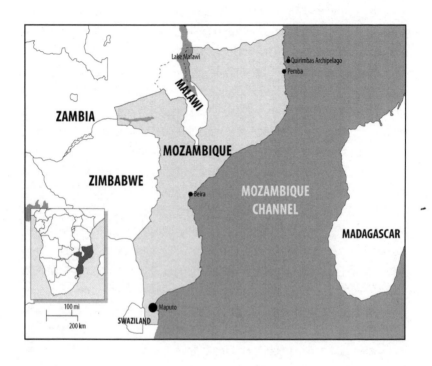

160

Mozambique

Some of you might be familiar with the name Norman Hunter, a former Leeds United footballer best remembered for a style of tackling that teetered on the fringes of sadism. Strangely enough he was a quiet, superstitious bloke when he wasn't snapping and crunching bones and it's always stuck with me that before every match he insisted on being the last man to emerge from the players' tunnel into the heat of battle.

As a regular user of airports and aeroplanes I have long since adopted Norman's approach. This doesn't involve damaging the limbs of fellow passengers but rather allows them to compete in line for early access to the cabin whilst I smugly watch the action unfold from a comfortable distance. At the moment the penultimate punter flicks open his passport and relinquishes a section of boarding card to the lipsticked lady I amble forward, flash what I hope is a sexy smile and…

"Sorry sir, this is not the flight to Maputo. Didn't you know it had been switched to gate A19?"

O.R. Tambo airport, Johannesburg is a very big place these days, particularly so when your flight is scheduled to depart fifteen seconds hence. It was a desperate, ungainly sprint past the duty frees and through the seemingly endless corridors of shops purveying biltong and pretend giraffes and all manner of enormous wooden carvings that would each surely require a plane seat of their own. Every stride was punished with the remorseless pounding of shoulder bag against thigh and I could sense the floodgates about to give way in what would doubtless be a sweat-fest of Victoria Falls proportions. So much for Norman Hunter. He was crap anyway.

I leapt aboard the transit bus as its door was folding and we were in the sky long before the panting had abated. The refreshment trolley

161

took most of the flight to reach row 29 but its eventual arrival helped nurse me back into life and encouraged conversation with Katie, my neighbour in seat C. She was quite some lady, a thirtysomething American whose desire to help those less fortunate had first brought her to Mozambique ten years earlier. She worked with children who had been abandoned by their mothers, women who themselves had been abused and then forced into prostitution as their only means of survival. Katie's conversation was compelling and her story a fascinating one, not least because she had just married a widower in South Africa and become a stepmother to her husband's four children. We agreed to meet for coffee the next morning.

The windowless, dimly lit, arrivals hall served as a sharp reminder that, unlike so many of Johannesburg's affluent northern suburbs, I was well and truly back in the real Africa. Twenty five minutes in a plane had rewound the clock fifty years and here I was waiting for my visa in a worn and broken room with its single conveyor belt, flaky walls and signs with missing letters. The corny posters from a bygone era advertised hotels and restaurants in peculiar and badly spelt English and I couldn't help thinking, perhaps unfairly, that they would probably be misspelt in Portuguese too.

The bureaucratic process was slow, disorganised and confusing, as though the arrival of foreigners at an airport was an unexpected scenario. But a system of sorts did eventually emerge, as it usually does, albeit one that clearly did not have customer service at the forefront of priorities. However many times one does it, and I have done it many, many times, the move from first world to third always comes as a shock to the system.

The Hotel Cardoso returned me to surroundings rather more stylish than I had imagined – or sought – when booking. Turning up at such a place with reservation in pocket is easy and convenient but to me never feels in keeping with the spirit of adventure and how embarrassingly middle class and middle-aged is it to have a porter carry your bag to the room and then run through the procedures for using the a/c and the TV remote. Could this be the same backpacker that once haggled for a mattress in an Indian doss house to share a room with a rat?

* * * * *

Mozambique is a Y-shaped landmass with Swaziland and South Africa to the south, Zimbabwe to the west and Malawi, with its magnificent lake, separating Zambia and Tanzania on its northern borders. To the east is the Indian Ocean, an immense two and a half thousand kilometres of Mozambican coastline and the capital city of Maputo perched aside a wide bay almost at its southern extreme. And here was I, Mr Privileged, sitting at a table on the hotel lawn, beer in hand, looking out across that spectacular stretch of water. It was nearing the end of May, heading into the southern winter, but the sun was still significantly warmer than a summer's day in England. I waited until late afternoon to take to the streets.

It was the trees that really struck me. Granted, my gaff was in an affluent area, lush and leafy with high walls and stylish villas but I was soon to find that Maputo's arboreal charm was not limited to the suburbs of the wealthy. The pavements were broken and the roads severely potholed but here was a city blessed by nature with thousand upon thousand of jacaranda and flame trees so cleverly distracting from the poverty, neglect and dilapidation that one sensed was just beneath the surface. It was such a pleasant place in which to wander, not only because of the greenery but the splendour of the old colonial buildings and stylish architecture of which the Portuguese can be duly proud. And if you haven't read the history of Mozambique, it seems they didn't have too much else to be proud of...

It was 1545 when their first ships arrived in this bay and the city would become known as Lourenco Marques in honour of the chap at the helm. The Africans from the west coast had already been in this part of the continent since the days of Christ and the Swahili-speaking Arabs from the east are said to have arrived some seven hundred years after that. But it was the Portuguese, led initially into the north of the country by Vasco de Gama, who claimed the authority. They took over the Arab trading ports, sold as many as a million Africans into slavery and then much later, three centuries later in fact, declared themselves officially in charge.

Not surprisingly, the locals weren't impressed. The Europeans did nothing to win hearts and minds, they overtly and unashamedly pillaged the country and abused its people at will. Resentment simmered beneath the surface for the next half century or so but the bubble finally burst in 1960 when the Portuguese authorities opened fire and massacred a peaceful group of demonstrators. That was the beginning of the end, a resistance movement gained momentum and after a fifteen year armed struggle, some 477 years after Vasco had first led his men on to the Isla de Mozambique, the Portuguese were finally kicked out.

* * * * *

I found a streetside café by the name of Chicken Piri Piri, reminding me that I'd read somewhere that this mother of all chilli peppers had originated in Mozambique. I took a seat, perused the menu and, as I knew I must, ordered a Chicken Piri Piri and a beer (in favour of the surprising offer of Vimto, that good old Manchester drink).

Very little time seemed to pass – one beer in fact – before a waiter emerged holding aloft a tray with a headless creature the size of a hippo. It looked well dead, well cooked and well spiced and, I figured, would be best enjoyed with a half decent drop of red wine. Would this be an appropriate request in such a modest eatery or would it equate to shouting up a bottle of Chablis at a KFC? Proximity to the vino-paradise of South Africa convinced me a glass of house red would be a safe enough bet, in hindsight a line of logic that suggests a burger van parked up in a Dover lay-by might be relied upon to offer a vintage Burgundy. The food was delicious but the wine so spectacularly repulsive that I couldn't even convince myself, though not for the want of trying, that a second glass might somehow taste better.

The streets were quiet and as I meandered vaguely homewards a young boy emerged between parked cars, eager to earn a few coins by selling me locally-grown nuts. Then a young woman with a very short skirt appeared only she was more interested in getting her hands on my British-grown nuts! Both were extremely polite and friendly (I refer of course to the boy and the woman), both were fighting for survival and both, I reflected sadly, were doing what they would probably do for the rest of their lives.

Other ubiquitous folk of the night were the security guards whose job it is to sit and watch the world go by, their workplace through the long hours of darkness just a white plastic chair on the pavement in front of the buildings they are employed to protect. I chatted to quite a few and noticed how happy they were to shake my hand and talk about their lives and their families and the difficulties they face. They were delighted to meet a visitor from UK and always surprised to come across a version of Portuguese that blended accents from the south-east of Brazil and the north-west of England!

Some were young, some had been sitting there for 25 years, all were wearing anoraks and bob hats against their version of winter cold (it sometimes drops below 10 degrees). Every night they would sit there in silence, stare at the ground and fight the overwhelming urge to drop off to sleep. At best a boring existence, at worst an exceedingly dangerous one and I have always wondered how these lowly-paid guys, most of whom have lowly-paid day jobs as well, would be expected to respond in the face of a gang of armed, masked robbers. But I decided it better not to ask.

In the days that followed I realised how much I liked Maputo, or Maputu as it's pronounced by the locals. It wasn't just the trees and the quirky buildings but the vibrancy of the small bars and restaurants tucked away on otherwise sleepy streets and – later in the evenings – the simple kiosks and mobile trailers that opened their hatches, turned on the music and cracked open the beers. A street party on wheels, Mr Whippy by day, Mr Wetherspoon by night... aaagh the pleasures and opportunities of life in the tropics.

It all reminded me so much of those bohemian streets of Botafogo in the southern suburbs of Rio where I'd once had the good fortune to work and live. A topsy-turvy world where rules and regulations exist in abundance but where daily life goes to prove, sometimes for better though often for worse, that few people have the will or authority to enforce them. An atmosphere of organised chaos and a carefree, happy-go-lucky, enjoy-it-to-the-max attitude to life that epitomises the "cariocas" of Rio de Janeiro but invites such pompous cynicism from the suited and booted of rather more serious Sao Paulo. I suppose within us all there's something of the crazy carioca and the pensive paulista and we are among the fortunate few that can choose to dabble with a little bit of whatever we fancy.

This in marked contrast to the world of Katie and her young colleague Amy who had turned up to meet me, as arranged, in the café across from the hotel. Two women dedicated to the work of charities, caring for young people who have no choices at all over the directions that their lives will take. These are children whose mothers have suffered sexual abuse long before reaching puberty, usually at the hands of their fathers or uncles, or both. They are all people without a voice, victims of an African tribal society that dictates young girls do not question the actions of their elders.

Victims too of the wacky rule of witchcraft that stipulates one member of the family must be sacrificed for the rest to succeed. And so these young girls are cast off into adulthood without a shred of dignity or self-esteem, forced into a life of prostitution, homelessness, and almost inevitably disease. They are damaged children who soon produce children of their own, often intentionally on account of the myth that pregnancy itself offers immunity to infection. It is a pitiful state of affairs, a cycle of abuse and misery and ignorance and it made me realise just how much the world owes to people like Katie and Amy.

* * * * *

There would never be enough time to do justice to a country the size of Mozambique. I'd given this a lot of thought and decided the best plan was to drive south for a few days then return to the capital to catch a flight to Pemba, right up at the top towards the Tanzanian border. From there I had hoped to head west into the jungle, possibly even across to (what we call) Lake Malawi but instead, for reasons I will later explain, would have to make do (!) with a chain of exotic islands known as the Quirimbas Archipelago.

I returned to the airport to hire a 4x4 and made straight for the ferry terminal on the shoreline beneath my hotel. To my delight and astonishment the rusty motorised platform loomed into view exactly in accordance with the timetable that had been relayed to me from a scribbled-on piece of paper in the manager's office. Sadly it was to loom immediately out of view again having cruised directly past the line of waiting vehicles and passengers. This being Africa nobody (except me, of course) expressed alarm or disappointment or even the slightest curiosity about the ferry's diversion and the consequent non-adherence to the sailing schedule.

In the end it was a two and a half hour wait for the five minute crossing of the bay, the refuelling of the trusty vessel having never been factored into the timetabling process. No matter, the views back towards Maputo made it all worthwhile and offered an entirely different perspective of this unusual two-tier city. I easily picked out the Cardoso, high up on the headland away to my right, and now saw clearly that the modest smattering of tower blocks that was the city's commercial hub – the "baixa" (pronounced bysha) – was very much down the slope at sea level.

Life across the bay was manifestly different. The town of Catembe was little more than a run down village, a cobbling together of roadside stalls either side of a gravel track that served as its main street. The only street, in fact, which after a couple of hundred metres widened out to form the main "highway" linking Maputo to the south of the country. Its surface resembled a clay tennis court, firm to a point but dry and red and dusty with the constant threat that an over-eager manoeuvre could result in disaster. I started slowly, built up speed and confidence then slowed down again when a bend provoked a mini skid and almost deposited man and vehicle into a roadside ditch. There was no hurry, I told myself, just enjoy the rural scenery, the wide empty spaces and the rolled-out carpet of blue sky.

Villages were few and far between but even remote areas were not without people appearing at the roadside: a man standing alone under a tree, a woman carrying an enormous bag on her head, a couple of children playing in a field. Where had they come from? Where would they go? What did their lives entail? What a peculiar existence.

An hour of crunching gravel was followed – against all expectations – by the delicious, silky smooth sensation of tarmac and almost at that same moment the scrub, barren landscape transformed into rolling green countryside. The window was down now, no longer essential to keep out the clouds of dust, and with top gear engaged and the breeze in my face life was starting to feel rather good. I was making reasonable headway towards Ponta Mamoli, a small bay just before the South African border and the image of myself with a foam moustache from that first beer was hanging in a bubble over my head like a cartoon caption. And so to a question only God can answer. Why, dear bearded one, did you decide that this lovely road should simply come to an end slap bang in the middle of nowhere?

The Toyota must have looked like a fly walking through a bag of flour as it battled through the last forty kilometres of soft, powdery sand. There were moments, scary moments indeed, when the wheels just whirred and screeched in protest and it seemed we were destined to go no further. So what would I do if I got stuck in the sand, miles from anywhere? I gave it some serious thought and realised with no small amount of disappointment that a Plan B of any sort was unlikely to be forthcoming.

Thankfully Plan A got me where I wanted to be with more than ample reward. The coastline was strikingly green and rugged and the only sound I could detect, once the engine had been cut, was the swirling of the ocean and the crashing of waves upon the rocks. The sheer brutality of it lured me down to the water's edge and I found myself standing alone on a beach that seemed to have no end. Virgin sand, miles and miles of it, not even a footprint, or any debris, or anything at all to indicate that man had ever set foot in this corner of the globe. Strangely it reminded me of Cornwall, yes... a tropical Cornwall without any people. This was why Ponta Mamoli had come so highly recommended.

I was offered a cheery welcome by the Mamoli hotel team and led to a wooden cabin set in a dense cluster of trees behind the beach. It was appropriately simple accommodation. Every care had been taken to preserve the environment and it quickly shone through that the South African owners managed their small resort with a sense of pride and professionalism. They assured me of their best attention and hoped I would enjoy my stay. It was never in doubt.

The home cooking was superb, the staff were brilliant and the small bar inevitably added the final touch. Scuba diving and horse-riding were always an option but there are times an alphabet traveller needs to have a rest, take it easy and spend a few days just to walk on the sand and – when the heat gets too much – dunk his head in the surf. You're probably thinking this job is a doddle, anybody could do it blindfolded, but then you don't yet know about the Maputo Elephant Reserve do you?

My map and guidebook had already drawn my attention to the immense nature reserve that was allegedly home to a few hundred elephants, to say nothing of hippos, crocs and a plethora of birdlife. Indeed it had been one of my reasons for deciding to head south and the rough plan was to pay a visit there en-route back to Maputo. So what a stroke of luck that I should get to hear of a short-cut to an unmarked park entrance, accessed along a track just a short distance from my cosy little haven. All I needed to do was get to Lake Piti, just half an hour away, follow it round to the right, and Bob would be my uncle.

I got up in the dark and set off as soon as dawn broke, ready to catch Africa's wildlife with its pants down. What a buzz of excitement, surely there's nothing that gets the blood pumping like a big toothy croc before breakfast. I followed the directions exactly as given but when the track split two ways, as it did several times, my only ally was educated guesswork and a vague sense of direction. An hour slipped by. All was lake-less, hopeless and very much Uncle Bob-less.

Just as misery and frustration were threatening a dual appearance I spotted that ubiquitous Solo African Bloke In Field, presumably on his way to or from somewhere. He pointed me towards the lake and sure enough, after another twenty minutes of lurching and rocking, I found myself on the bank tucking into a hard-earned breakfast. I'd silently attacked the 4-metre crocodile from behind, karate chopped it across the back of the neck then choked it on its own tail before scooping out its warm innards with my Swiss Army knife. I also had some bread, cheese and fruit courtesy of the hotel.

OK so I didn't really see a croc, except on the warning sign that offered a subtle picture of one with its teeth bedded into the side of a child's head. Of hippos, statistically the most prolific man-killer, there was no mention yet I did manage to spot a family of them through my bincs where their backs were raised above the surface of the water. More surprisingly I was also able to pick out a park ranger just beyond the lake, and found him standing in front of a wire somewhat curiously rigged up between two posts. In return for my hearty "Bom Dia!" he explained that this was an official park border, that his job was to collect the entrance fee, but that today it wouldn't be possible on account of his not having a receipt book. Thankfully he seemed content with the suggestion of my settling up at another gate on departure and having offered his apologies for the park maps also running out, he unhooked the wire and allowed me to pass.

A map would have been very handy, or perhaps the odd sign to indicate where the many sandy tracks might eventually lead. The countryside was blissful, particularly above the dunes looking back along that wild coastline, but it could only be enjoyed in short bursts given that steering demanded so much concentration. The first hour was a novelty but the second started to be tiring and by the third hour I was seriously fed up. Where exactly was I, what was I doing here and…. most importantly of all, how the bloody hell was I going to get out?

The only sign of life came in the form of a few monkeys, the occasional antelope and then my best catch of all: two ladies carrying heavy bags upon their heads. They were typical African females with large breasts and protruding bottoms but with thin legs and wrinkled faces that made them look twenty years older than they probably were. They spoke no Portuguese – less educated women tend to learn only their tribal languages – but made it clear they too wanted to get to the main entrance and would show me the way. Smiles all round and no wonder, it took another hour and a half to drive and would have been a two-day walk.

The tiny grocery shop by the main entrance of a seldom-visited park had to be struggling for trade and the lady standing within those four bleak walls was entitled to look unhappy. Her fridge was empty except for a few bottles of Coke and the dusty shelves displayed little more than a few bags of rice and tins of sardines. We both enjoyed the opportunity to have somebody to talk to and the cold fizzy drinks she snapped open gave a welcome lift to mind and body. On reflection, how much did I really care about seeing an elephant anyway? The old lady was much more interesting than was her place of work. She told me the story of how in the 1980s she and her five children had been forced to escape to Maputo on account of the war that had gripped the country almost as soon as independence from the Portuguese had been won.

It was a war that I'd read about but struggled to properly understand. After eleven years of battling against the colonial masters the freedom fighters (Frelimo) had become the new government and turned east to Russia and East Germany for support and guidance. But there were many countries to the west who had no wish to see communism come to Africa and an opposition group rose up under the name of Renamo. Civil war ensued, the country's fragile infrastructure was smashed to pieces and Frelimo's leaders kept on dying in mysterious circumstances.

Mozambique, already a mess, became a bigger one. The first seventeen years of independence were dominated by war and the communist ideal proved (as usual) to be less than ideal after all. A few years of Marxist nonsense drove the country into bankruptcy and from 1975 to

1992 there was nothing but chaos and destruction. And then the world changed. The Soviet Union fell apart and South Africa suddenly had bigger fish to fry: rewriting its own history was far more important than fighting a war for its impoverished neighbour. Mozambique was left alone, desperate and destitute, but at least, at last, peace could finally break out.

* * * * *

I was happy to be back in the city. The pre-ferry lunch at the Catembe Gallery Hotel had been a perfect end to the excursion, not only for the quality of the seafood but the unforgettable views from the balcony out across the bay. I'd sat there in the sunshine for almost two hours looking out towards Maputo's unusual skyline and watching the small boats weaving patterns on the surface of the water. An idyllic setting and a rather pleasant way to spend an afternoon, don't you think?

Though Maputo traffic is light by the standards of most cities and, unusually for a "foreign" colony, drives on the same side as UK, it was easier to spend the last day exploring the "baixa" on foot. I called in at the railway station at the city's far end just to admire the stunning architecture of the white and green building, and then, reflecting that I might be turning into an anorak, dropped into a couple of small bars for cold beer and tapas style snacks (petiscos): cod balls, prawn rissoles, crab in the shell, steak and onions chopped and ready to eat with toothpicks. Always yummy, always fried, and always best followed with a generous swig of Gaviscon.

It was a typical balmy Maputo evening and I was heading home through the quiet streets, admiring the silhouettes of the trees when – quite suddenly – all hell broke loose. Car horns blared in every direction and people of all ages appeared at their windows, most screaming frantically and many waving flags. A strike? A protest? Surely, please, not another war? I watched and I listened, utterly bemused. Then a local gentleman came over and explained the situation. The football match beamed from Lisbon had just finished and once again, for the sixth time in seven years,

FC Porto had won the league. So they didn't need José Mourinho after all.

I was still smiling about it as the plane took off for Pemba the next morning, a two hour twenty minute flight to the northernmost state of the country. It was a journey that promised to follow almost the entire coastline of Mozambique and one that I'd been rather looking forward to. But why Pemba you are itching to know?

It all started some months earlier with a session of internet research and a closer look at the map. The north of the country had seduced me with the tantalising eastern shore of Lake Malawi (known as Lago Niassa in Mozambique) on one side, a chain of exotic islands on the other and a vast swathe of jungle in between. The latter was almost virgin territory – the long bloody wars had kept out investors and tourists – but I'd seen that a South African company called Rani had recently opened a lodge way out in the middle of the bush. It sounded very different, so I dropped them a line.

The response was immediate and more comprehensive than I had expected. Yes they could fly me from Pemba in to their wildlife hideaway, I could also stay at one of their properties in Pemba itself...and then they would fly me out to the islands to soak up some luxury in one or two of their other establishments! All I had to do was give them my credit card details and authorise a payment equal to the cost of a five bedroom house in Mayfair.

This was above the budget of an Alphabet Traveller by a ludicrous distance but it didn't stop me dreaming of what might have been. Maybe I could find equally interesting places for a lower price, or plead poverty and try to negotiate a backpacker's rate? I couldn't let it rest. The internet offered inferior alternatives and even higher prices, confirming an ever-growing suspicion that northern Mozambique was amongst the most expensive places in the world for visitors despite being one of the poorest for the folk that live there. I contacted Rani in search of a compromise.

In the end we struck a deal and I convinced myself that the financial sacrifice would one day be justified. The itinerary was to be exactly as first offered but when it came to finalising the dates it turned out the jungle lodge had been booked out by a hunting party from Russia. A disappointment, though one that had long since passed as I peered down at the turquoise ocean through the window of the aircraft.

"Been in Maputo long?"

The voice of my neighbour, a South African guy on a connecting flight from Johannesburg. His introduction prompted an exchange of stories and thoughts about his homeland and then moved on to the reason for his trip to Mozambique. He was a professional photographer on his way, as he described it, to the middle of nowhere.

"My mate up the plane has all the details. All I know is we've been hired by a group of Russians for a hunting trip."

The flight was as spectacular as I had expected. The detail of land and sea was clearly discernible from six miles up and the mirror images of the white puffy clouds cast strange dark shadows on the ground. It brought home to me how much of the country I was missing out on as we crossed the major landmarks: the islands of the Bazaruto Archipelago, the port city of Beira and the mouth of the Zambezi. One of my favourite African names, there is something exotic about the word Zambezi isn't there? This is the great river that David Livingstone set out to explore in the 1850s, to chart its course from the highlands of what is now Zambia to this point on the Indian Ocean more than 1500 miles downstream.

And so to Pemba. Not to be confused with Tanzania's island of the same name, I'd already noted that this small coastal town claims rather boldly to be built around "the third largest natural harbour in the world". Sydney, Rio....Pemba. Getting the idea? It is at best a highly dodgy assertion but I have to admit, as we swooped in over the vast kidney-shaped pool of water, it was every bit as impressive as the locals would have us believe.

The Pemba Beach Hotel was equally impressive. Peach in colour and built in the style of an Arab fort, the sheer magnitude of the wooden doors at its entrance was a clear indication of the splendour that was to come. I was led into a courtyard replete with fountain and palm trees, offered the customary welcome drink and steered towards the staff at reception. Everywhere was cool yet bright and airy; there were few doors, open spaces in the place of windows and wide cloisters leading out to the restaurant and the gardens. A series of archways introduced the views and the welcome breeze of the Indian Ocean and I was feeling far too damned pleased with myself to even concentrate on filling in the forms.

Rui The Manager had a Portuguese name, a South African accent and a charming manner. He would be available at any time to offer help and guidance though apologised for the fact that he would have to go out later that day. A big occasion at the nearby orphanage he explained, a party thrown by the missionaries to extend a hand of friendship to the local communities of the town and the villages beyond. Would I care to go along and join in the fun?

Three hours later, somewhat at odds with my original plans for the afternoon, I found myself sitting on one of the many rows of chairs in a large community hall. On the stage before me two young men with drums and a guitar bashed out a distinctive, unchanging African beat whilst an unusual assortment of people danced to the rhythm with remarkable energy. African children, teenagers and adults were throwing themselves frantically into the action, always ready with the right moves and seemingly unconcerned by the heat, sweat, and odour levels that were cranking up by the minute. Added to the mix were the representatives from the West, the white men and women of varying ages who were clearly at some disadvantage but gamely determined to offer their support and join in the fun. It was still only 5 o'clock in the afternoon and as the music got louder, the line of people on stage grew ever longer. Please God, don't anybody try to get me up there.

I probably looked, and definitely felt, like a miserable old fart but at least tried to seem polite and upbeat as Rui introduced me to the (mostly) American people running the show. They all greeted me with warmth and friendship and a level of enthusiasm that I must confess was mildly unnerving and not easy to reciprocate. I was hugged and welcomed, my every comment deemed to be "awesome", and on more than one occasion reminded that we were all there as friends of Jesus.

I was sorely tempted to put the record straight and say I was actually a friend of Rui's but sensed that Manchester humour might fall on stony ground. (Would they have thought Bernard Manning was "awesome"?). They were indeed a peculiar bunch but no question that these were good people whose sole purpose in life was to bring love and happiness to children who had never experienced either and many of whom would never recover from the torment of their early years. Sad, lonely kids who had never known what it was to be hugged, had never woken to a dry mattress, had never seen a smile or ever felt able to produce one of their own. Such were the heartbreaking stories of their short lives, relayed to me in bursts over the beating of the drums.

More and more people of all ages filed in and headed directly for the stage. The music and dancing was frenetic and unceasing, occasionally supported by communal chanting or a random high-pitched shriek from one of the members of the band. There were happy faces all round and the kids in particular were, quite literally, having the time of their lives. It was impossible to distinguish between those that lived there and the many hundreds from the surrounding areas but every one of them was king for a day and had enjoyed a free lunch thanks to the hard work and generosity of the team at the orphanage.

Rui had had to return to work and we'd agreed I would follow on foot. The party had been a wonderful, touching experience but I sensed it was time for me to leave when it entered the trance and worship phase in preparation for the guest of honour. Top of the bill was an American missionary who, I was assured throughout the day, had oft taken awesome to new levels by curing the terminally ill and even – when really on his game – restoring life to the deceased. To miss his gig was an unthinkable act in the eyes of the true believers so I didn't make too much of a fuss of my departure when I slipped out of the door and headed back to the hotel for a poolside snifter.

The events of the day had given me much to contemplate. I couldn't have faced an evening of wailing and chanting or the stomach-churning spectacle of able-bodied people crawling on their hands and knees in the name of the Lord. My cynical side struggles with these bizarre displays of devotion and positively rebels against the concept of adults seeking to brainwash the young and the vulnerable. Yet without the love, kindness and dedication of these missionaries what would happen to these kids and the other half million orphans in a country with no resources? It is often said that the world would be a better place without religion but I suspect that's not the view of a homeless Mozambican child or the many poor souls around the world who would otherwise be left to suffer in silence.

* * * * *

Pemba sits on a peninsula that is roughly a mile and a half in width with the open sea on one side and the world-famous bay on the other. The land in between is dominated by a steep hill so it stood to reason that a walk from "coast to coast" would be challenging in the heat but rewarded with fabulous views of the water on all three sides. I weighed up the options and decided to take a taxi to the top.

My best photo of the bay, from the highest point I could reach by car and foot, was taken while standing on a wall in the cemetery. Even then the camera struggled to do justice to the majestic expanse of turquoise water down below or capture the length and shape of the coastline as it curled away and then back on itself to almost complete a circle. Guinness Book of Records or not, the Baia de Pemba had made a valiant effort.

It was a beautiful morning... but then most mornings are beautiful just twelve degrees below the equator. The air was clear and the rich colours of the trees and the flowers more than held their own despite the dense mass of blue sky and the stunning colour of the water in the background. All was as silent as the photograph itself. There was only one other person around, a gardener dressed in green overalls and wellies, and he was thrilled to lead me on a tour of his remarkable graveyard.

It seems an odd thing to admit but I've become quite fond of cemeteries. They always bring a sense of calm and a measure of dignity to the world and, more often than not, a lesson in local history. This one was a beauty in every sense. The gravestones reflected the country's (almost equal) mix of Christians and Muslims and even in death highlighted the extremes of rich and poor. I was shown the marble tombs of the wealthy and then taken around the lower, slightly unkempt, field where wooden sticks marked the burial sites and the names of the deceased were simply scratched on by hand.

But it was the smallest, tidiest compound that captured my attention. It held around a hundred well-maintained graves and the crystal clear inscriptions caught my eye from quite some distance: Ferguson, Riley, Lowe, Robinson..... men of the South Lancashire Regiment who had fought in the First World War battle of Porto Amelia (as Pemba then was) and lost their lives fighting for the King and the British Empire. Young lads, probably from Manchester, that came by ship to Africa and paid the ultimate sacrifice. For all I know, they might even have gone to school with my granddad.

I walked on in search of something less sombre and indeed I covered most of Pemba on foot in the days that followed. I watched the kids on the beach digging for worms and fishing in rock pools for prawns and wondered how much of their toil was for fun as opposed to a means of survival. And I watched artists with the simplest of tools and the widest of smiles carving beautiful ornate pieces from lumps of raw timber, single items that would take several months to complete to be sold on the market for just a few dollars. Another reminder of the poverty of Mozambique and the fact that its north-east is the poorest region of all.

The last stop in Pemba was Wimbi Beach, the jewel in the crown, the magnificent sweep of sand that pulls the tourists in. Yet this day it was almost empty. I made a point of walking its entire length, childishly touching a rock at each end to signify completion, and stopping on the way for a bottle of coke (supplied free of charge as the bar had no change) and a chat with a security guard. He stood very formally in a booth in front of three beachside chalets and confirmed that times indeed were tough, tourism was suffering and the properties he was supervising were nearly always empty except for the period leading up to elections.

"Elections?" Had I heard him correctly?

"Ah yes, the owner always come to Pemba just before the elections. He is the President of Mozambique," my friend added matter-of-factly.

The reputation of the Dolphin restaurant took me back to Wimbi for the farewell (to Pemba) evening. It was a safe recommendation in that dinner under the palm trees, caipirinhas made with vodka and fresh limes and three flowery-shirted blokes knocking out a tune is rarely a disappointing combo. The owner, Humberto, one of a steadily diminishing number of white Mozambicans, was pleased to have a European guest. He came over to chat at every opportunity, kindly treated me to drinks on the house and even insisted on driving me back to the hotel at the end of the evening. Pemba brings very few customers from overseas, he lamented, and he would never be accepted as one of the locals even though he'd lived there for all of his sixty plus years. He was a fish out of water, not by any means a racist but – as he saw it – a white man trying to make his way in a black man's world. A nice bloke and what a desperately sorry tale. Here's to you Humberto, meu amigo.

Speaking of fish, my host the next evening was a totally different kettle of. A handsome Frenchman with the unusual name of Elder had some years earlier been so charmed by the island of Ibo that he bought a house there. As with most of the neighbouring buildings it had been no more than a decaying shell, abandoned by the Portuguese who had used the island as an administrative base in their colonial heyday. Together with his business partner and a team of locals Elder had – slowly but surely – transformed the property into a fabulous little guest house and la piece de résistance was the bar in the back garden and a dining gazebo beneath a large solitary tree.

He loved to chat, in any one of a number of languages, and his enthusiasm was inspiring. Not surprisingly he was well accepted by the island community, his staff looked up to him as a father figure and the local administrators welcomed his proposals to introduce programmes of garbage collection, sewage disposal and sexual health. He was sensitive to tread carefully in more ways than one given that the island folk had for so many years used the street as a dustbin and the beach as their toilet. And as for sex, one of the island's booming pastimes, how could he change the local perception that condoms are insulting to women and dispel the wacky myth that they are a major cause of disease?

The bar in the garden had become the focal point for the local community and its popularity a measure of the respect that Elder had earned. I was introduced to Joao Batista, a fascinating old chap who explained over handshakes that he was born in 1927 and was undisputedly the oldest man on the island. He had seen a lot in his long life and, a little to my surprise, held no grudges against the former colonial masters. His mother had cleaned the properties of the men sent out from Portugal, he had been treated as one of their own and neither he nor the folk of Ibo at large had put up the resistance that had happened elsewhere. The island had been well known as a trading point for slaves, he added darkly, the three forts on the edge of the village serving as a constant reminder of the places innocent men were incarcerated, tortured and – if they complained – executed. Ibo was no place to start getting rebellious.

I'd travelled to the island on a plane no bigger than a London cab, sitting next to the pilot and pointing at the vast array of dials on the dashboard as one might expect of a seven-year-old kid. To my astonishment I was even offered a spell on the joystick and for the first time in my life experienced the thrill and the fear of making a plane go up and down in the sky. We landed smoothly on a grassy airstrip (I didn't do that bit) and no sooner had my bag been removed from the small hold than it was balanced on the head of an elderly man who set off briskly along the only path I could see.

I had no idea who he was or why he was carrying my bag on his head or even where we were going for that matter but there seemed no good reason to offer a challenge. We moved quickly along the sandy track and I struggled to keep up with him despite the fact that he wore no shoes, was handicapped to the tune of 12 kilos and old enough to be my father. Fifteen minutes later, in the centre of the village, he pointed out the Miti Miwire guest house, explained through a toothy smile that he was 75 years old and that how much I chose to pay him was entirely up to me.

Ibo was weird. The grid of streets that were once graced with fabulous colonial buildings today resemble the aftermath of an earthquake, or at least an emergency so dire that most of the residents flee and never return. As I wandered in the half light of the early evening there were few signs of life, just the ghostly silhouettes of crumbling walls and an eerie, surreal silence. Of the houses that were still standing it was difficult to distinguish between those that were inhabited and those long since abandoned, save for the precious few, including Elder's, that had been restored to their former glory.

By day it was a livelier picture as children paraded off to school and men wandered around carrying bunches of small fish on S-shaped hooks. Aside from a handful of silversmiths still smelting down old coins for a living the sea provides the main source of employment and, owing to the poor soil, almost the only food for which the islanders are not dependent on the mainland. But it was the ladies that caught my eye. Many of their faces were coated in a yellow-grey paste that they make by rubbing a certain tree bark against a rock and adding water. It's known as musiro and according to Maconde tradition it enhances the beauty of the womenfolk and offers their skin protection against the tropical sun. At first I found this visually quite shocking but after sharing a laugh and a joke and eliciting a few of those lovely wide African smiles it became very much easier to see the person rather than the mask.

Yes it was weird alright but Ibo was fascinating, a walk through time, and my inaugural flying (!) visit will live long in the memory. What the island lacked in beauty it more than made up for in history and what a very different proposition from Matemo, my next port of call, a five minute hop to the north.

The tiny aircraft delivered me in to the welcoming arms of another Rani team and this was the moment that The Alphabet Traveller from Ancoats, Manchester, with a huge smirk and a slightly itchy bottom, officially became a newly signed up member of The Jet Set. At least that's how it felt to me. I had landed on an alien planet and was about to share a feast of natural beauty on a scale beyond my comprehension, to experience a world of luxury and privilege far in excess of anything my humble contribution to society had ever merited or genuinely deserved. It was strange, embarrassing, even mildly disconcerting. Now I knew how it felt to be Peter Mandelson.

The open air lobby spilled on to a deck and views of an empty white beach that ran almost as far as the eye could see. The designing of the resort must have been the fulfilment of an architect's dream, the completion of a mission to create a hotel worthy of a small slice of paradise. Away to my left I picked out the circular bar that hovered above the ocean, the rainbow of colours of the bottles beneath its thatched roof standing out in marked contrast to the constant, vivid turquoise water upon which it all seemed to float. To my right a ramp led up to a gourmet restaurant spread across the veranda: breakfast served until 11, lunch 11-3, dinner from 6 until late. It wouldn't take too long to settle in.

From my luxury air-conditioned chalet I walked to the far end of the beach to the point that it curved away to the right, after which it held a straight line for at least a further two kilometres. I had it all to myself, not counting the thousands of crabs that scrambled awkwardly along the sand and disappeared back into holes as quickly as they had emerged. The wind created patterns on the surface of the water and caused the trees to bob and weave, more than a welcome breeze against the unrelenting sun.

Every few hundred metres I spotted signs that separated the beach from the bush behind and when curiosity got the better of me I wandered over to see what they were about. "Beware of land mines" had been my guess or perhaps a simple warning not to trespass. What I hadn't expected was a cartoon picture of a man in squatting position with trousers round his ankles and a spectacularly large triangle on the ground beneath his naked buttocks. And below, lest the message had been lost, the words almost identical in Portuguese: "DEFECATION IS PROHIBITED".

Twenty minutes later I reached one of Matemo's six villages. It was no different from a typical cluster of mud huts found anywhere else on the African continent except that the group of ladies sitting under the tree all wore the striking – and still somewhat unnerving – musiro face masks. They waved excitedly, beckoned me over and insisted I sit down for a chat. Their language was a version of Swahili, they explained, but they spoke with me in Portuguese and reserved their own tongue for private comments (and sexual innuendo) that always resulted in girlie giggles. I asked them about musiro so they mixed up some of the paste and then howled with laughter as they slapped in on all over my face.

Everything about that northern tip of Matemo was so delightful that I couldn't force myself to explore its other forty square kilometres. Time was short, too short and for a few days of my life I was determined to savour the millionaire lifestyle. Come on, fair dos, I did spend almost a week in soaking wet clothes freezing my nuts off in the mountains of Kyrgyzstan!

When the plane came to transfer me to Medjumbe Island, the final destination, my mind went in search of a logical reason for leaving. What more could I possibly hope for? How could one surpass the insurpassable? Surely anything, everything from here on, would have to be a backward, downhill step.

The flight took no more than twenty minutes and the island turned out to be a leaf-shaped slither of land just long enough to land the small plane. The meeters and greeters I'd now become used to led me on an introductory tour of the sumptuous bar, lounge, and restaurant before delivering me, and my excruciatingly scruffy bag, to one of the twelve guest suites. More villa than chalet, I would say, this time a private deck and jacuzzi all that divided one's quarters from the beach and the gentle lapping of the ocean.

It took only a quarter of an hour to walk the circumference of Medjumbe and confirm that I'd already seen everything there was to see. The beach, the sea, the hotel, the runway. Every last detail a work of art.

The villas stood in a line and all looked identical though this didn't seem to go down as an acceptable explanation when I walked in on the naked Italian lady sitting atop her husband. It was a mistake anybody could have made and I still don't follow her logic that I should have knocked before entering a room I felt sure was my own.

The only other guests were a rowdy group of men accompanied by a blonde lady with very long legs and a breathtakingly short skirt. She seemed to belong to a man twenty years her senior who sported greasy hair, a permanent three day beard and a beer belly that drooped pitifully over the elasticated waistband of his shorts. He was the loudest of them all and the more he drank the louder he got. Much of his day was spent slumped almost horizontally in a chair, he ate like a pig and picked at his teeth in the moments he wasn't eating or swilling. His behaviour was as rude and aggressive as his appearance was obnoxious and it was with a certain embarrassment that the South African manager came across to explain what was going on.

"They are Russians, they've been in the bush all week on a hunting expedition and have flown out here for a break. Sorry, sir."

* * * * *

At first I had thought it was a joke when told that Medjumbe time was one hour later than the rest of the country but the Rani management had been absolutely serious about selecting their preferred time of sunset. And why not? What else was important? There were no shops, no offices and, beyond the hotel, there were no people either.

The population was made up of herons and egrets and other graceful, long legged birds that would stand at the water's edge for hours on end. And I would sit and watch them for hours on end from the silence of the deck, all parties motionless but entirely at peace unless the eagle flew over and gave us all a scare. Survival of course was the name of the game and the birds' heads would bob occasionally into the water in search of food, sometimes producing results but more often yielding no reward for their inexhaustible patience. For me on the other hand it was rather more simple: a thrice daily walk to the restaurant and an obligatory pause at the bar to share a joke with the Italian couple with whom I was on intimate terms.

When the Russians were drunk enough to go to bed I would follow the staircase up from the bar to a sort of attic, the one room that was quite different from the rest. Its wooden beams and thatched roof were more in keeping with an alpine lodge than a tropical hideaway, as indeed was the eclectic assortment of gorgeous, floppy armchairs. At the end of the evening this was my chosen spot to luxuriate in the almost silence, to pick books from the many shelves and turn pages without really reading. An ambience that elsewhere in the world would include a crackling log fire but here the senses were touched by the breeze drifting in though the openings in the walls, the view of the stars peppering the night sky and the barely perceptible whoosh of the water below.

It was the sound of the metal bird that brought the dream to an end. I knew it was going to happen, it had to, but I wasn't quite ready. Not just yet. It was a haunting reality that I would almost certainly never come back to Medjumbe and here was a memory that demanded to be cherished. The price in the end had been worth every penny and if you are lucky enough to have one or two pennies, or you win the lottery, then please let me give you a word of advice. Life is short, terribly short, so don't die with money in the bank. Call Rani, book out the island, choose two dozen of your favourite friends and enjoy a few days, or weeks, on Medjumbe time.

* * * * *

During my stay on the island of Matemo I received a phone call with the sad news of the death of Annette Farrer. She was a lovely, kind, warm-hearted lady whose generosity touched the hearts of so many people. This chapter is dedicated to her memory. x

Azerbaijan

History was made on the sixth day of September in the year 2006 and repeated exactly nine months later to the day. The ten-letter countries of Azerbaijan and Kazakhstan twice found themselves on opposite sides of a brutal conflict and those proud, newly-independent oil-rich nations were prepared to leave no stone unturned in search of the ultimate prize. The stakes were high. The winner of Group A would go through to the final stages of Euro 2008.

Had results gone differently over the two years that followed (the above matches both ended 1-1 you will recall) football fans around the world might have been treated to an all Ten-Letter final in Vienna. Ladbrokes offered tempting odds but alas it was Poland that topped the group and the eleven defeats suffered by Luxembourg in Group G completely scuppered the punters' chances of an unlikely TLC double.

But that's not really the point, is it? The big issue here is that Azerbaijan or Kazakhstan COULD theoretically become the champions of Europe and I wonder how we really feel about the possibility of the coveted prize being paraded on the borders of Outer Mongolia. Could Azerbaijan's winning of the 2011 Eurovision Song Contest (and hosting of the 2012 event) prove to be the thin end of the wedge? One mustn't get one's knickers unduly twisted over such matters but it does perhaps beg at least two important questions: 1. Why doesn't somebody tell FIFA that Kazakhstan is in Central Asia? 2. Where exactly is Azerbaijan anyway?

That answer lies between two seriously large expanses of water that sit almost side by side on the map: the wide oval of the Black Sea, with Europe to the west, and the long, dangly Caspian Sea (almost as big... but actually a lake) that opens the door to Asia and all points east. Both stretch for a

187

whopping 700 miles at their widest points but it is the three hundred miles that separates them from each other upon which our attention must focus.

This relatively small slither of land is dominated by mountains that span east to west, "coast to coast", two parallel ranges known as the Greater and Lesser Caucasus. The former, to the north, is significantly higher than even the mighty Alps and as the entire region is known simply as "The Caucasus" we are all spared the daily worry of whether the three small countries comprised within – Azerbaijan, Georgia and Armenia – actually belong to Europe or Asia.

* * * * *

It was Sunday lunchtime, Heathrow Terminal 1, and there was something suspiciously unremarkable about the group of people waiting to board the flight. From past experience unusual destinations generally attract unusual passengers wearing unusual clothes, adorned with unusual jewellery and invariably weighed down by a large number of unusual packages. Not so BMI flight BD 929 to Baku. It could have been the afternoon shuttle to Manchester.

So it was reassuring to hear that we were flying over Belgium and could expect to reach the Black Sea coast less than three hours hence. Two hours beyond that I would be landing in Azerbaijan, a country to which, as far as I could recall, nobody in my class (school or social) had ever been known to go on holiday.

It felt more like sitting in a spa than on an aeroplane with a whole row of seats to myself, the Sunday papers scattered freely and the afternoon sunshine spilling in through the porthole. It all seemed rather jolly actually. Was I going to have fun like this in Azerbaijan? I now considered, albeit somewhat late in the day.

Having leapt four time zones it was midnight when I arrived at Baku's "Old City Inn" with the pain of handing over a stonking US$ 100 for an airport visa only just starting to abate. The rumbling of a stomach running on GMT at least helped override this deep sense of self-pity and it was with a vivid mental picture of a ham and cheese toastie, possibly a gherkin on the side, that I enquired of the night porter as to the availability of some nosh. His response was to smile politely, speak a few foreign words, point to the clock and then count up to 8 on his fingers. The time at which breakfast would be available. Sleep well sir.

I can only assume it was hunger that prized me awake at 7. All was silent and daylight had yet to appear but curiosity won out over common sense. I pulled on my jeans and a sweater, bade good morning to the grinning, well-fed night porter and headed out of the Old City Inn into a dark alleyway of what looked rather like an old city.

The wind was strong and biting into my face and the cold air forced a defensive self-hugging as I scuttled along the cobbles. It could have been a November morning in Middlesbrough, a thought so bleak that I banished it instantly from my mind. When shapes became discernible in the half light a vast, high wall – jagged and fort-like – introduced itself as that which divided the old city from the new. An arched opening and a set of steps led me from one side to the other, to an impressive boulevard surrounded by lawns, fountains and statues of famous people I might soon find out about. Park benches were numerous, every one vacant. There was almost nobody on the streets except a team of ladies with brush in hand searching for something to sweep.

Further exploration found me on a pedestrianised street looking at names that included Benetton, Pierre Cardin, Boss....even Mothercare had made it to the Caucasus. The architecture above the glitzy windows at street level was regal and stylish and as I walked along in the silence thinking that this could be a street scene from Vienna I spotted a restaurant opening up for breakfast. The name, I then realised, was Café Mozart.

I resisted the temptation of food and warmth and instead walked on to reach the shores of the Caspian Sea. And back came the image of Teesside. The grey mass of still water with the silhouette of cranes on the horizon offered precious little to get excited about, but who knows, I might have thought differently if I was in on a slice of the 12 trillion dollars that its oil is said to be worth. Ugly or not, a geographical phenomenon on this scale merited at least a few moments contemplation however brutal the wind blowing across it.

To my left the suburbs of the city stretched and curved, an urban skyline of rectangular tower blocks expanding far along the peninsula that shapes Baku's enormous natural harbour. There was little to report in the other direction, save a TV tower up on the hill and the obligatory panorama restaurant looking down over the world's largest lake. A body of water the size of Japan whose 7000 kilometre shoreline visits Kazakhstan and Turkmenistan in the east, Russia in the north and Iran to the south, just a few hours' drive from where I was standing. No wonder the region's early inhabitants mistook it for a sea.

The day had eventually dawned, the wind no longer quite so harsh and Baku was coming to life. People and cars emerged in numbers and noticeably the thudding and piercing sounds of hammer and drill filled the air in all directions. It was 8 o'clock and, at long last, time to break the fast. I headed swiftly back through a urine-free underpass, across another fountained square and entered the labyrinth of steep slopes and winding passages on the opposite side from which I'd emerged. Against all the odds, to my absolute bewilderment, I stumbled right into the door of the Old City Inn.

* * * * *

I spent the next three days in Baku, time enough to recognise it as a city moving through a period of profound change. But then "change", from what I could gather, has always been the norm in Azerbaijan. Surrounded by former empire-building bullies such as the Turks and Mongols and Persians this tiny little country has been invaded time and again over the last two thousand years. The most recent aggressors were the Soviets who took control for most of the 20th century and it was only when that union collapsed in a heap in 1991 that Azerbaijan gained full independence. Yet despite all that has happened the Azeri language, a spoken form of Turkish, still prevails and the Islamic religion has held its ground for well over a thousand years.

Amidst the cranes, the boutiques, the Hyatts and Sheratons, the karaoke bars and take-away pizza joints, it was hard to imagine that no so long ago this was just a small city in the desert. I saw nothing except the occasional mosque to indicate that this was a Muslim country. The men, a uniform mass of pale brown skin and jet black hair, dressed no differently from men the world over, though in this part of the world designer stubble, fag and phone come as standard accessories. Perhaps the suits are just a little more shiny, shoes a little more pointed. For the girls it's large earrings, large sunglasses, large heels and the smallest of skirts. And all this less than two hundred miles from the Iranian border. What would the bearded folk of Teheran make of all this, not to mention their thoughts on Harry's Bar, The Red Lion, The Brewery, The Phoenix and – home of the Baku Bears – The Clansman?

The fact that brown bears have always roamed the Caucasus was no doubt an influential factor in the naming of the Azerbaijan branch of the Glasgow Rangers Supporters Club. I'd read in the Baku Weekly that The Clansman Pub was their adopted HQ so when I spotted the sign on a small street running off Fountain Square – the local equivalent of Piccadilly Circus – I couldn't resist popping in for a cold one.

It was essentially a large room with identical shaped bars in the left and right corners, an interesting symmetry and unlike any pub I'd ever been to. I took a stool on the right where the only two customers were drinking beer and soon found myself in conversation with a blonde, blue-eyed barmaid name of Anna. She was Russian, clearly a very well-educated lady and through a heavy accent she told me of her life in Baku, the city in which she had always lived. She explained that she'd never learned to speak Azeri as Russian had been the dominant language in schools in the pre-independence years and, in her case, it was also the mother tongue. Had she ever ventured north to her parents' homeland?

Her eyes seemed to turn to ice. Yes, she had travelled with her mother, a train journey from Baku that had necessitated crossing Russia's most southerly state of Dagestan. After the collapse of the Soviet Union this had become a wild and lawless region, predominantly Muslim and dominated by ruthless tribal warlords. Anna told of how, as they sat on the train, her mother was warned that females with blonde hair were very much a rarity and that her daughter could be kidnapped, taken as a prize and never seen again. And so the young woman was forced to spend the entire journey hiding on the luggage racks, unable even to use the toilet for fear of what might happen. Then she stopped talking, smiled at me and changed the subject. She wrote down the name of a must-read book on the history of Azerbaijan, thrust the piece of paper into my hand and headed off to serve the Scotsmen at the other end of the bar.

The far walls were covered with photos of sporting memorabilia but my half of the room, the right hand bar, was entirely given over to Glasgow Rangers FC. Azerbaijan had become the land of oil and money and the men with kilts had been drawn like moths to a flame. Every two weeks they would fly out to the rigs for fourteen days hard labour and every two weeks they would return to The Clansman to drink beer, whisky and watch their beloved team on the big screen.

I was introduced to Ralph, Anna's colleague.

'Are you from here Ralph?' I asked, having never a met a Ralph so far from home.

'Aye, shure. From Baku. Ets no' exactly ma neam tho, if ya ken wot a mean.'

'You are..er.. Azerbaijani?'

'Aye.'

'But..erm…you speak...'

'Aye, wi' a Scorts arccent'…. he offered proudly. 'Been werrrkin' here a couple o' years the nu.'

What a funny world we live in.

* * * * *

Drinking with Jocks was one thing but I was eager to keep to local food and more than happy with a lunchtime regime of lentil soup and salad from the wide range of cheap cafés. By night Baku offered all the cuisines of the world and at the risk of being sucked into a tourist gimmick I decided to indulge in a "traditional local" restaurant. The menu brought back memories of Central Asia and from an entertainment perspective it certainly didn't disappoint. The laminated pages of the magnificent leather-bound tome had been translated into somebody's idea of English and the 227 dishes on offer conveniently divided into 14 sections, "Cold Collations" and "Meals Baked in Sec" to name but two. To read through the menu AND eat a meal all on the same evening would have been nigh on impossible so I plumped for a dish entitled Baku Boulevard on the basis that "Sturgeon with Nut, Cheese and Smetana" was something my Mum had rarely served up when I got home from school. The moment of recklessness was rendered complete with a side order of potato and mushrooms in sour cream and a glass of local red wine.

All in all it turned out to be a decent nosebag, though it would have helped to know in advance that smetana is in fact sour cream and that chilled Azeri plonk falls some way short of delicious. The people in the restaurant, as with all the locals I had met, spoke very little English (I was always taken for a Russian) but their patience and kindness shone through. This was a city that felt warm and civilised, where the streets and squares were kept spotlessly clean, where the folk gave off an air of being honest, decent members of society. Slushy I know, but that was how it felt to me and at no stage did I ever feel threatened or intimidated.

The weather changed to the delightful autumn sunshine I'd left behind in London and conditions were perfect for exploring the winding lanes of the old city that are said to have been there for at least a thousand years. I visited the splendid Shah's palace at the top of the hill and at sea level climbed the spiral staircase of the peculiar Maiden's Tower, a short fat building that resembled an open-top lighthouse. Was it built by the Zoroastrians, like the Towers of Silence I'd found in Iran, where the dead would be left exposed to the elements and the vultures invited to do the rest? One of many theories, no-one seems quite sure.

I looked out to the cranes of the Caspian in one direction and, in the other, amidst the cranes of the city, was the ancient caravanserai, the remains of the roadside inn where men and their camels used to take rest after weeks of crossing the desert. And back I went through the streets of the ancient quarters, spookily quiet save the sound of drilling and a handful of carpet vendors who would repeat the usual mantra of "hello my friend, just come and have a look". Then they would smile, knowing it was hopeless, and leave it at that. This was gentle, easy travelling and when I'd walked enough I found a bench by one of the many fountains and read Ali & Nino, the book that Anna had recommended, which also turned out to be the name of the shop.

As jet lag started to slip away the blue skies encouraged a forward plan. I would follow the line of the Greater (more northerly) Caucasus in a north-westerly direction taking a road that seemed to run along the foot of the mountains all the way to the border with Georgia. From there I would find a way to get to its capital city of Tbilisi and possibly, with a following wind, continue further south into Armenia. Calm down Jenks, one step at a time. I must have had a very good sleep.

The final day in Baku would take me by taxi on a dual mission to the north of the city. An investigative visit to the impressive, state-of-the-art bus station revealed coaches and minibuses sensibly lined up in numbered bays and I soon got the confirmation I wanted that transport to Ismayilli would be easy to come by next morning. Simple answer, no hassle, I was again taken aback by the modernity and sophistication of a country that was obviously going places in more ways than one.

But there was nothing remotely modern or sophisticated about my other port of call, it had been there since before the days of Islam and this, without question, *was* linked to the strange world of the Zoroastrians. Theirs is said to be the oldest religion still in existence, a devout worship of fire and flames that originated in Persia more than two thousand years ago. The Fire Temple wasn't easy to find, tucked away in a drab industrial suburb, but it was well worth the effort.

The taxi driver dropped me at the arched doorway and when I stepped

194

into the tidy courtyard it came as no surprise that there were no other people in sight. I was drawn instantly to the flame flickering away in the centre and I must have been standing there for some minutes wondering how long it had been burning when a voice from behind my right shoulder leapt out of the eerie silence. The young woman with spooky waist-length hair spoke good English and introduced herself as my guide.

The temple had been built in the 18th century on the same spot that the last of the Zoroastrians had been chased out a thousand years earlier. They had originally arrived from Persia, where it all first started, and were forced eastwards to India when the Arabs brought Islam and pushed all other religions aside. A few thousand fire-worshippers still exist in India today, known as Parsis, and it was their community that returned along the ancient Silk Road to rebuild this place of worship on the outskirts of Baku. The land itself is not considered sacred, it is the natural gas vent beneath the ground that offers the chance of an eternal flame.

Today the site is essentially a museum and the pilgrims that regularly walked across the mountains from India no longer appear. I was given a tour of the twenty or so rooms off the courtyard, all of which were cool and dark and some of which were positively sinister. Life sized models depicted wizened old men chained and scorched by the flames that they worshipped, many lying almost naked upon a bed of hot coals. The devout would refuse food and drink only water, such was the purity of their lives and the sacrifices expected of the true believers. No wonder the mad buggers stopped coming.

* * * * *

The minibus was full by 9.30 and within half an hour it was climbing into the mountains along a good tarmac road. The male passengers all wore suit jackets though odd pants, I noticed and the ladies dressed in clothes of the countryside: black cardigans, long skirts, black tights and socks. Few people spoke to each other or on telephones and the smokers waited to disembark before lighting up. A quiet, comfortable, pleasant journey that I

195

was in no hurry to come to an end.

It took just three hours and 5 Manat (£4) to travel almost half the width of the country. Azerbaijan is only about the size of Scotland and even though it is the largest of the three Caucasus countries the whole region from Black to Caspian would fit comfortably inside the UK. I baled out at a roundabout on the entrance to Ismayilli where a posse of Ladas taxis lay in wait.

The drivers guessed correctly that the mountain village of Lahic was my intended destination and opened a bidding war for the privilege of taking me there. That I couldn't understand Russian was a mystery they weren't able to fathom and my ongoing failure to comprehend despite a) constant repetition and b) a substantial increase in volume I'm sure led many to assume that I was being deliberately obstructive. They had probably never come across a non-Russian speaker but the more creative won the day by displaying numbers with his fingers and confirming them on the keypad of his mobile phone. We settled on 12 (two fully opened hands plus two fingers), not big money considering the punishment the stony track had in store for his ancient little motor.

The twenty kilometres deep into the valley took a full hour. Second gear was the best we could hope to achieve and the flocks of sheep and goats always claimed right of way over the solitary Lada. The village was eventually announced where a river cut across the road and a large incongruous sign pointed to the nearby Garden of Paradise guest house. I had read that such a place existed, a deciding factor in my plumping for such an outlandish location.

From the custody of my driver, whom I felt morally obliged to slip a few extra Manats (surely some of his car would need replacing after two legs of that journey), I was handed over to a young man who'd emerged from the adjacent orchard. He introduced himself, in surprisingly good English, as the owner of the guest house and directed me through the trees to where two other men sat under a canopy cooking chicken kebabs over hot coals. Have some lunch and a glass of red suggested Jesse – and then we'll get you a room sorted out.

The food was extremely tasty – served as per custom with a bowl of fresh salad and Frisbee-sized discs of warm bread – and thankfully I managed to sidestep the wine and the vodka. (*Thankful* to miss out on a sesh? How very grown up). We were sitting behind a small café at the foot of the garden and to my chagrin our makeshift shelter blocked out the lovely sunshine that was illuminating the autumn colours on the far side of the mountain. The air was noticeably much cooler up here and I guessed that this would be the only part of the day to deliver any natural warmth. Jesse explained that the "tourist" season had ended on the last day of September, which is when they'd closed the café and started to prepare for the long hard winter ahead. Strangely he made no mention of the fact that today was the first of October and the time to which he referred was just the day before.

When lunch was over and the bottles drained we walked through the orchard and climbed the wooden steps leading up to the veranda of a tired-looking property. The five guest rooms behind each of its doors were all unoccupied (and likely to remain so for the next six months) and I still have no idea why Jesse ushered me into the one that he did. It looked like a cell designated for exceptionally dangerous prisoners; there was no window, no heating and the temperature was already in freefall. There was no furniture of any sort, no anything, just two sagging single beds against each side wall.

I was formally invited to utilise both sets of bedding and indeed any supplementary materials from adjacent rooms, none of which was locked. Thus the prospect of my being cold and miserable was instantly downgraded to just plain miserable and Jesse had clinched himself a deal. "What time would you like to wash by the way?"

I quickly returned to the veranda to look out over the orchard and the glorious shape of the tree-covered mountains beyond, fresh snow already visible on the peaks. This was more important than a warm, cosy room I had to start believing though in truth I'd already decided that what might have been a two or even three day stopover was getting shorter by the minute. It was late afternoon, the sun was getting weaker, I needed to get on the move and keep warm. And so, with the promise of hot water upon my return, I headed off to downtown Lahic.

The entrance to the village proper was announced by a small square where four elderly gents, clad in the universal square-goers uniform of jackets and caps, huddled together on a short bench. This thriving hub gave way to a narrow cobbled street lined with tiny shops and a tea room, the latter identified by an urn sitting on the ledge of an open window. There was no sign of any customers, or for that matter, anybody else at all. I assumed this to be the main thoroughfare but on spotting a flight of steps climbing up to my right I decided to see what a change of level might bring.

I hadn't expected to find an old mosque converted into a museum, even less an English-speaking man sitting quietly within. He wasn't speaking English when I found him, you understand, in fact I sensed that he hadn't been speaking anything for quite some time. He was a lovely chap and eager to tell me the story of his village but sadly for all concerned his collection of ancient pottery and farm implements was somewhat underwhelming.

I had already read that Lahic was famed for artists and artisans, coppersmiths in particular, but hadn't grasped the extent to which this valley had lost its people. The gentleman informed me that not so many years earlier 36,000 hardy folk had lived along the banks of the river and in those times, even as recently as the 1960s, there had been no road to link them to the outside world. For almost two thousand years this community was isolated – the only way in and out of the village was to cross the mountains on the back of a horse – and the language they have grown up with is entirely different from that spoken in the rest of the country.

By the time I rejoined the main street the sun was sinking fast, the coppersmiths had downed tools for the day and the only sign of life was from the ladies in dark woollen clothes who scuttled back and forth to fill their containers with water. There was a rich supply with spouts poking through the walls every few hundred metres directing the flow from the side of the mountain into ornate receptacles below. Or in some cases it simply gushed onto the street, formed a pool and went off in search of the lowest point. With no mains water anywhere in the village the women fetch and carry all day long to cook food, wash pans and ensure their husbands and children can wash before sleeping.

I dropped down another level and walked back home through the river bed, a fat snake of rocks and boulders that must have been a quarter of a mile across yet – strangely – carried only a skinny worm of water through its middle. Something of a pity as the landscape all around was stunning and it deserved a spectacular torrent rather than a sorry, muddy trickle just a couple of metres wide.

Meantime, as promised, Jesse had been preparing for my evening ablutions. I was all set for a bucket to be deposited outside the cell but instead my host led the way across the orchard to an outhouse I hadn't even noticed. Beyond the heavy door was a large tiled room that connected to another of a similar size, this one very much hotter and dispensing steaming hot water via a tap in the wall. It was once the village hammam, Jesse explained, a sort of Turkish bathhouse for all the local residents, but now owned by his family for the use of his guests. Or should I say, guest.

There was something rather spooky sitting there alone in what felt like a damp dungeon but a few of my Rod Stewart solo renditions and some extreme dunking with the help of a plastic bucket averted a potentially sombre mood. It was the prospect of returning to my icy chamber that hung like a dark cloud overhead but at least I had a dinner engagement to look forward to – Jesse's mother was preparing her special home-made cabbage and carrot soup.

Still glowing from the steam and several gallons of brutally hot water I emerged into the chilly night, grabbed a fleece from my even chillier parlour and presented a bright purple head at the door of Mrs Jesse's. She was probably in her late forties but looked thirty years older, as with so many people whose lives have been more a question of endurance than pleasure. She waved me into the room and pointed at the small dining table at which her son was sitting. There was also an armchair, evidently Mother's, an ancient TV, two beds, and a coal-fired stove in the corner upon which our dinner was cooking. It was a living room in every sense and the only part of the house that wasn't freezing cold.

She ladled, we ate and the TV brought us a report from the southern, mountainous region of Nagorno-Karabakh. The two-word caption alone was enough to get Jesse's blood boiling. He'd been a teenage lad when Armenia, their smaller – and significantly, Christian – neighbour, had laid siege to this disputed territory and in the five year war that followed 30,000 people had lost their lives and half a million Muslims were forced to flee. It was, and still is, a massive blow to Azeri pride and the reason the two countries haven't been speaking for the last two decades. For the record it had probably belonged to the Armenians in the first place, Stalin having wrestled it from them sixty years earlier, but this was a detail Jesse didn't seem to care for.

Sleep came surprisingly easy that night despite the crushing weight of two thick quilts beneath which head and body had been entirely submerged. The mind must have also relaxed following the wise decision to depart next day and the win-win deal with Jesse whereby he would drive me to Qabala, the next town west from Ismayili, and thus earn some cash towards fuel for his winter hibernation. We would hit the road after a tea and bread somewhere around 9.30am, giving me chance to pop down the high street again for a pre-breakfast gander.

* * * * *

It all went to plan, a seldom-used phrase in the world of travel. Those coppersmiths tapping away early morn had been happy to pose for my digital camera and another ninety minutes spent chatting with Jesse brought home to me the harsh realities of life in the mountains. We talked of his annual battle for survival during the winter period from October to May and the stockpiling of food and fuel that was needed to keep families alive, in many cases with no income at all. Even those with money have limited opportunity to spend it; snow can cut the village off for weeks on end and the bridges that span the rivers too often collapse.

Despite all the hardship he had chosen to return to the quiet life of the village after his university studies in Baku. Not easy for a man of 27 he confided, given that rural life had failed to move with the times and thus any relationship with a girl would have to become marriage within weeks. He intended to choose carefully (his face had noticeably become very serious) and he was too smart to fall into the trap of taking a wife to whom he would not be suited. That he had reached such a ripe old age without a bride had set local tongues wagging but that was their problem, they would just have to wag. A wife isn't just for Christmas is it, or words to that effect.

Once we'd reached Qabala Jesse drove up alongside a Mercedes taxi parked amongst the Ladas and haggled over a fare to take me to Sheki. In truth the bus would have suited me fine but his kindness, initiative and bargaining skills resulted in an offer too good to refuse. Where else in the world could I travel forty miles in a chauffeured Merc for fifteen quid? The empty road was a pure delight with the trees and the mountains, viewed from the comfort of my black leather seat, putting on a show in the autumn sunshine. Yet again I had that Austria feeling.

Sheki, when written in Azeri, has a squiggle under the s and the e appears back to front, the only letter that differs from those that we are used to. As a measure of its independence Azerbaijan dumped both the Arabic and Cyrillic scripts that were imposed by the regimes of the day and implemented a far more sensible, traveller-friendly Latin alphabet. A blessing indeed compared to Georgia and Armenia, both of whom have invented unique and complicated writing systems to complement their unique and complicated languages. I could live with an e being the wrong way round.

Not only was it easy to say, Sheki was easy to like. The orderly town with smart streets and tidy shops came up with a sparkling modern hotel right on its central square and within three hours of my leaving a primitive mountain village I was poured out of a limo and into the lobby of a luxury four star establishment. How very embarrassing, this isn't really how an explorer is supposed to behave is it?

The view from my private balcony (yes, I even had a fucking balcony!) was of mountains in all directions with billions of rust coloured trees glowing in the afternoon sunshine and snow sitting atop the peaks like icing on a cake. Nature doesn't get much better than that and rarely does an alphabet traveller feel so overwhelmingly chuffed with his morning's work.

The square was a large shady affair where men in their hundreds gathered around to drink tea and play backgammon under the trees. Most wore jackets and some form of headgear, most smoked, none brought their wives. It was a far cry from the cosmopolitan cafés of Baku.

"That's how it is" confirmed Ilhama, an intriguing lady whose life story came my way the following day.

She had married and bred, fulfilling her obligation as a female, but now in her thirties had been determined to learn English and, much to the consternation of the local folk, had even had the audacity to learn to drive. This in a society where men do men things and women do women things and God forbid anybody who meddles with, or so much as questions, the system. Ilhama was a feisty renegade, and proud of it.

Her job was that of tour guide at the gorgeous little church up in the mountain village of Kish. As always the countryside had quickly lured me from the town and the cute little building with its dome shaped roof and pretty gardens had turned out to be the star attraction. Ilhama explained that the site had been a place of worship dating back to the first century – proof that the Caucasus was where Christianity had first begun – and that this temple had been painstakingly reconstructed as recently as the year 2000. In Azerbaijan the religion has long since been replaced by Islam but the church, now a museum, will always be preserved as a national treasure and all thanks to a Norwegian gentleman name of Thor Heyerdhal.

Yes, it's the same incredible man that sailed the Kon-Tiki raft across the Pacific way back in 1947. Thor visited Azerbaijan frequently in the last twenty years of his life (he died in 2002, aged 87) and was convinced by the rock carvings he'd studied, particularly those of ships, that his countrymen originated from an ancient people of these parts who eventually moved north to populate what is now Scandinavia. Hence the funding, the international co-operation, the restoration, and the reason Ilhama has her job to this day.

She was engaging company and determined that I should sample the nearby restaurant for lunch and stay in the local guest house the next time I visit. It then became evident they were one and the same, it was the house opposite the entrance to the church not thirty metres from where we were sitting. Her house, in fact.

We struck a deal whereby I would go for a long walk while she prepared the food and I returned as agreed two hours later a very happy old Hector. She showed me to one of several tables amidst the flowers and the fruit trees of her courtyard and I sat contentedly in the sunshine admiring my newly acquired photos. Shot after shot of the orchards creeping up the mountainside, the fresh snow on the peaks (so much closer now) against the rich blue sky, the Japanese style houses with pyramid roofs, old ladies in country costume bent double as they walked along the cobbled lanes, the ubiquitous water spouts jutting out through the walls. It could indeed have been rural Japan I now decided and for somebody who barely knew which way up to hold the camera the pictures looked like a work of art. Should I apply for a job with National Geographic Magazine?

A large, ornate teapot was placed before me together with an 8-man portion of mashed potatoes and parsley, freshly picked tomatoes, hot bread (that looked like flying saucers) and home-made blackberry and white-cherry jam. The sun was warm now and the only sound was that of the insects hovering around the flowers. It could not have been a more idyllic setting. And then they arrived.

Now I have nothing at all against American folk, they are amongst the friendliest people in the world but what a terrible shame that the power and energy of their voices can't be harnessed to provide a defence against tsunamis or to counter the threat of nuclear attack. The Peace Corps and their family took up camp in one corner and I found a pretext to move to the furthest point away but it really made no difference in an area so small. Every word came my way, though one in three was actually the same. If only they could avoid using the world "like" (pronounced lake) all sentences would be thirty percent shorter and a 100 minute, 100 watt mega-drone could be over and done with in little over an hour. Better still, why not dedicate Tuesdays and Fridays as "lake" days and then have five days off for normal conversation? What really concerns Grumpy Old Man is that the annoying habit is moving like a hurricane across the Atlantic and is already on the verge of wiping out what is left of British civilisation.

So where was I? Having eaten as much as my body needed and then, all too predictably, the same amount again I took out my wallet and went in search of Ilhama. She was chatting in the kitchen with her staff, a couple of jolly ladies who spoke no English but nonetheless were eager for me to sit and have a natter. My chance to get a female perspective of a woman's life in Azerbaijan.

The picture they painted was an all too familiar one wherein the sum of their experiences involved little more than the drudgery of basic family survival. But did they have any sort of social life at all? Had they ever had boyfriends before they got married? These were completely alien concepts in the rural life of Azerbaijan and how they laughed their heads off on hearing stories of our promiscuous European world. Could they really be expected to formulate an image of a girls' night on the toon in Newcastle?

I was invited to make a donation as opposed to being billed for lunch, a nice touch by my hostess whose trusting approach would win her lots of friends and no doubt more money than she would ever have the nerve to charge. The enterprising lady did however stipulate a fixed 5 Manat fare for a taxi back down to Sheki, a service she could now perform herself having recently passed her test.

A few heads turned on seeing a lady at the helm of the Lada, a situation no doubt made even more gossipworthy with a lone foreign man as her passenger. But Ilhama was too busy concentrating to notice, her eyes staring wildly and tiny hands nervously pushing the steering wheel back and forth to negotiate the steep, twisting road.

"I've only driven down to town a few times and am really quite scared" she eventually confided.

Then a pause as we both wondered what best to say next.
"But it will be OK", she finally added. "It will be OK".

* * * * *

There are three marshrutkas (minibuses) leaving Sheki every morning for the town of Zaqalata, a two hour, two Manat journey. The 9am one nudged out of the depot as the hour struck and how I struggled to get used to the good fortune of Zurich efficiency at Zambia prices. The road was good and, as ever, traffic-free, the driver performed his duties courteously and without risk to his passengers, there were no trussed animals, smelly fags, or vomiting children. The countryside was lush and lovely and like every other journey I'd made in Azerbaijan there was a sense of disappointment rather than relief when the time came to disembark.

Zaqalata sits in Azerbaijan's north-west corner, little more than 40 kms from the Georgian border. I stepped from the bus into a cauldron of activity where the early risers were returning from market, laden with bags and burrowing into the mass of humankind that moved in the opposite direction. Every man in the town seemed to be leaning against a Lada taxi, the cars parked three deep and evidently far outnumbering the volume of paying customers. I had a quick wander then took one such vehicle to the neighbouring village of Car.

My pronouncing it Car caused some confusion but anyway we headed towards a quaint old part of the town, through a world of narrow streets and gas lamps and on up the hillside to a place that sounded like Char. Then past a pristine and apparently brand new stadium that had real stands and gleaming bright blue seats and which would have graced any of the major footballing cities of the world. But what on earth was it doing in north-west Azerbaijan in a town of twenty odd thousand people? There was obviously some serious money here, could I sense a bid to host Euro 2024?

We climbed into the foothills of the mountains along an idyllic country lane where the houses were large and sturdy and Mercedes cars outnumbered the usual doddery Ladas. The sign that I had hoped for was lashed to a telegraph pole on the right, an arrow pointing along a track that led over a gushing white river and deep into the densely wooded hillside. According to my guidebook the obscure guest house was somewhere under the canopy of trees but as the road fizzled to a premature end I had no choice but to pay the driver and seek it out on foot.

The steep steps led me into a world of semi-darkness where the sun and the sky were entirely blocked out by the roof of the forest. I looked all about me in search of a good reason to be there and my eyes eventually adjusted to pick out a wooden, open-fronted booth at the base of two large trees. Inside it was an old table and two chairs – evidently somebody's idea of a romantic place to take tea – but judging by its decrepit state no tea-drinking had taken place for many a long year. My neck craned and swivelled and picked out another, and then another, and eventually I spotted quite a few of these abandoned tree houses semi-camouflaged like a puzzle in a children's comic.

Higher up, in a clearing, stood a spooky house and a low, flat building with a Coca-Cola logo and the word Restoran on a rusty sign. I stood there in silence and bewilderment wondering what to make of it and beyond the caff spotted a cluster of cabins amongst the trees. In Soviet times it might have been construed as a holiday camp but today there was no indication of human life, in fact a dead body or two would not have come as a great surprise. I felt like a character in a horror film and could almost hear the background music stoking up the drama as I reached out a hand and slowly pushed the door that led into the house...

It opened and the radio was on somewhere inside. I called out but nobody came. I did more standing, pondering, wondering. What was I hoping might occur? And then, just the way it happens in horror films, I turned round to find somebody standing in complete silence right behind me. A young lad, high teens, who showed no surprise or interest at my arrival and who understood not a single word of English.

What would I have said to him anyway? Has the rest of your family been butchered to death? How much is one of your cosy cabins? Instead I smiled and gestured a request to dump my bag inside the back door then headed, rather quickly, back down to the river to gather my thoughts.

It didn't take long. Three hours later, with the help of a minibus and a taxi, I was in the queue at the border, passport in hand. Rather than spend a night at the House on Haunted Hill I'd settled for a long walk along that most English of country lanes and lapped up the visual beauty of a wealthy corner of rural Azerbaijan. The camera couldn't get enough of the sprawling farmhouses amidst the orchards or the cute little calves grazing in the open meadows with the snow-capped mountains always in the background. A glorious rural scene to grace any calendar.

We all stood patiently at the immigration office wondering what might happen next. A line of vehicles formed a parallel queue, their owners leaning against open car doors and peering forward at the enormous gate and the stretch of no-mans land beyond. There had been no interaction between pedestrians and drivers until a fat, dishevelled looking man leapt out of a minibus, ran towards where I was standing and rather inelegantly tugged at my arm. "Tiflis, Tiflis?"

I guessed it was a question because he jutted his chin out in the hope of a response and, as it wasn't instantly forthcoming, he sighed heavily, tutted with frustration and jogged back towards his vehicle as though worried it might suddenly pull away without him. He had been touting onward transport to Tbilisi, I then realised, but his sales patter had let him down badly. I'd been spoilt by the gentle, polite Azeris.

The rubber stamps hit different pages of my passport and Azerbaijan was behind me long before I was ready to leave. It was a sad, surreal walk through the border posts and I wasn't really in the mood for the gangly Georgian man who wanted to bum a lift to anywhere I would pay to take him. He had enough English to feign friendliness and create an excuse to follow me around and it didn't take long for my irritation to rise above good manners. I found myself ducking and weaving and walking in figures of eight as though trying to shrug off a wasp but each time I thought he'd given up his annoying Mr Bean face would reappear above my right shoulder.

The first taxi in line was manned by a scruffy character who barked at me in a language I couldn't follow. He waved his calculator under my chin and bashed out numbers to indicate his charges while Mr Bean lowered his neck between the two of us like a giraffe nibbling at leaves on a tree. The nasty, aggressive little taxi driver was just starting to get truly het up when a van pulled up alongside to deliver a torrent of abuse at him through the driver's window. I couldn't understand a word but guess it went something like:

"Step back from my customer, you bounder, for it was I who first spoke of a journey to Tiflis."

"Away with you scoundrel. 'tis no such system. Long hours have I waited and toiled…"

And thus voices grew louder and tempers more frayed, two skunks in a pissing contest that neither had a hope of winning. Mr Bean was fully engrossed in the show so I slipped away, changed some money and headed off to Tbilisi in another taxi, feeling strangely discomfited by all the shenanigans and a little mean at having left him behind. Maybe he wasn't such a bad bloke after all.

The introduction to Georgia was further soured when my chauffeur twice handed me his mobile phone for a voice to translate his messages. The first was to say he would have to take on board another passenger to help with the cost, the second to advise that there would be a surcharge unless I agreed to be dumped on the outskirts of the city. What a very different world I had entered.

It was early evening when I climbed out of the taxi at Rustaveli metro station deep in the heart of Tbilisi. A new city, a new country, the sun was shining, I was safe and well and a few days ahead of schedule. It should have been a satisfying moment but the sense of sadness at leaving Azerbaijan and the unsavoury events of the day had left me feeling surprisingly low.

The taxi driver took his stash of dollars and drove away with a smile as I glumly fiddled with my bags at the roadside. All I wanted to do was to get to a hotel, lie on the bed and admire my photos, the collection of which

I was unusually proud. Azerbaijan with all its surprises had put on a display of stunning colour and magnificent contrast and from what I'd already seen of the pictures the camera had more than succeeded in capturing those flavours. And with those thoughts I instinctively looked down towards the pocket of my daypack where the camera always resided … and that was the moment I realised it was no longer there.

Repeated searches confirmed it must have escaped because I hadn't fastened the zip properly and I felt sick to the pit of my stomach. There was absolutely nothing I could do, it had gone, end of story. Obscenities were tempting but instead I settled for a long, hard stare at the ground. And then I started walking.

Pointless, thoughtless, mindless, aimless walking entirely focused on the passing of my beloved little camera. Where the hell was I? Where was I going? Why was I here? The city was busy, this was their Oxford Street and there was nothing at all therapeutic about lugging my bags up and down it. I decided to do some swearing after all and then found a Lada to take me to a hotel.

An interesting hotel it was: perched on the rim of a huge bowl with fabulous big windows looking down over the city of Tbilisi. It was there to be enjoyed but I was in no mood just yet to contemplate enjoyment of any sort. I resolved instead to finish the book I was reading – Ali & Nino – ironically the story of an Azerbaijani who fell in love with a Georgian girl at the time of the First World War. He too had suffered a culture shock on his travels to Tbilisi and how his words seemed so poignant almost a hundred years later:

"Lazily I dressed. I felt dizzy. All this Georgian hospitality was so completely different from the quiet, dignified receptions at my uncle's house. There we drank strong tea and talked of sages and poetry. Here they drank wine, danced, laughed and sang, were pliant and hard like a steel spring. Was this the gate to Europe? No, of course not. This was part of us, yet so very different from the rest of us".

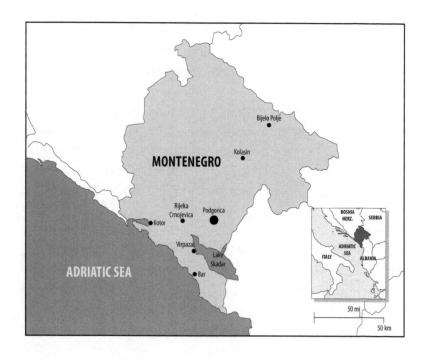

MONTENEGRO

I was the only living person in there, a sort of glass pavilion tucked away in the museum gardens. It was a bright and airy building, once famous for its flowers; a green and pleasant corner of the city of Belgrade that Josep Broz had chosen as his final place of rest. There was no fuss or fanfare, just a marble tomb in the centre of the room with a rectangular glass plaque stating the years of his life and the name by which he was better known. Tito. 1892-1980.

It was a chance finding and one of three landmarks in the city that would help me piece together the history of this troubled region. This was the man who had fought off the Nazis, kicked out the Italians and steadfastly refused to be pushed around by the Russians. It was Tito who had formed a left wing resistance – the anti-fascist Partisans – and ultimately brought together the feisty Croats, Serbs, Macedonians, Bosniaks, Slovenians and Montenegrins. Under his leadership the Slavic people, for so many years dominated by others, had become a force of their own. It was in 1943 that they officially united as the Socialist Federal Republic of Yugoslavia and thanks to Tito another ten-letter country was born.

He held the federation together and ruled Yugoslavia with his own brand of communism for the next thirty seven years. What a life he must have had, I found myself thinking, as I read the dates again on his solitary tomb. Not just him but all those people who'd been plunged into a world war at the age of twenty something, only to find it happen all over again a couple of decades later. Strangely the mausoleum tells nothing of his struggle against the dictators of the 20th century but instead records that his funeral was attended by 31 presidents, 4 kings, 6 princes and 22 Prime Ministers. 128 countries in all were represented and there is a simple shaded map on the wall that highlights – somewhat ominously – those that were not.

* * * * *

I waited for the bus to take me back into the city centre. Standing at the roadside was a challenge against the blazing afternoon heat but my mood was positive and the decision to start the journey to Montenegro from here in neighbouring Serbia had already been vindicated. The itinerary had been shaped by the convenience and economy of a Wizz Air flight from Luton to Belgrade coupled with the prospect of an onward adventure by train but how right it now seemed for the action to commence in what was, after all, the former capital of Yugoslavia.

I looked up and down the dual carriageway as people do when waiting for buses. Then I carefully mopped sweat from the side of my face, slugged water, assessed the waste bin (a 40 litre job, I guessed), admired the trees..... and spotted the floodlights poking out above the high branches. Across the road, almost obscured by the summer greenery, I was treated to the thrilling surprise of a football stadium and how appropriate that it should turn out to be the home of Partisan Belgrade. Was this mere coincidence, at the graveside of the partisans great leader? Could I resist the temptation?

Heading in a straight line – road, trees, field, car park – my first point of contact was the club souvenir shop. Black and white Partisan regalia hung from the windows but there was nobody around, not much happens at football grounds on a Thursday afternoon. It didn't stop the adrenalin kicking in though, in fact it just increased the burning desire to get inside.

I proceeded clockwise around the circular walls, read the graffiti and studied doors and gates and padlocks as a criminal might prepare for a heist. My patience (and stupidity?) was to be rewarded in finding a metal door slightly ajar and no sign of security staff to prevent my passing through unnoticed. But what if I was collared? I figured they (who?) wouldn't speak English and was sure I wouldn't speak Serbo-Croat so mentally cobbled together a plan whereby I would smile matily, shake hands with great enthusiasm and say the words "Manchester City". It would give us some common ground, so to speak, and who knows, they might even think I'd been sent over on official business from Eastlands.

It opened into a concrete corridor which led to a laundry room and a flight of steps. Go for it lad: in for a penny, in for a pound. Quiet as a mouse I climbed the stone spiral staircase, gaining height quickly and swinging round and round back on myself several times. Suddenly, unexpectedly, daylight flooded the shaft, I raised my hand instinctively against the glare and had to trust autopilot to carry me blindly up to the top.

When my eyes had adjusted to the brightness I realised, with childish excitement, that I was standing almost at the entrance to the players' tunnel! One of those long, retractable canvas thingies, a sort of tube that spills over the touchline and onto the grass. On my right was what looked like the visitors changing room and in a corridor to my left, unlit, was a series of doors behind which, no doubt, the Partisans would prepare to do battle. I'd better just have a quick look down there.

It was a long hospital-like corridor with lots of metal doors bearing words I would never understand. Just a quick peek inside the physio or weights room would have been enough for me but everything was locked, every handle I turned drew a blank. The further along I walked the darker and more pointless it became so I decided to turn back, make for the players tunnel and, as any self-respecting middle-aged man would, jog casually out on to the pitch to the imagined roar of the crowd. The ticker was pounding away big time and it moved up a notch further when I started to head for the small circle of light at the far end and saw the man swinging the iron gate across the opening.

The chap about to turn the key had no idea he wasn't the only person in the stadium and it must have been a scary moment for him. I tried to seem in control. "Hello there!" Loud enough to do the job but with the matter-of-factness of addressing a fellow rambler on a country path. The elderly gent shouted something back and waved his arm but I sensed minimal aggression and saw no weapon. It was crucial to profit from his state of shock to avoid the risk of incarceration so I jogged briskly from darkness to daylight, fixed a beaming simpleton smile in place and led with an outstretched arm as though about to hand over a relay baton. "Manchester City".

He looked extremely puzzled and responded with what was almost certainly Serbo-Croat for "who are you and what the fucking hell do you think you are up to?" There was nothing else for it than to upgrade the handshake to a little hug, give him one more "Manchester City" and make the humblest possible gesture to indicate my desire to get onto the field of play. To my great relief, it worked. Slowly but surely we became mates though sadly all I could follow from our long conversations were the words Arsenal and, inevitably, Manchester United (the Reds were beaten there in 1966, I later noted and gloated). Then he let me walk out alone to the centre circle, to play my game of make believe.

* * * * *

I made the train reservation for two days hence and set about enjoying Belgrade. The weather in UK had been the usual summer flop so a flight from the Chilly Chilterns to the Balmy Balkans (you saw it here first, Wizz!) had been just what the doctor ordered.

No city of two million people can boast more squares, parks, statues or orthodox churches. Belgrade was interesting and for the most part pleasant though the old city, the hub of the action, is still blighted by graffiti and carries more than a fair share of communist concrete. The new city, a soulless commercial park of hotels and shopping centres, is uncannily reminiscent of Welwyn Garden City, so the less said about that the better.

The jewel in Belgrade's crown is the Kalemegdan fortress that sits on top of the hill, built on an old Roman site by the Austrians and Turks who between them dominated the region for the best part of five hundred years. It commands a fantastic view over the rivers Sava and Danube where they come together in the heart of the city, a unique vantage point that drew me back several times during the short visit. What a joy it was to sit there in the sunshine with a bird's eye view of the capital, looking down over the barges that become nightclubs in the hours of darkness and – in the distance – the seemingly soundless movement of cars shunting back and forth across the bridges that link the old city to the new.

It was almost time to head south to Montenegro but not before an important photo en route to the station. The bombed and hastily abandoned nine-storey building that had once been the army headquarters was an horrific sight, a disfigured windowless shell desperate to collapse but somehow hanging on more than ten years after the attacks. It had been left untouched, right there in the middle of a main thoroughfare in the centre of the city (and just round the corner from the British Embassy). For good or for bad, a constant reminder of 1999.

The 1990s was a decade of tragedy in the Balkans. Four of the six republics abandoned the Yugoslav federation in favour of independence leaving Serbia and Montenegro as the only remaining partners. The Serbs, under Milosevic, were determined to gain more influence and didn't waste much time in picking fights with their own province of Kosovo, the (predominantly Catholic) Croatians and – to the west – the Muslim dominated region of Bosnia-Herzegovina. Six years of bloodshed resulted in the loss of more than 100,000 lives, mostly Muslims, and in March 1999 NATO finally gave the order to bomb strategic points of the city of Belgrade. The assault lasted for 78 days. It was a clear message to the Serbs that enough was enough, the civilised world was not prepared to sit back and watch ethnic cleansing any longer.

The Montenegrins had already grown tired of the Serb hunger for domination and effectively severed ties in 1996. They switched currencies from the Dinar to the Deutschmark, later adopted the Euro, and formally filed for divorce ten years later. Independence then came quickly and on June 3rd 2006, fourteen years after the collapse of Tito's Yugoslavia, another ten-letter country had taken its place.

* * * * *

There is a certain charm to long-distance train travel which intensified the moment I stepped aboard the 13.10 bound for Montenegro. The carriages were again in that old-fashioned Hitchcock-thriller style with separate compartments feeding off a long corridor and the fact that passengers were few in number allowed me the luxury of total privacy behind the sliding door. So I made myself at home, scattered my possessions, put my feet up, and waited to be murdered.

The journey from Belgrade to Bar on the Adriatic coast is surely an assassin's dream. It can take anything up to twelve hours, there are 254 tunnels in which to do the deed and a choice of 435 bridges over which to dump the victim's body. In all it covers a distance of just under 300 miles at an average speed, according to my calculations, that would not be beyond the scope of a reasonably well-fed donkey. No wonder it's billed as one of the great railway adventures of the world.

My ticket was to Kolasin in the centre of Montenegro, the highest point of the track above sea level. The scheduled arrival time was 20.30 assuming a constant gallop of 27 mph but I had been warned that even this was an optimistic guess. No matter, this was my twentieth country as an alphabet traveller and the first time to cross the threshold by rail. I was determined to enjoy every minute.

And enjoy it I did, though by 20.30 we had only reached Bijelo Polje just over the border. Serbian immigration officials had earlier wandered through the train and now came the drama of a team of heavily uniformed Montenegrin policemen raiding my corridor. It all felt very second world war and the stern-looking characters sliding doors back and forth added a slightly sinister edge.

"Passport". No smile. Inspection of face. Inspection of photo. Face again.

"England?"

'Yes sir, England' (cringeingly polite)

216

"Blackburn 1, Arsenal 2. Just been watching it on TV. Welcome to Montenegro".

He stamped a middle page and I examined his handiwork as the door slid and clunked back into place. And you know what really made my day? Pathetic for a grown man you probably think but the new inky rectangle had a little picture of a train in the bottom left hand corner. A permanent reminder of what had been a perfect journey: gorgeous Serbian countryside, the bridges and tunnels, the pork schnitzel and chips that the buffet man had cooked up for my lunch, the cold beers and the little shot of clear liquid that had brought a smile to his face and tears to my eyes.

The further we travelled the more dramatic the scenery became and it was bad luck that darkness snuffed out the north of Montenegro (hence the introduction of beer and dodgy brandy). It was 22.20 when I finally clambered down on to the tracks of Kolasin station (was there even a platform?), just nine hours after departure and two later than scheduled. The air was cool, worryingly so in light of my gung-ho decision to wear/pack only shorts, and I was pleased to find a taxi next to the railway shed. The driver must have been there all evening, probably a familiar scenario, and who could blame him for requesting a price hike in view of the lateness of the hour. He apologised for charging three Euro instead of the usual two.

* * * * *

Kolasin is a small town in the mountains, a ski resort struggling to attract tourists outside of the winter months. That was my conclusion based on the almost empty hotel and the fact that I was the only be-shorted person wandering around the square on an overcast Sunday morning. A pleasant but unremarkable place it was except for the incongruous triangular building at its centre, a (once) modern design that wanted to be Sydney Opera House but had failed so miserably it resembled a very large, decaying public lavatory. This community centre of sorts held my curiosity for quite some time until the wind started whipping my knees and the flapping canopy of the rent-a-bike marquee lured me over to the far corner of the square.

There was a lovely road to cycle up to the ski centre, I was assured and (very believably) there would be little in the way of traffic. It was a piece of advice for which I was grateful and which resulted in my puffing and wheezing up the side of a mountain for the rest of the morning. On reaching the final goal there was little to see other than a hibernating ski lift, a map of 31 kms of closed pistes and a large empty car park with a small wooden hut at its entrance. It was, in truth, something of an anti-climax but I was glad to plonk the bike on the ground, stretch my legs and take a few photos of a ski resort at rest. What happened next was the last thing I expected.

The door of the hut swung open, out stepped its sole occupant and the grumpiest of outbursts was accompanied by a series of elaborate arm movements. We had a problem, a serious problem: my bicycle was obstructing the highway and under no circumstances could it remain there a single moment longer. There was no smile, no sense of irony, just another volley of Serbo-Croat and a further gesticulation. Imagine landing on Mars, going on a walkabout to collect dust and stones then returning joyfully to your spacecraft to find a parking ticket on the windscreen.

The highlight of the bike ride was the large thatched conical hut on the edge of town. Only on the return leg did I realise this was a *restoran* and it was curiosity more than hunger that inspired me to poke my head inside. A ready smile and a proffered menu charmed me into a seat and the kindly lady proprietor did her best with limited English to explain the list of dishes. I followed her recommendation and ordered Kacamak, the house speciality and not, as you might be tempted to think, a raincoat for the incontinent. It was then just a question of sitting quietly, reading the no-smoking signs and observing my fellow diners, all of whom except a six-year-old boy had a fag on the go at the same time.

The dish of melted cheese and potatoes was rich and tasty, an old-fashioned recipe from the days when you'd had a good innings if you lived to the age of 45. I ate just half (perhaps I would live to be 90?), tried to pedal it off in the afternoon and resumed the feeding frenzy six hours later with a bowl of boiled lamb, a peasants stew and a side dish of beans and roasted vegetables. Another charming wooden shed of a restaurant, this time with a log-fuelled stove at its centre and how I enjoyed my first few glasses of Vranac, the very drinkable local wine that was almost as purple as my face.

Life in the mountains generally involves as much exercise as the weather permits and as much hearty food as the body can burn. This a sensible balance but one which can tip quite dangerously if the rains arrive and a spot of boozing is introduced as a late substitute. So when word reached the hotel reception that dodgy weather was imminent I had no choice but to scrub plans for trekking in the nearby national parks – Biogradski and Durmitor – and consider new options. North and west had effectively been ruled out so should I head east to the small Muslim towns over by the Albanian border or south to the capital and the treasures beyond?

The particular treasure that caught my eye was Skadar Lake in the south-east and according to the guidebook it would take just two hours and two buses to get there. This the great advantage of travelling in a country even smaller than Northern Ireland, with what seemed a well established public transport system to serve a population of only 625,000 people. On the face of it, getting around would be a doddle.

So, after breakfast next morning I boarded the 09.30 bus to Podgorica (rhymes with pizza), a contender with Nouakchott and Dushanbe for the least famous capital city in the world. We headed west out of town then followed a long series of hairpin bends in a southerly direction, always keeping the Moraca river to our left-hand side. It was a landscape of astonishing beauty and every twist and turn was rewarded with a stunning mountain vista.

The road clung on to the side of a steep, heart-stopping gorge exposing the snake of crystal clear water far below. The river was forceful in places but in stretches reduced to no more than a trickle, the stony islands in midstream telling the story of a long dry summer. Contrary to the forecast

219

the weather was glorious, the bright sunshine lit up the huge valley, and high in the distance I spotted one of the many viaducts that carry our famous train from one tunnel to the next. Once again I was enjoying one of THE great rail journeys of the world, except this time it was from the back seat of a bus.

If a city can be measured by its bus station (perhaps not a bad benchmark) one would describe Podgorica as clean, tidy, well-organised and exuding confidence. Such was the efficiency of the customer-friendly terminus that within two minutes of arrival my holdall was stored in left luggage, a computer-generated ticket had been issued for the next leg of my journey and the precise departure time and platform had been verbally confirmed against the information that appeared on the electronic board. Would the day ever come, I wondered, when all Ten-Letter Countries could offer this level of service?

I had a couple of hours to kill and nothing by way of a plan. The capital seemed a pleasant enough place with its mountain backdrop and grid of tree-lined streets but I had neither the time nor inclination to seek out anything in particular. So I went for an aimless plod around Pod and on reaching a crossroads was drawn by a large building away to my left advertising itself as the Hall of Montenegro. What could this be?

I ventured Hallwards only to discover on entry that it was a large, new shopping centre of zero interest but with a traditional old market building alongside. Therein I was treated to a colourful display of fresh produce and a tour of the cheese room where cheery ladies in aprons scooped samples of white salty stuff from vats that were often larger and wider than they were (no small achievement in some cases). This traditional cheese – known as *sir* – all seemed much the same but I moved from one vendor to the next just to make sure and the cross-cultural banter brought lots of laughs all round.

The need for a mouth-rinsing coffee led me to the edge of the building and a small booth where two men stood by a table. One was the café owner enjoying a lunchtime tipple with his mate (the small, empty brandy glasses by the cups and saucers always a tell-tale sign) and my arrival seemed a welcome diversion to what was probably a regular scenario. We shared no common language but the friendly boss was eager to slice and share his newly bought peaches, offer shots of *rakija* each time the bottle re-emerged and go to great lengths to explain in mime, and with considerable emotion, how his sister had long since departed for Adelaide. The two men were great fun, lovely people, and it was a shame I had to leave in a hurry so as not to miss my connection. We parted company with handshakes and hugs, a piece of paper with an illegible address and the absolute promise that I would send Vejnovic (the first word of his spidery scrawl) a photo of our brief and unlikely encounter.

The tidy little bus departed on schedule and headed south through the city past the Mall of Montenegro. That I had misread it first time round brought a smile to my face and I was still feeling pleased as punch half an hour later when the road sign announced we had reached the village of Virpazar. The scenery was just as striking as it had been earlier in the day and I was already starting to get a sense that stunning natural beauty was the rule of Montenegro rather than the exception. Would I get through the chapter with my limited supply of superlatives? Or would I have to resort to making a few up?

The Hotel Pelikan was on a narrow street at the entrance to the village where the proprietor, an eccentric character sporting a funky straw hat, was handing out bags of his fresh herbs to passers by. Assuming it to be the only accommodation available I took one of the tiny rooms overlooking the square and signed up with the owner's son for a trip on the lake later in the day. A hasty and amateurish move in hindsight as a short walk soon revealed that rooms and dining options were plentiful and every man and his dog had a boat to explore the beauty of Skadar.

The lake is 10 kms across and 43 kms long though a third of its area, at the opposite (south-eastern) end, is on the Albanian side. Montenegro protects it as a National Park, a twitcher's dream home to almost three hundred species of bird and the Dalmatian Pelican the king of the castle with a body length equal to the height of a man. So a sense of excitement prevailed as our little vessel chugged through the channel of lotus lily leaves to reach the open water. The sun was strong now, the breeze only that from the motion of the boat and the surface of the lake was sparkling like an enormous floating diamond.

I can think of no more pleasant a way to spend an afternoon. The birdlife was less than hoped but the majestic egrets and herons, standing gracefully and motionlessly in the shallow waters, more than adequately compensated for the paucity of pelicans. The mini-cruise also helped in terms of general orientation and with map in hand I was able to identify the scattering of villages clinging to the edge of the lake with the vineyards and the mountains beyond.

Such was this beguiling landscape that I set off on foot next morning, in the direction of Albania, with just my daypack and as many water bottles as it would hold. There were more country lanes than I'd imagined and they climbed up high, dipped into the valleys and traversed hillsides where tiny communities had evidently managed to survive over hundreds of years. At the roadside figs and grapes and pomegranates hung from the trees in abundance, I passed isolated farmhouses offering bottles of wine and *rakiya* on makeshift stalls and the lake popped back in to view every few minutes just to remind me of its sheer magnificence. If there is a place called paradise, surely it must look something like this.

Except for the occasional passing vehicle I saw no-one until reaching Zabes, high up in the mountains. Here in this tiny hamlet the narrow road was lined with parked cars whose owners and passengers, perhaps twenty five in number, sat at tables under a canopy in the garden of one of the properties. They were mostly elderly folk, talking quietly in groups and sipping on drinks and some nodded politely at the foreigner wandering by with a bag on his back. How very weird, we were all thinking.

The path I decided to follow left the road, climbed the steep hillside and led, rather unexpectedly, to a small church with a pretty graveyard. As you may recall, I like cemeteries for their sense of local history but when I wandered into this one there was something of a surprise in store. It all started quite routinely, reading through the family names that were repeated over and over and the sad tributes to the lives of those that died young but then I spotted a grave in the far corner that was very noticeably different from the rest. In fact, was it a grave? There was no headstone, there was just a mound of earth and… and an empty space with a hole in the ground. Please God tell me somebody hadn't escaped!

The silence and the spookiness was suddenly overwhelming. I was tempted to retreat and it was only after giving myself a severe talking to that I started tiptoeing vaguely towards the corner. My steps noticeably shortened as the hole approached and taking great care not to get too close to the edge I tilted my upper body forward ever so slowly, ready to jump back in case something leapt out from within. Then I peered inside.

And there it was, six feet below, the shape of a person beneath a crisp white sheet. The latest arrival, probably that morning, and no doubt the reason for the gathering at the farmhouse below. Or were the mourners here, right now, a row of white faces behind me, fifty eyes staring silently at my back? I turned quickly like a startled bird, found to my enormous relief there was nobody in sight and ran like buggery back to the land of the living.

Reaching the pretty village of Godinje I found a café, completely empty except for a fat lady stretched out on a sofa. You can imagine my relief when I observed that her large frame was moving slowly up and down and as she sensed my presence her eyes opened and she swivelled awkwardly into an upright position.

"Salat?" I asked, pretty much exhausting my knowledge of the lingo.

Her response was unquestionably positive, the demeanour that of a thoroughly nice person and no further words were needed except to choose coke over beer. Ten minutes later the smiling lady brought forth the expected bowl of freshly diced tomatoes, cucumber and onion, a plate of salty cheese and prosciutto ham and later some smoked fish she insisted I try. She fussed around like mother to son and tried to call a cab to speed my return to Virpasar. Alas a mission that resulted in failure due to the fact that, as she explained through a series of comical gestures, all taxis were booked for a funeral on the other side of the mountain.

* * * * *

Safely back at the Pelikan, thanks to a lift from a French couple, I plotted the onward route. The executive decision was to hit the Adriatic at Kotor, stay there for a few days, then continue north up the coast into Croatia to fly home from Dubrovnik. My next stop would be the town with the catchy name of Rijeka Crnojevica but not before I'd called in at the Lake Skadar Visitor Information Centre across the bay in Vranjina. Not easy names to remember, hence they were, and always will be, logged in my mind as RC and Vagina.

The mourning traffic (!) had evidently subsided and I had no problems this time to locate a taxi and negotiate a ride across the mountain to RC. A half hour in Vagina was part of the deal and just about enough time to fully explore the delights within …. the excellent Centre covered not just the Lake Skadar National Park but the four other designated parks elsewhere in the country.

The journey to RC entailed climbing high above the lake and thanks to my chirpy driver, unable to acknowledge my zero grasp of Serbo-Croat, a running commentary was offered throughout. Bless him, his enthusiasm could not be faulted and he even stopped at his favourite viewing point so we could get out and marvel at the splendiferous body of water below. This was his home – a born and bred Lake Man – he knew every village, every town, every peak and he proudly pointed out what was where. Straight ahead Albania, diagonally left Kosovo, due left the towering mountains of Kolasin.

To say the scenery was stupendous is in danger of becoming a bore to us all, so from now on I'll just let you know when it wasn't. We followed the line of the River Crnojevica (which translates as Rijeka Crnojevica, I then realised) and crossed over the bridge to reach my destination of the

224

same name. Not so much a town as a street by a river, a few shops, a couple of restaurants and a bar with rooms to rent.

The *Perjanic* was owned and manned by an unshaven, bespectacled man of around sixty. His name was Ivan, he had just returned from Melbourne after twenty years of living there yet his command of English was fragile to say the least. Good enough however to explain his life story (he was born in Serbia) and introduce the different coloured brandies in the specimen jars behind him as though each was a cherished member of his family. He was clearly quite a character and talked all the way upstairs as he led me to the only room (of three) available that evening.

The bed was a mattress of sorts covered with a black nylon sheet, the walls were bright orange and the curtain was a torn piece of material that covered half the window. The scant bit of furniture could have been plucked from the local tip and the bright green paintings were at best mysterious. It was truly hideous. The only redeeming feature was that the room boasted an en-suite with a shower and a toilet though the sink had long since been removed and, on that particular afternoon, a dead grasshopper had taken its place.

"It's 40 Euro" Ivan ventured, shrugging his shoulders as if to acknowledge that he couldn't possibly ask any more. That he was the only show in town helped his cause enormously so I shook hands on the deal and promised to join him in the bar later.

My fellow guests got there first. A Belgian couple, so charmed by Ivan's hospitality that they'd returned for the second time in a week, were sipping on beers with two men from Innsbruck. The Austrians turned out to be father and son who were heading towards Albania on a trans-European motor bike adventure and they had many an interesting story to tell, as indeed did our gregarious host. I sensed we were in for an evening of fun.

The wacky Ivan convinced me that his eel was the finest money could buy and his wife would prepare it for my dinner. At least I thought he said eel. Or was it veal? Or even heel? The assembled drinkers encouraged me to go for it anyway and sure enough, several beers and a few glasses of wine later, the plate was delivered.

The fish, if that's what we call it, was neither long nor slimy but looked much like a pile of spare ribs. A preliminary, self-conscious, tinkering around with the cutlery suggested that it was also best consumed in a rib-like manner and so, reluctantly, hands and teeth were engaged to prize the oily meat from the central bone. It probably tasted OK but was smothered in pieces of garlic the size of pineapple chunks, as was the potato and cucumber that completed the feast. As an event it kept everybody well entertained, particularly the lucky folk whose choice of food had enabled them to enjoy dinner without being immersed from head to toe in grease. I decided drinking was more fun.

It was the moment Ivan had been waiting for. He grabbed his beloved specimen bottles from the shelf behind the bar, painstakingly lined them up on the dining table around which we all sat and set about a passionate presentation of each and every one. These waters of fire derived from apricots and plums and quince and figs and apples and walnuts and a baffling assortment of other things that you or I have never even heard of. The liquids were mostly clear but there were also yellows and greens and even a bright red to lure you on board.

To our host's delight we all chose a few different ones and those that went unchosen he poured out anyway. Each shot would be taken back in one go, as is the norm with these schnappsy concoctions, the displeasure so intense that no sane person would seek to prolong the experience. You neck it in one, everybody claps, your eyes water, boiling acid consumes your innards. And then you do it again.

It is a form of insanity that could be considered socially acceptable around midnight but how would you feel about a couple of shots with your juice and cornflakes in the morning? When I noticed Ivan had one on the go at breakfast next day I knew he would enjoy my raising the subject:

"I never, ever drink until afternoon, he announced very earnestly, but today my friend came for coffee at 6am. He takes a drink, I must drink also. This is Montenegro".

The conversation moved on to the Montenegrin breathalyser, a subject that provoked howls of laughter. It was important to understand that Montenegro is a small country, everybody is related to one another and no policeman would ever want to make a problem for a member of his own family. At which point my taxi driver came into the bar, ordered a large bottle of beer, lit up a smoke and announced that we would be leaving in ten minutes time.

* * * * *

Those final ten minutes had been very interesting. Ivan talked of the history of the town, how it was once the royal capital and how his little bar had in those days been exclusively for the use of the King's security guards, to which the name *Perjanic* relates. And he explained how the earthquake in 1979 had all but destroyed RC and reduced the population to a shadow of its former self. Most of the victims had been forced to seek refuge elsewhere and, as the government had failed on its promise to finance the rebuilding, they were never able to return.

The historic theme was about to continue. I was heading for Cetinje, the city that became the country's capital when Montenegro final wrestled free from Turkish domination in 1878. Strangely, the Turks never actually gained control of Cetinje but it suffered heavily in the second world war when the Germans and Italians took over and 20% of the local population was killed.

It struck me as an elegant city and the five smart museum buildings at its centre evidently attracted a substantial number of tourists. I bought a bumper ticket to gain access to all five and realised after ten minutes what a cavalier investment it had been. The cultural feast was far too bland from the perspective of one so easily bored and after another token trudge around I gave up the ghost in favour of a corner table in a nearby café. And even that didn't cheer me up. The service was glacial, the soup when it did arrive was lukewarm and the foul smell of cigarette smoke made me want to retch. One of those Mr Grumpy days, it was time to smile and move on. Sorry Cetinje.

The deal with my taxi was E50 from RC to Kotor with this lunchtime stopover thrown in. It would constitute a third of my overland expense from Serbia but a price that had to be paid to travel roads not served by public transport. And so we headed across another sweeping valley, through the Njegusi region (famed for its dried ham, I remember seeing *Njegusi prsut* on a menu in Belgrade) and into the foothills of the country's most famous mountain. Mt Lovcen at 1749 metres is far from the highest (my cycle ride in Kolasin had taken me to that altitude) but it was the most distinctive feature to the Venetian sailors that ruled the waters of the Adriatic in the 15th century. They called it *Monte Negro*, the Black Mountain and this is how the region, and later the country, would come to be known.

We passed the entrance to Lovcen National Park and by now the road was dropping and curving steeply round a series of hairpin bends. The driver seemed very pleased with himself and with a clever use of his hands indicated that a photo opportunity was imminent and that he would know the best place to stop. He was right on both counts.

Now if I was an American actress prone to outbursts of hysteria I think I would have thrown my arms in the air and very slowly, very loudly and very deliberately yelled OH....MY....GOD! But as I'm a male, extremely British and only a humble alphabet traveller I just stood by the car, upper lip as stiff as you like, and gently nodded my approval at the scene below.

The Bay of Kotor creates the illusion of a vast sparkling lake imprisoned by a claw of mountains. A wall of sheer grey rock, at times almost vertical, seems to block the water's escape though hidden from the naked eye is the narrowest of channels forming the link to the Adriatic beyond. From high above, represented by red rooftops and church steeples, the town of Kotor occupies the tiny space between the cliff face and the water's edge. Similar but smaller communities adorn the circumference of the bay, some perched on the coastline, others nestled high up on the mountain slopes where the land is significantly greener and rather more gentle.

I gave my word not to bore you about spectacular landscapes so my hands are tied. I am a hostage to my promise, kicking and screaming, straining every sinew. But a deal is a deal. You really need to go there.

* * * * *

It took twenty five more steep, consecutive bends to drop down to Kotor, an explanation for the absence of a public bus. The town that had promised so much from above looked equally intriguing at sea level, the ancient wall surrounding it adding a certain charm and mystery as ancient walls do. This one a thousand years old, twenty metres high and five kilometres in length, an incredible achievement given the rugged and complex terrain. It would tease me into reading up on the history of Kotor and discovering that it was quite a different story from the rest of the country.

I checked in to my pre-booked hotel which turned out to be in the area known as Dobrota, a chic residential neighbourhood 4 kms north along the bay. The elegance of the buildings, the palm trees and the glorious colours of the bougainvillea eased me through the disappointment of not being more central and the gorgeous "lakeside" walk to get back into town confirmed my good fortune. This was the land of villas owned by millionaires and palaces of those far richer still. The architecture was square and sturdy, simple and symmetrical and the Italian influence further betrayed by the shutters at every window.

And here's why. In the four hundred years that most of the region was dominated by the Turks it was the Venetians that held the power in the Bay of Kotor. They ruled the roost from 1420, developed trade, restored churches, enlarged the Romanesque city walls and kept the monster of the Ottoman Empire at arm's length. It was only in the 19th century that Kotor first attached itself to independent Montenegro but then fell under Austrian rule until the world wars of the 20th century and the eventual formation of Yugoslavia.

The old town is a mouth-watering cocktail of tiny streets, winding alleyways, narrow passages and flights of steps that sometimes, but not always, link them together. The cute squares and courtyards provide a perfect setting for the cafés and souvenir shops and the tourists duly arrive in their thousands to soak up the history and the glorious ambience. You can't knock it, but if you're not into the tourist scene, you probably can't do it for too long either. My instinct was to seek out the grimier side, to follow the smell of frying garlic or faulty sewer; to head towards the laundry that poked out from the upper windows.

And in so doing, I came upon a small shop that rather tickled my fancy. It was almost entirely empty except for a lady encased in a booth, a television suspended from the ceiling and a shelf on one side supporting a large stack of crudely stapled pamphlets. What could this be? She didn't seem to mind my wandering in, nor was there any reaction to my picking up the paperwork. But whether or not she looked up as I burst out laughing I'm afraid I can't be sure.

The first thing that caught my eye was Akrington and yes it was spelt with a K. The odds on them fighting out a draw at Tranmer were quoted at 5-2 whereas, a little further down the page, Volsol, Jeovil and Maklsfild were being offered at almost even money to secure home wins. I couldn't believe my eyes. I was in a Montenegrin bookies shop and the document in my hand was not only a list of every football match to be played at the week-end across Europe, South America and Asia but a phonetic translation of each team into Serbo-Croat! And to think how many tourists were swarming in to the churches of St Luke and St Nicholas yet not one of them would get to enjoy the raw pleasure of a Sruzberi, Stivenedz or Rocdejl.

Kotor is pretty and very pleasing on the eye and the restaurants at the waterside offer a panorama over the bay as delightful as anything your mind could possibly conjure. The water is crystal clear, the mountains resplendent, the scattering of tiny communities on the far shore seductive and intriguing. But, as Chris Tarrant might say, we don't want to give you that. We want to erect an enormous TV screen in every restaurant and give you the opportunity to exchange nature at its finest for a mindless fucking soap opera or a basketball match without any sound. And to make absolutely sure you don't get a single moment's pleasure we will impose a non-stop, never-ending, never-changing, never-anything flow of rap music, the most unpleasant phenomenon since the invention of marzipan. And on that note my latest rant comes to a close. How happy was I to be based in Dobrota.

* * * * *

The charm and serenity of this sea that pretended to be a lake demanded at least two days of quiet contemplation. The early September sunshine made for perfect conditions yet all the reclining chairs on the hotel deck were unoccupied but for mine. It was a joy to devote time to this unique vista, to read, to write, to sit and observe the light playing tricks on the surface of the water. There was barely a ripple; it was so clear that the fish venturing close to the edge were visible on the sea bed. Several times I swam amongst them though the breath-catching coolness always forced a quick return to the chair.

I sat there for hours, reflecting on the events of the week, watching the boats bobbing up and down on the water. Small vessels in the main, probably chained to moorings for most of the year, but as the sun was starting to dip on my final day a large cruise ship emerged into view. A hotel with funnels, the word Thomson in large letters moved slowly from left to right across the bay, temporarily blocking out the silhouettes of villas and churches on the peninsula beyond. Its passengers, a row of several hundred dots from where I sat, lined the decks and hung over the rails to catch a final glimpse of paradise before cocktails and dinner and the next port of call. They had done Kotor, no doubt loved every minute, but that would be the beginning and the end of their trip to Montenegro. If only they knew what they'd missed.

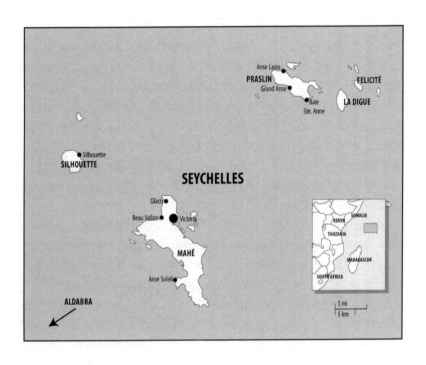

SEYCHELLES

It was just after nine in the morning, the headphones had been collected and a gloved hand, careful to avoid all contact, had pooper-scoopered away the remnants of the polystyrene omelette. The captain confirmed we would shortly be landing, on schedule, in the Seychelles and that in line with expectation it was already 29 degrees Celsius on the ground.

A hundred voices, mostly unheard throughout the previous ten hours, hummed into life. And no wonder, rarely would anybody's Monday start this way. It was as though the dazzling sunlight had brought new energy to the weary passengers and real life entertainment had replaced the misery of cartoons in the darkness. Each dip of a wing filled the cabin with a feast of colour, the Indian Ocean in all its glory, an absurd shade of pale green not normally associated with water. Had buckets of the stuff been poured on our heads the impact could not have been greater.

There were islands too, often no more than a few clumps of trees, like bunches of broccoli poking up from the surf with a beach wrapped around the base where a rubber band should be. Would such tiny specks in the ocean be marked on the map? What does a bit of land have to do to be accorded "island" status? Mid-spectacular-descent was hardly the time or place for scientific contemplations but this did have a certain significance given the claim that Seychelles is a nation of 115 islands.

Out of this daydream appeared yachts large and small, their chains and anchors clearly visible in the sparkling, transparent water. Then, seemingly from nowhere, swapping places with the sky, a dense diagonal wall of dark green, a tree covered mountain with a scattering of villas. It all seemed to happen so quickly. The undercarriage wheezed and clicked and we were ready to land on Mahé, the largest and most important island of all.

The Seychelles (I *do* feel happier with a definite article) is listed amongst the world's smallest countries and if all its component parts were stuck together the total area would still only equate to one sixth of tiny Luxembourg. Yet, fascinatingly – to a weirdo like me, anyway – the archipelago is spread across an expanse of ocean more than twice the size of France. And there's more to come. As I waited to disembark the aircraft, to set foot on this north-easterly Seychelle (I'm just teasing now), I calculated that the islands of the Aldabra group in the south-west of the country were a staggering 1150 kms away. That's further than John O'Groats is from London.

The in-flight magazine had had much more to say about Aldabra. This remote chain supports over 100,000 residents, not one of whom will ever venture to another part of the country or even have an inkling of life beyond the reef. These island dwellers eat all day long and their bodies eventually become so large and heavy that movement becomes difficult and painfully slow. Yet against all the odds, some live for more than a hundred years. It could indeed be the American Midwest except we are not talking people here, in fact... there are no people here. These are giant tortoises and there are only two places on Earth where they live in the wild.

In contrast the human population of the Seychelles is a smaller number, just under 90,000, and all but a handful live on Mahé and two other islands close by. Praslin and La Digue would be easy for me to visit but what would be the chance of my making it to Aldabra? The story of this World Heritage Site, a remote place I'd never heard of until now, had really captured my imagination. More information could be obtained from the Seychelles Islands Federation and with that thought in mind I made sure their e-mail address was safely in the bag.

The other article that had caught my attention was that written by a lady name of Soraya Mitchell who had recently moved from UK to live in the Seychelles. Her experience as an ex-pat in a tropical paradise had made for entertaining reading and it was during that industrious phase of the flight that I made a mental note to try to track her down.

The plane was all but empty now, the only people left on board were those in need of assistance and a strange man with a head full of trivia and a list of unusual projects to pursue. I stepped out into the blazing heat, tired as hell but very excited.

* * * * *

Bliss Hotel could not have been more aptly named. Thanks to the Trip Advisor recommendations my first hours in the Seychelles were spent upon a bed bedecked with frangipani petals in an all-white room on the side of a mountain. Set amidst the trees and flowers and tweeting birds its simplicity was utterly charming and the view over the bay out to Silhouette Island exactly what a visitor would dream of waking up to. I'd planned to stay for three days and quickly extended to five.

The village of Glacis sits just below the most northerly point of Mahé on the thumb-shaped promontory at the top of the island. Up here only a couple of miles separate the west coast from the east, or more specifically, the resort of Beau Vallon from the capital, Victoria. (*Capital*?! It's the only town in the country). The communities of this peninsula are linked together by the number 22 bus and as luck would have it the bus stop was right at my door.

I resisted climbing aboard for the first couple of days. An alliterate regime of sleeping, snorkelling and sipping on sundowners snuffed out the jet lag and a few sessions on the laptop were yielding some satisfying results. I joined the Social Seychelles network, arranged to meet Soraya for a beer, received an invitation from an author by the name of Sandra Hanks and set up a meeting with Lindsay Chong Seng, the Science Co-ordinator of the Seychelles Islands Federation (SIF). Not a bad return for two days on the beach!

Beau Vallon, considered the main resort on the island, was not the place I had imagined. I counted three shops, three hotels and three restaurants adjacent to a sweep of beach that must have been a mile from end to end. Visitors were here and there in small clusters, as were the local souvenir vendors, but as tourism goes this was about as low-key as it gets.

It was a hot and sticky late November day with a pre-rainy season heaviness in the air so I opted for a paddle along the water's edge and carried on to the village of Bel Ombre, dropping in at the small grocery store to buy a local paper. The shopkeeper was keen to chat and especially eager to offer his thoughts on the person whose photo appeared on the front page of The Nation. It was to prove an educational encounter.

The man that stirred his emotions was Albert René, the country's president from 1977 to 2004. An arrogant, loathsome man (according to my new friend) who had declared a coup the year after independence and appointed himself as the country's leader when President Mancham was in London for a Commonwealth meeting. More damning still, eight years later, René's main political rival was brutally assassinated on a London street. Gerard Hoarau's body was pumped with 39 bullets from a sub-machine gun but the Seychelles government refused to co-operate with Scotland Yard and the crime has never been solved. Hecky Thump – and I'd only popped in to buy a paper!

Back at the beach I found shade by the trees and sat upright in the warm, powdery sand, knees clasped tightly under chin(s). A thoughtful pose to watch the waves roll in and to imagine what it must have been like for the first settlers arriving in the bay with precious little idea what lay beyond the shores. So when exactly was that? I realised how little I knew of the island's history and it seemed like a good time to dig out the guidebook and force myself to learn a few basic facts.

Apparently it was 1756 when the French claimed the islands and back in those days the beaches were infested by enormous saltwater crocodiles. (I think I would have been inclined to turn the boat round and look for somewhere else to live but, don't forget, these are people who pull the legs off frogs and cook them in garlic.) They moved in, got their slaves to do the hard work, killed all the crocs and generally got the place up and running. During this period the Brits would sail in from time to time to make their presence felt and on such a visit in 1810 they explained ever so politely that the Tricolour would be coming down and the Union Jack going up. The Frenchman in charge, like a true hero, responded with a shrug of the shoulders and a few Oogh La La's then changed the spelling of his name to make it look more English. He was kept on as boss of the island for the rest of his life.

Britain had no real interest in the Indian Ocean Islands, which at the time also included Mauritius, so they left the French to run the show for most of the 1800s. Only "a few eccentrics from London" would arrive on Mahé though the Brits were instrumental in sending several thousand men who had just been released from slavery. A few Indian and Chinese merchants also sailed in to ply their trade but it was only in the early part of the 20th century that Britain made a serious effort to populate – and anglicise – the country. By then, it could be argued, it was too late.

Aaagh, now it was starting to make sense. It had initially struck me as odd that a country ruled by the French for 40 years and the Brits for the next 166 actually seemed more comfortable with the language of the former colonists. The man on the bus, the people at the hotel, the ranting shopkeeper, they had all spoken English but sounded French!

By 5.30 the beach was all but empty and the sun had reached its most important position in the sky, that critical distance from the horizon that dictates the timing of the first proper drink of the day. The only bar was packed with a crowd of tattooed men and mini-skirted women, most of whom seemed to be American and all of whom seemed to be in very high spirits. To a boring and (almost) middle-aged man armed with a local newspaper and preparing for sunset such a loud, chaotic ambience seemed rather incongruous and, I have to confess, just a tad irksome. What on earth was going on?

The sweet, demure and not unattractive lady with the chilled bottle of Seybrew on a tray came up with all the answers. They were off the US naval ship, they were here to protect the world from the Somali pirates and this raucous partying had become quite a regular scenario. Clearly it wasn't her scene either so we smiled at each other and shook our heads conspiratorially, just one step away from away from a tut.

The front page of the paper brought stories of Albert René and the introduction of VAT but it was the article in the sports section at the back that made my eyes light up. The Seychelles Football Federation had appointed former Manchester City player Andy Morrison as national coach and by way of self introduction his pledge to the country was to bring discipline to all levels of the squad. I'm not sure what surprised me more: their choice of leader, that Morrison would know the meaning of discipline or that the squad had several levels that needed knocking into shape. Was this that wild character from Scotland with legs like tree trunks? The bloke I'd watched at Wembley in Manchester City's finest hour of the nineties, a Division 2 play-off final victory over the mighty Gillingham?

* * * * *

Lindsay Chong Seng turned out to be a man and a very engaging one at that. We met in his small office close to the hospital in Victoria and he talked with passion and eloquence about Aldabra, the second largest atoll in the world. By definition this is a coral island surrounding a lagoon and only Christmas Island Atoll, way out in the middle of the Pacific, can rival it for size. The UK and USA got their hands on that one for nuclear testing and wanted Aldabra to go the same way but thankfully international ecologists fought hard enough to ensure that it didn't happen. The remote atoll was granted World Heritage status in 1982.

You might be surprised to learn that the main threat to Aldabra's huge giant tortoise population is posed by goats. They are relatively few in number but chomp away at the island's greenery and thus compete with their crusty co-dwellers for limited resources. Lindsay's challenge therefore is to eradicate the beardy beasts from the islands and he was preparing to hire an experienced gunman, a contract killer, to do just that.

"So how often does anybody get out to Aldabra?" Carefully selected words and a golden opportunity for the extending of an invitation.

Lindsay scratched his chin and paused for a long time as though what was to follow might be too painful to hear. Then he explained that ecology cruises, at one time very popular, had dried up because of the threat of piracy and thus an important source of income had been lost. Nowadays just six to ten scientists are based there for half a year at a time to carry our research programmes on behalf of SIF but he, the man in charge, can only get there once every two years. It remained unsaid that Jenkins, four days in the Seychelles and writer of silly books, would not be making the trip.

The second prize, however, was still up for grabs. I was right next door to the Botanical Gardens which I knew from my research would afford the opportunity to revel with giant tortoises and see that other great natural phenomenon of the Seychelles at first hand. The Coco de Mer is a palm tree endemic to the country and its fascination I suspect is more a consequence of the distinctive shape of the double coconut that grows upon it. The (Y) has become the symbol of the Seychelles and I am not the first person to have noticed its similarity to a pair of shapely female hips and that mysterious region from which wee-wee and babies sometimes appear.

The well-kept gardens were calm and silent in a way that public libraries *used to* be (rant suppressed) and I must confess to having given more time to watching the airborne creatures than admiring the palms or those huge, ugly steak and kidney pies crawling around in their pit. It was the tiny red birds I found most fascinating, the plucky male Madagascan Fodys who would sing in the trees and dance at your feet and show no inhibitions whatsoever despite their lack of camouflage amidst the dense greenery. And at the opposite end of the beauty spectrum, fruit bats by the thousand squawking and circling or, worse, hanging from the trees and waving their fleshy black capes. Horrid looking things but, according to the locals, absolutely delicious in curries.

Downtown Victoria is of a certain Commonwealth ilk. New office buildings sit alongside old colonial masterpieces which are sometimes nurtured and cherished but more often decaying and waiting for something to happen. Some shops are bright and modern but far more are dark, pokey, even a little bit smelly; rather than entice you in they implore you to leave as quickly as possible. Not so the Creole Travel Agency however, the spiffy office that issued my ticket for the Saturday boat to Praslin – 45 Euro a pop for the short crossing was evidently maintaining a very nice lifestyle for Cat

Cocos ferries and all who sell for her.

I saw *the* country's set of traffic lights, *the* roundabout and *the* road junction at the centre of which stands Victoria's only defining feature. Big Ben is the capital's pride and joy, a silver grey replica of the clock tower in London's Victoria all but for the part that makes the bells ring. Unfortunately that bit was lost overboard back in 1903 when the clock was shipped to Seychelles to celebrate her separation from Mauritius and new status as an independent colony. Chimeless though it was, I found something immensely satisfying about this tin-foil landmark, enough to convince me to find a seat on the balcony of the adjacent restaurant and raise a toast, in silence, as the hands formed a perfectly straight line at 6pm. May the sun never set on the British Empire.

* * * * *

A Daihatsu 4x4 is the first vehicle I've ever driven that is narrow enough for a man with short arms to touch the passenger window while sitting at the wheel. This is not in itself a guarantee of a great day out but ideal, as I was to discover, for the twisting roads of Seychelles along which buses hurtle at frightening speeds and where there are few kerbs or pavements to offer any margin for error. The deal with Seycars was E40 for the day, delivered to Bliss, and the deal with myself was to make a plan for my return a week later having had a quick butcher's at the rest of the island.

Mahé is roughly eighteen miles from north to south and less than a third of that at its widest point. There's a road that hugs the shoreline for most of the way round and several short ones that cut across the mountain to link the east and west coasts together. I started out with a couple of such traverses: the short hop from Beau Vallon to Victoria and then the climb up through the dense forest and welcome shade of the Morne Seychellois National Park.

The highest point of the road was a spot on the map marked Ruins, a remarkable location for a school that the British had once built to educate the children of the newly liberated slaves. Little remains today other than the plaque that tells the story but the small slice of history and spectacular views over the island were well worth the effort of parking up and taking a short walk through the clearing.

Ten minutes of zig-zagging dropped me back onto the west coast and according to my maps (just the two) a right turn at this junction, northwards, would soon lead to a dead end. The otherwise continuous coast road would fizzle out at the Port Maunay Marine National Park and I figured any bay with a title so grand deserved to be checked out. It turned out to be a smart move. The only vista more endearing than a white beach meeting turquoise water is a wrap-around bay with a copse of palm trees in which to take shade and park vehicles.

I stopped the jeep so the fronds dangled onto the bonnet and gazed at a curve of sand the colour and texture of sifted flour; it had even been raked as a service to the guests of the nearby hotel. All beaches in Seychelles are open to the public but this bay was so utterly magnificent I questioned my entitlement to be there. I felt like an impostor, an intruder, surely nobody deserved such privilege without having given something in return. The sparkling water was as flat as the surface of a mirror, a three-sided, almost transparent swimming pool that – unbelievably – formed part of the Indian Ocean. Impostor or not, I was going in for a dip.

It was to be the highlight of a memorable day out. The west coast brought rugged, dramatic scenery, bays, coves and empty beaches of all shapes and sizes. And in between, or tucked in behind, tiny communities supported by a grocery store, a church, sometimes even a small school. The east side, by comparison, was more developed and relatively featureless though what passes in Seychelles for simply OK would still make your eyes pop out in most other parts of the world. But it was the south-west that would charm me back a week later and I made a note of a couple of places to head for and people I would try to get to meet.

The loop completed, I was back at Bliss an hour before dark and ready for my 6pm sundowner with Soraya, the ex-pat lady of the in-flight magazine. By a happy coincidence her apartment was just round the corner and once we'd made the introductions and husband Mark had charged our glasses we were to find that the coincidences didn't stop there. She was from Manchester, he was from Stockport and we'd both been to the same school just a few years apart. So early conversation was as much about our sadistic geography teacher of three decades earlier than life in Seychelles where Mark himself was a teacher at the International School.

As we sat on the balcony drinking wine, looking out over Glacis Bay and Silhouette Island in the distance, Soraya confirmed they were enjoying Seychelles more than they had Mark's previous posting in south-east London! It had given them a unique opportunity to see the country from a local's perspective and understand the difficulties the Seychellois face earning an "African" salary to meet a "European" cost of living. The last two years had been particularly tough for the country. Seychelles no longer merited grants from international agencies, it had been forced into cutting the value of its currency by half to remain competitive and it was desperately seeking investors with ready cash to pump in. The world recession had hit tourism badly but business was flowing in from wealthy Russians, Chinese and of course Arabs, one of whom had just built a five-block seven-storey mansion on top of the mountain above Victoria.

We had a great evening and laughed a lot, particularly at Soraya's expense. She would have to make a trip back to snow-covered UK that week-end while I was heading off to Praslin and Mark stayed home to run in the annual round-island marathon. It was unanimously decided that Praslin sounded the most appealing of the three.

* * * * *

Ferry crossings are fantastic for amateur sleuths. You can home in undetected on fellow passengers, study physical characteristics, take a quick peek into people's lives and make up the bits you can't work out. There's always that predictable mix of families travelling with kids or ageing parents, couples holding hands, men with briefcases, tourists with backpacks. There are people who sit in silence and rarely move. And there are those who fidget and never, ever shut up.

Looking around, I reckoned at least half of my subjects on board that morning were Seychellois. Their skin colours spanned the entire coffee spectrum from rich black to milky cappuccino – perhaps not surprising in the middle of an ocean that separates Africa from Asia – but their facial features, I now realised, were not dissimilar to the white Europeans who sat alongside. (Or *grey* Europeans, in the case of the group carrying coats and scarves and the wild, exhausted demeanour of the "just landed from snowy Germany".) This was, is, after all, a place where everybody is a foreigner, an island that two hundred and fifty years ago was inhabited by only crocodiles and bloody huge tortoises.

I made for the rail to feel the breeze and chart our position. To my left was the mountainous Mahé, to my right Praslin with a silent s, a quarter the size and noticeably lower in the water. This the country's second island, home to 6,500 people and if you look at the map you'll see its shape is remarkably similar to that of a flattened frog. We were heading for Baie St Anne, that inviting gap between its bowed legs.

The harbour was a picture postcard of bobbing boats and tropical fish and the water a breathtaking version of pale green even by local standards. It was clear enough to pick out the detail and vivid colour of the marine life that swarmed around the jetty and the lenses of my sunglasses exaggerated that which already seemed surreal. The amphibian's rectum was an impressive introduction.

Setting foot on land I made a charge for the public bus pulling up at the end of the pier, not always the best tactic when moving home in a tropical climate. Whether the driver spotted the arm-waving foreigner, or heard his foolish noises, I can't be entirely sure but the vehicle remained in place long enough for me hurl myself on board and collapse in a sweaty heap on the first row of seats available. Thank Goodness I'd made it, imagine having to wait ten minutes for the next one to come along.

The road from the bay cut across the Vallée de Mai National Park, a protected forest and home to the naughty vulva-esque coconuts that draw in the tourists. I knew this from my chat with Lindsay – SIF manages this park too – and the revenue from entrance fees is used to finance the research projects on Aldabra. After a couple of miles, a third of the island, we emerged from the trees and followed the coast around Grand Anse.

An "anse" is a cove, a smaller version of a "baie" I guess, and almost every stretch of Seychellois coastline is known as Anse something or other. I counted twenty five of them on the Praslin map and I was going to tally up the number on Mahé but then stopped in my tracks to consider where research ends and autism kicks in. So, anyway, here we were on the south coast at the big anse, at the door of Le Relax Hotel, a recommendation from the lovely ladies at Bliss who had kindly booked me in at a very reasonable price.

My chalet was cool, quiet, and fragrant. The shower was fantastic. (A Grohe. I love Grohes.) On the wall at the foot of the large comfy bed was a TV with satellite channels and the promise of sport night and day from around the world. Fifty metres from my door was the beach but before reaching the sand there was the bar, the outdoor Indian restaurant and the swimming pool. There was only problem as far as I could see. How would I ever persuade myself to leave the premises?

One obvious temptation was the 18-hole championship golf course just up the road but the certain heat and probable price told me a gentle walk would be a smarter move. I could head towards the western end of the island, find the path to the famous Anse Lazio (supposedly the best beach in the Seychelles), cool off with a swim and then carry on round the corner to have a look at what the other side had to offer. It sounded a satisfactory week-end plan and deemed worthy of a minor celebration so I treated myself to a couple of Seybrews, devoured a chicken curry and went home to watch Roger Federer devour Andy Murray.

* * * * *

Two days later I was back at the jetty enjoying the company of the parrotfish.

The Praslin Plan had worked a treat, Anse Lazio* was every bit as beautiful as predicted and a bus had turned up to deliver me to Cote d'Or on the north side of the island. I realised immediately this coast was more attractive than the disappointing Grande Anse where the beach had turned out to be coated in seaweed and effectively off limits to tourists. Was it worth relocating to the "other side"? In truth I was more interested to seek adventure than just another stretch of sand so in the taxi back to my curry house (driven by a FIFA linesman with many a story to tell!) I took the decision that had brought me back to the harbour. I would move on to the island of La Digue.

Whereas you could cover Mahé in a single day by car you could do Praslin on a bicycle and would have no trouble getting round La Digue on foot. I'd studied the geography and read a fair bit about this diamond-shaped island and part of its appeal was that it measured a mere 5 square miles, there were very few vehicles (none at all until recently) and that bicycles and oxcarts served as the main form of transport. It was accessed by ferry several times a day from the jetty in Praslin and would take half an hour to make the short crossing.

All of which proved to be correct though I hadn't expected to see a line of glossy 4x4 Toyotas sitting on the quayside to greet our vessel. Their function was to transport passengers and luggage to the twenty odd hostelries on offer and from what I could see on the map, and soon through the tinted windows, the average journey distance would be somewhere in the region of 800 metres. The ferry lands on the north-west side of the island, the only village or community of any sort is directly adjacent to the jetty and, to keep life simple, the hotels and guest houses are clustered together just behind its main street.

I had expected the regally-named Chateau St Cloud to be hopelessly beyond my modest budget but wanted to see it nonetheless. Its entrance gate was suitably imposing but the reception area comprised a very small room with a very small desk, behind which sat a very large lady. Her name

* In August 2011 two men lost their lives in separate shark attacks off Anse Lazio, the first recorded fatalities since 1963.

was Miriam, she was the first white Seychellois I had knowingly come across and she was proud to explain that her (French) family had bought the building, an old vanilla factory, in the 1820s and had been there ever since. She went on to tell me that she was closing up for renovations at the end of the week and would offer me a competitive rate to stay half board. It was a deal I was more than happy to accept.

I rented a bicycle from Miriam and stayed with her, so to speak, for five days. It hadn't been part of the plan but La Digue seemed to have a special charm that grew with familiarity. It was somehow different, slightly bohemian, with a feel of the Caribbean and a pace of life to match. Shirtless men with rasta hair cycled around the "town" – La Passe – though where they were going or why was not easy to deduce. It felt a happy place, like a model village with its own hospital and police station and library and school and a supermarket so well-stocked it had earned the nickname Dubai. A self-contained community of 3000 people most of whom had been born there and will probably never leave.

Rain fell heavily at night-time, the first proper downpours La Digue had seen for four months, but after a couple of windy, humid December days normal service was resumed. The sun was hot from early morning but it made for pleasant cycling on the coastal tracks and the single road that crossed the island offered abundant shade from the many thousands of flowering trees. There were plenty of Anses to swim and sunbathe, all within a twenty minute cycle ride, and a scattering of restaurants meant there was always somewhere to stop for lunch and a drink. Center Parks comes to the tropics.

When it all got too much I'd play at being a local, call into the internet café to connect to the real word and grab lunch from that popular Seychellois institution, The Take Away. For less than a fiver a plastic tray would get filled with fish and curry and noodles and all sorts of stuff that tasted far better than it looked; it was a great deal and for most residents the most they would be able to afford.

In contrast the ice cream parlour was definitely aimed at the punters even though the poster on the wall inside was written in the local Creole, a sort of pidgin French. How the Parisians must cringe when they see what has become of their beautiful language:

Creole: Manz omwen 5 porsyon fri ek legim par zour!

French: Mangez au moins 5 portions fruits et legumes par jour!

Getting five fruit and veg a day is not as easy as you might think for the people of these tropical islands. Banana, coconut, mango and papaya grow in abundance but much of the fruit goes directly to hotels to meet the tourist demand and most other produce is imported at vast expense. What an odd situation in a climate that guarantees sunshine year round and plentiful rainfall, albeit that the latter tends to be in the form of a feast or a famine. It's not a subject that had ever really fascinated me but nonetheless one that I resolved to delve into a bit further. Was I having a mid-life crisis?

The fruit situation aside the only disappointing feature of the three islands had been the paucity of coral and the absence of any decent snorkelling. Roughly half the islands of the Seychelles group are coralline but the populated ones are granitic which means, as always seems to be the case however far one travels, a day trip is needed to get out to a reef. Not surprisingly La Digue's leading entrepreneurs have invested in small boats for this very purpose and I somewhat reluctantly agreed to pay Eddie E80 for half a day aboard his craft. Or at least the privilege of swimming around next to it.

He was a pleasant chap, born and bred on La Digue and, as one might expect of a Seychellois boatman, a keen supporter of Arsenal (at least he didn't say Man U). We moved at speed across the bay with Eddie pointing at islands and yelling out names over the sound of the twin outboard motors and within half an hour we'd moored up on the edge of Coco, a small island that looked no different to any other. Had I been taken, quite literally, for a ride?

The answer lay no more than a foot below the steps of the boat. Once masked and flippered an inelegant reverse plunge thrust me into a parallel world, a psychedelic underwater garden inhabited by fish of shapes, sizes, colours and designs too diverse and complex for my simple human mind to process. I swam in circles, giddy with excitement and then hurried to gain more depth on realising how close my chest was to the razor-sharp coral. It was important to calm down, I told myself, to expend as little energy as possible and to concentrate on what would have been pure silence were it not for the eerie, rhythmic thud of my own breathing.

The new technique was to let my body just drift where possible, gently sway with the movement of the water, follow a single fish as it moved from one piece of shiny coral to the next. I picked a big green and purple wrasse, one of those fish that always has a grumpy face and managed to follow him around without pissing him off any further. He never stayed long in the same place I noticed, just gave three or four pecks on the cheek of a piece of coral before moving on to the next. And thanks to my newly controlled breathing pattern I could actually pick up the sound of each kiss.

I have been lucky enough to visit a few coral reefs over the years but the sense of wonderment never seems to diminish. The sheer number of fish is in itself quite overwhelming and the fact that they seem oblivious to a human presence utterly remarkable. Where wild animals scatter in fear these creatures carry on regardless, even allow us to play a small part in an underwater extravaganza that is nature at its finest.

Nature at its very worst, or perhaps spookiest, was my encounter later that day with a creature in a cage. I spotted the metal basket hanging in front of a roadside souvenir stall but as I cycled by it wasn't immediately obvious what resided within. So I hit the brakes, did a U-turn and parked the bike directly underneath it. It was then that the large black cape unfolded and, to make matters considerably worse, the small angular face of the fruit bat poked out through the mesh to run its tongue across my saddle.

Stallowner cum batkeeper explained that she had found it lying on the ground as a baby and cared for it ever since as though it were her own child. She feeds it fresh fruit several times a day and for all I know, as it is the only mammal on the islands, she might even poke a nipple into the cage from time to time. We got onto the subject of bat curry as a local speciality, a dish she agreed was harder to find these days as the men with large nets just don't go out and catch them as they once did. Perhaps, she suggested, I would have more luck in the restaurants on Mahé.

Seychelles

* * * * *

The Marie Antoinette restaurant is perhaps the country's most famous. In 1972 the entrepreneurial Mrs Fonseca converted a charming colonial house into a place where visitors and locals could go to sample traditional, good quality Creole food. She ran the place herself for over thirty years and though she died in 2008 her legacy and the reputation of the restaurant lives on.

It was easy to find, high up on the road just outside Victoria and on that Saturday lunchtime, after a hard morning's ferrying, I was the first guest of the day. The set menu was noticeably batless but I wasn't going to kick up a stink given the offer of aubergine fritters, parrotfish goujons, chicken curry, vegetable curry, tuna in tomato sauce, Creole fish, mango salad and papaya salad. This wasn't either/or, it was all or nothing.

I chose all and it was superb. The ambience was equally impressive, as much museum as restaurant, and once the banquet had been cleared I sauntered around the spacious fan-cooled building, out onto the decking and into the gardens. I read the story on the wall of Oliver Levasseur, known as La Buse. The notorious pirate was said to have had a gang of 500 men who, in the 1720s, repeatedly attacked British, Dutch and Portuguese vessels crossing the Indian Ocean. (Has much changed in three hundred years?). He left the French alone, and vice-versa, and was said to have amassed millions of dollars worth of treasure which he buried on Mahé. When he did eventually cross swords with the French they tracked him down and captured him but offered to spare his life in return for divulging the whereabouts of his booty. He chose to hang and, according to the legend, threw a map and a note into the crowd as he went to the gallows.

Out in the garden I met Abraham, the victim of a nasty accident some years earlier. His penchant for sexual intercourse of an afternoon was apparently well known to the restaurant staff so when a wall collapsed on his back there was widespread concern that the old boy's pleasures would have to be curbed. But no. According to the notice on the wall all was well and indeed Abraham had frequently been seen performing out the back, in the midday sun, and even with several different partners. Such is the life of a giant tortoise. (Surely you didn't fall for it again?).

Much as I would have enjoyed it there just wasn't enough time to wait and see if Abe or any of his pen friends (!) were in the mood. I had places to go, people to visit, and having been re-united with my bijou jeep it was time to set off for the south-west. By a stroke of good fortune the address of my new internet friend Sandra Hanks was Anse Soleil, in the same region I had earmarked for further exploration, so I followed the east coast past the airport and hopped over the mountain in search of that very Anse. We would meet at her home the next day.

The best deal I would find anywhere in the country (E80 per night) was a large one bed apartment with its own garden and a sweeping view that took in half of Mahe's west coast. Anse Soleil Resort fitted the bill perfectly and my joy was complete on hearing that the beach was only a two minute drive away and thereupon I would find a restaurant for a beer and evening nosh.

Well, almost complete. I was into my second well-chilled Seybrew when I spotted something on the menu of which I had entirely given up hope. Not only was the famous yet elusive Bat Curry at last featured but there was also the entirely unexpected alternative of a plain, straightforward Grilled Bat. Now it has to be said that the prospect of tucking into one of these beasts was extremely unappealing but having done horse and camel and guinea pig and crocodile and God knows what else over the years of alphabet travelling I was determined to give it a go. At least in a curry it would come in slices or chunks or a format to disguise its identity, wouldn't you think? Yes, this would definitely be my choice and it would also remove the awkwardness of not knowing how to respond to the waitress if she were to ask "How would like your bat done sir?" (Definitely no blood.)

I took a long swig and a deep breath then boldly called the lady over to place my order. She was French and despite her tender years had already mastered the art of surliness.

"Non. We av no bat."

'No bat?'

"Yes. Les catcheurs are not coming since a long time".

I smiled, she shrugged. Then she let out a short sigh, looked at her watch and gave me the stare one normally reserves for the discovery of dog mess upon one's shoe. My time was running out. Don't push your luck lad, just order something she's likely to have.

My faith in human nature was restored upon a visit to the village shop next morning. The smiley Indian lady took me to her bosom and it was with a sense of pleasure that I stocked the jeep with breakfast ingredients for my debut foray into self-catering. A Sunday morning deserves a Full English but three eggs in a plastic bag, a packet of Kraft cheese slices and the only ripe tomato available was the nearest I was going to get.

Sitting in the sun-drenched garden, eating scrambled eggs and reading the week-end paper had never seemed so good. There were no football results in my copy of The Nation but the Ministry of Tourism had come up with a statistical analysis that was almost as compelling as the Premiership table or the racing results from Kempton. Despite the world recession 158,000 visitors had landed in Seychelles in the first 11 months of the year, an average of almost five hundred a day and the highest number the country had ever seen. The article even gave volume by nationality which, thanks to the calculator on my phone, I was able to break down into percentages to give to you now. 20.2% French, 15.1% Italian, 12.5% German and 7.2 % British. Perhaps I am a bit autistic after all.

I had planned to drop a few of these tasty morsels into my conversation with Sandra but the moment never seemed to present itself. We drank tea on the veranda of her house and I was entertained from start to finish with a rolling dialogue that she warned me would be loud, opinionated and unashamedly packed with expletives. Sandra was raised in California, had established a career as an author and married a man who was half English and half Seychellois. Her experience of living in UK was "an absolute fucking disaster", they moved to Anse Soleil in the mid 90s and now she is divorced and raising two adopted children. She still keeps busy as a writer, working on commissions from all over the world and she hosts a blog which is as forthright and funny as the lady herself.

"It's an interesting place", Sandra assured me with just a hint of cynicism. She talked of the massive problems of heroin addiction and alcoholism that had swept into the country and how the more sinister side of Seychelles life was always pushed quietly under the carpet. How the Russians with money were buying favours and, the most astonishing of all, the tale she'd heard about the Arab palace on top of the mountain. It comprises five adjacent buildings each with five storeys above ground and two below but it has not been furnished like a palace. It is more in the style of a government building and the word on the street is that the ruling families of UAE will have a base from which to operate if and when the Middle East really kicks off.

Sandra wasn't the only one with stories of espionage and intrigue. I spent a fascinating couple of hours at the workshop and home of Tom Bowers, a gentleman and a sculptor who had fallen in love with the islands twenty five years earlier and decided, at the age of 49, to relocate with his family from Glossop in Derbyshire. Theirs was a true adventure. When they arrived in the country there was only one suitable house available on the market, there was no electricity and no telephone. But there was a "listening station" on Mahé, a fact well known to the island's government. It was the time of the Cold War, US spooks would come here to monitor activity in Moscow and in the interest of impartiality the Seychellois would invite a KGB agent for every CIA one. All day long the spies would follow each other around the islands and no doubt it was easy enough for the boys from Langley, Virginia to spot the ones with the fur hats.

Tom's art is as interesting as his conversation – particularly if you share his passion for women with long protruding nipples – and a visit to his open workshop (marked on the tourist map) is highly recommended. Ditto the studio of The Adams Family. Michael and Heather, a charming couple who left UK ten years ahead of the Bowers have spent their years in Seychelles painting colourful island landscapes. I popped in to their gallery for ten minutes but found it impossible to leave within the hour; this was some art collection, vibrant, enchanting, as indeed was their genuine hospitality. Heather insisted on my staying for a chat and a glass of fresh juice while she introduced her other guest, Catherine Olsen, a writer from Brisbane who had spent time in Seychelles and chosen it as the setting for her latest novel. How uplifting to be in a country where people have the time to be kind to one another and the humility to treat a stranger as a friend.

By way of a contrast my evening meal was consumed at a table adjacent to a group of four people from Russia. They evidently had lots of money but were destitute in every other department of life and determined that their own unhappiness be shared. Their arrogant, obnoxious treatment of the kind Seychellois staff was truly embarrassing and a sad, dispiriting reminder of just how vile the human race can be. They had turned a pleasant evening on its head and something needed to happen to make us all feel happy again. That's when the diving instructor walked in.

The dude with the rasta hair, jet black face and shining white teeth had enjoyed a few hours under the water and a few more sitting at the bar. He was full of booze-induced fun and laughter and came over to me (of all people) to announce that he was a Manchester United fan and that the happiest day of his life was when Ryan Giggs scored the winner in the Champions League Final of 1999. Well, I suppose I should have let it go but football people will understand that some things cannot be messed with. It was Sheringham and Solksjaer on the scoresheet the night they scraped through against Bayern and if he really was a Red (nothing to be proud of) he should have known better!

No amount of persuasion would convince him of his error. So certain was he of his facts that he re-enacted the Giggsy goal as it lived in his memory and then insisted we have a friendly bet to settle the score. I was to come to his dive shop at nine the next morning and if able to prove my facts his wall chart of tropical fish would be mine. If proved wrong, I would agree to abandon the jeep and walk the length of the island, returning to Glacis on foot. He really had had a very full day.

The decision to spend time in the south-west of Mahé had been a good

253

one. It was a region of few tourists, few anything, yet the rolling landscape and twisting roads had offered an extra dimension beyond the ubiquitous greens and blues. I'd met some lovely people and learned a lot but the time was now right to head back north for a final, Blissful, couple of days.

As the winner of the bet I was able to use the jeep for the return journey to Glacis. At 9am the dive shop was locked and the hanging wall chart still visible within, a not unexpected scenario, so I popped a note under the door with full match details, verified on-line, and a promise to return to Seychelles one day to collect my tropical fish.

The only other stop on the road north could be described as rather more "fruitful". My embarrassing obsession with fruit and vegetables had once again sparked into life on spotting a sign in a field bearing the words Seychelles Agricultural Agency and such was this sense of arousal that I found myself bouncing along a track to knock at the door of the building.

"Bonjour – just over from UK to see how your fruit production is going" was all I could think to say.

Roy and Marcel introduced themselves and were no doubt thinking I was a knob but both smiled warmly, stopped what they were doing and walked me around their fields to explain the latest developments. They had just been to Syria to talk irrigation, they were running all sorts of tests to get the best out of their difficult soils and they were erecting canopies over the crops to stop torrential rain from destroying their harvest. The government was desperate to improve yield, lazy farmers were being booted off precious land (most of the country is too mountainous to grow anything) and every home in the country was getting a visit with advice on growing fruit and veg for home consumption. It was all very interesting, positive stuff and I was able to continue homewards feeling far less anxious about the five a day prospects of the islanders.

* * * * *

Mark came over to Bliss for my last evening in the Seychelles. We drank beer and wine, ate one final (batless) curry and watched the sun go down over Glacis beach. If only we'd been gay it would have been very romantic but we just talked about schooldays in Stockport and I recounted my newly acquired snippets of intrigue and football. Little did I realise there would be a final twist in the tale.

Soraya had been in touch to say all was well in UK but a story had surfaced from the little-known Cheshire town of Northwich. The manager of its local football club was none other than Andy Morrison and the local press had been chasing for interviews about his exciting new job. New job? What new job? Phone calls were made, e-mails were sent and it turned out another Mr Andrew Morrison, a holidaymaker with very little football pedigree, had hoodwinked the Seychelles Football Federation into giving him a two-year contract. Rather than cancel it, they had reduced it to six months.

* * * * *

There weren't many books to peruse at the airport shop and the name Catherine Olsen jumped out from the shelves. The baffling title was Sweet Seduction and the Third Mermaid but more reassuring were the palm trees and the waterfall on the cover, unmistakeably the work of Michael Adams. I was sweetly seduced.

It was an interesting novel, a fireside read in sub-zero England, but it was the back cover snapshot of the author's life that took me by surprise. Catherine was born in Brisbane, had lived in London and during her time as a journalist had chronicled the lives of interesting people. Her role had been to interview the rich and famous, one of whom was Sir James Mancham, the former president of Seychelles. She had married him six weeks after he was deposed.

I have been keeping an eye on Sandra Hanks' website and have since discovered that she hails from a family of entertainers. Her younger brother, Tom, is an actor.

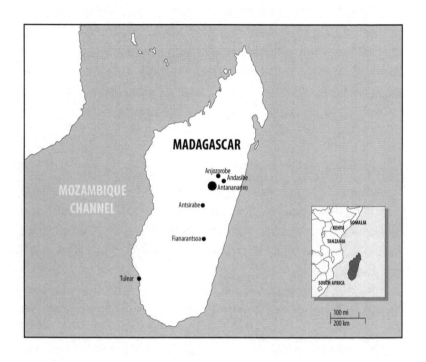

MADAGASCAR

One hundred and thirty five million years ago alphabet travelling would have been a very different business. There were no countries in those days, no people either, just two "supercontinents" to which an Austrian scientist would later apply the (eight-letter) names Laurasia and Gondwana. They occupied north and south of planet Earth respectively and at that point had already co-existed for the best part of a hundred million years. But then, it would appear, all hell broke loose.

Gondwana fell apart at the seams. One chunk of land became two, two became four (70 million years later) and these odd shapes floated in opposite directions like leaves on a pond. The land that held firm would go on to be known as Africa, a sub-continent would drift north to become India and the landmass that headed south is the icy Antarctica of today. The fourth and smallest piece of the jigsaw, though still a formidable thousand miles in length, had been cast adrift just a short distance to the east. And there Madagascar would remain, untouched, for the next sixty five million years.

A unique animal kingdom profited from the island's glorious isolation, constantly developing without the competition it may have encountered elsewhere, and abundant forests adorned the hillsides thanks to the rich land and generous climate. For all that time, that unfathomable length of time, everything in the garden was as rosy as could be. Then Man arrived.

It was just two thousand years ago, a blink of the eye. He has since eradicated every bird and animal larger than himself and of every ten trees he has chopped down nine. He has distorted the contours of the land, meddled with the climate and endangered the existence of the many unique species of plants and animals that remain. Yet these actions were not, for the most part, driven by greed or the urge for malicious destruction; this was Man struggling against the odds to ensure his own survival.

And still he does today. So what now, what happens next? What hope is there in the 21st century as the world's eyes focus on the mysterious island of Madagascar?

* * * * *

It was 11.30 in the morning, seventy minutes out of Johannesburg, when we crossed that much-loved coast of Mozambique. A ruler-straight line of empty beach and foaming surf somewhere south of Beira, I calculated; a sweet, lingering vista thanks to the angle of our north-easterly routing. Then another seventy minutes above the Indian Ocean, the post-Gondwana channel, to the first sighting of Madagascar's western shores. South African Airways was doing me proud.

I spotted a river, a big bugger, the width of a British motorway, its water a murky, ruddy brown. It twisted and looped extravagantly across the flat terrain and wholly convinced me that, with map in hand (as of course it was), I would not only calculate our position but be able to plot the flight path from coast to capital. Alas, a plan that crumbled all too quickly as we crossed another major river, a few small ones, then another monster. In fact there seemed to be almost as much water as land, the brick-red colour constant to both. I decided to chill out and let the pilot sort the navigation.

In contrast to the bland and rather daunting west, Madagascar's central plateau, upon which we were about to land, was awash with colour. Rolling hills, fields, dotted houses, more fields, a patchwork quilt of pinks and greens. Workers with hats and bright shirts: squatting, digging, carrying. I caught a glimpse of Antananarivo, the capital, a kaleidoscope appearing through the porthole then vanishing from view with the banking of the aircraft. Click. Thud. Welcome to the fourth largest island in the world. The twelfth and last of The Ten-Letter Countries.

* * * * *

Au Bois Vert is a hotel set in the woods just a short drive from the airport. It was my opening move within a game plan which I hoped would take me north for a few days, east for three or four more, and south for as long as I could manage. I would also spend time in Tana itself, the four-letter nickname of the twelve-letter capital, but for now, a quiet country retreat would fit the bill nicely.

It was more than quiet, it was deserted. The tourist season had yet to get started according to the waitress, who spoke in French, as she poured my first ever Three Horses Beer (THB) from a satisfyingly large, old-fashioned bottle. March is the end of the summer, the rainy period, she added, and there were still two days left in the month. She couldn't however explain why a former French colony would choose an English name for its beer.

Three sunny days and wet nights offered time aplenty to research and prepare in more detail. I was in the middle of a large island with an infinite number of attractions but a fragile infrastructure: air tickets were expensive, public road transport limited (journeys anything from 1-10 days according to season!) and rail options restricted to two lines built for shunting produce between the plateau and the east coast. So I arranged to hire a car and driver to cover the shorter distances, reserved a seat on a tourist bus to go south and enjoyed the peace and tranquillity of the hotel to read up on the wildlife.

Not that I am what you would call an animal lover. I'm prepared to say good morning to a well-groomed dog, a labrador say, but for some prudish reason tend to back off when the relationship threatens to extend to the licking of, or drooling over, my genitalia. (Despite the Welsh name, two legs is an absolute maximum for me when it comes to physical contact.) It came as great relief and a certain surprise to learn that the flora and fauna of Madagascar is rarely dangerous and that even snakes and spiders pose minimal threat. Only two creatures in the country, excluding mosquitoes, can cause serious damage to humans – one lives in the forest, the other in the rivers – and although they exist in large numbers it would be highly unlikely that I'd encounter either in the wild. So I took a cab along a bumpy road to see them in captivity.

Crocodiles terrify and fascinate me in equal measure. There is just one species in Madagascar, the Nile crocodile, ranked two in the world (after the saltie) for size and aggression. Particularly vicious as winter approaches, explained Tatah, a boiler-suited and booted chap with an appropriately toothy smile and fifteen years service under his belt at the Croc Farm. The beasts were preparing for three months of winter hibernation, their period of fasting, and would soon be seeking extra food to build up reserves. He suggested with a knowing smirk that I return at 1pm, feeding time, but when I got there at the appointed hour he had already lobbed half a bucket of dead chickens over the fence.

The fun and games was well and truly under way. The lucky crocs, those with birds dangling from either side of their jaws, were desperately trying to sidle away to a quiet lunch spot but their hungry comrades attacked in numbers, leaping on their backs, teeth exposed. Perhaps they weren't so lucky after all. There was much snapping and splashing and tails lashing out in retaliation. More chook was launched into the pen, new fights broke out and Tatah gave me a "told you so" wink as we watched the water turn into a soup of blood and feathers. Shameful to admit it but I loved every minute.

My own lunch in the calm of the restaurant was inevitably a crocodile kebab (looked like chicken, tasted like fish) after which I went on another tour of the lakes. Therein the scaly residents were grouped by age and, according to signs on the fences, many of the crocs had been rescued from injury and probable death. Hence the kindest course of action was to bring them here to the delightful Croc Farm where the young could be converted into handbags and the older ones sliced on to a skewer.

From there I went to meet an animal that seemed to dislike me intensely. The fossa is a fearsome cross between a dog, a cat and a rat with chunky legs and a horrid long tail. This nasty piece of work was pacing furiously from one end of its cage to the other until my appearance prompted it to let out a blood-curdling screech and hurl itself like a lunatic at the double wire fencing. Two layers or not it still caused me to back away and the reinforced mesh did little to dissuade it from a series of further wild lunges. It represented nothing but evil and the sight of it scared me to death, as it does the people of Madagascar's countryside and the animals that live in the trees. Picture a four-legged Roy Keane, former captain of Manchester United.

* * * * *

We headed north-east out of Tana on the RN3, direction Anjozorobe, another long name beginning with A. (I was soon to realise Madagascar has many of these so the town you are heading for will often sound much the same as the one you've just left.) My destination, an estimated four-hour drive, was Saha Forest camp, a new initiative promoted on the internet as being run by the community, for the community. Sounded interesting.

An hour of punishing city traffic and the stop-starting of Mercedes minibuses taking on passengers was rewarded with two hours on a pleasant country road. There were few cars to negotiate, just a steady flow of bullock carts and mats laid out on the tarmac every few hundred metres covered with rice grains drying in the sunshine. In all directions people worked the fields; some of them old-timers yet just as many young children no more than seven or eight years old. Three quarters of Madagascar's 21m population live in the countryside and it seemed to me that a passing vehicle, particularly with a white face on board, was always good reason to stretch, smile and wave one's heart out.

In the village markets fruit and vegetables were varied and wonderfully displayed, raw meat was plentiful (as were the flies crawling over it) and sausages of all shapes and sizes dangled from wooden struts. We stopped at the heart of one such community where I wound down the window to get closer to the action – all very charming until Daniel, the driver, slipped away to buy some water and a group of young men headed towards the car brandishing long, sharp knives. My heart lurched.

They flashed big white smiles and each then hoisted aloft what resembled a section of tree trunk, gesturing their readiness to cut me a fresh slice. It was a peculiar shape and an unfamiliar purple/brown colour though whether animal, mineral or vegetable I couldn't quite fathom. With perfect timing Daniel returned, three litres of Eau Vive in hand, to unravel the mystery and negotiate a couple of pieces. It was koba, a local speciality made from pistachio nuts and we sat there and nibbled on the sweet, sticky dessert as a crowd gathered around the vehicle to watch us in action. And then to send us on our way with a cheer and a wave. Whatever problems Madagascar faces, however destitute the economic indexes show it to be (the world's 11th poorest), it struck me there was no shortage of food or remarkably cheerful people.

When the RN3 came to an end we bounced along a potholed track for another hour. We crossed mountains and forded small rivers and when it finally came to an end we got out, stood in the field and looked enquiringly at one another. Daniel, my new friend, only friend, spoke first:

"Will there be much for you to do here?" It was one of the few sentences my dodgy French grasped in entirety.

I wouldn't have thought badly of him if he'd added a grin but the question was sincere, his face that of a worried parent dropping a child at a new school. We were both unsure of the next move until a resident of a thatched hut not 100 metres away waved his arms at us and purposefully turned side on to holler down the valley. Saha, whatever Saha was, was somewhere beyond the mountain. Somebody would be along to meet me.

We sat together and enjoyed the views. Fifteen minutes later two men dressed in boiler suits appeared, we all shook hands, they spoke to Daniel in Malagasy. Then they picked up my bags and we walked in Indian File along the mountain path.

* * * * *

Madagascar is almost a thousand miles long and three hundred wide. A spine of mountains and rainforests dominates the eastern half of the country with the highest points, around 2800m, at each end of the long range. The section in the middle, at half that altitude, is referred to as the high plateau (Hauts Plateaux) and this is the home of the Merina tribe.

It was their king who built the capital city 400 years ago and the Merina ruled the roost until the French took over at the end of the 19th century. They still dominate the region that surrounds Tana, considered to be the most advanced in the country, and almost a quarter of Malagasy are said to be of Merina stock. It was their ancestors who first populated the island but they didn't originate from nearby Africa, they travelled 4000 miles across the ocean from Indonesia. It was a remarkable achievement that baffles experts to this day and it still remains a topic of debate whether they stopped en route in India or perhaps somewhere on the east coast of Africa. Indeed Indians and Africans, as well as Arab sailors, did eventually follow in their footsteps and today these ethnic groups populate much of Madagascar's long 3000 mile coastline.

The men that led the way along the path had straight hair and slightly narrowed eyes, confirmation that this was Merina country. I was unsure what they were leading us to and Daniel wasn't going to drive home without finding out. We traversed the mountain and took a bridge across the paddy fields whereupon we saw the main building perched on the slope and several smaller ones adjacent to it. A flight of steps led to a wide, polished wooden veranda furnished with large sofas and tasteful lamps on the left side, a cocktail bar and reception desk in the middle and a cluster of dining tables to the right. Each was covered with white linen table cloths, flowers, candles, and wine glasses of varying sizes. "Bonjour Monsieur Jenkins, welcome to the camp."

Daniel, as astonished as I, accepted my offer of lunch and agreed to come back and collect me three days hence. He was still curious to understand my self-imposed isolation but could rest easy knowing that I had a comfy chalet to sleep in, spectacular rolling scenery to enjoy and a silver service restaurant to cater for my every need.

Every day I walked, read, slept and took three meals on the luxurious deck, always entirely alone except for one lunch when a man arrived from Tana with his family. Serge spoke fluent English with the confidence and accent of a Harvard education and it became evident that he had been instrumental in setting up the Saha Project. His business card gave FANAMBY as the name of his organisation and beneath it a punchy slogan that told much of the story: "a non-profit Malagasy group whose emphasis is a dynamic participatory process to sustainable conservation in partnership with women and men working on management of terrestrial and marine landscapes". Wow! But what did it mean exactly?

Serge explained the four points of the virtuous circle. Saha recruits, trains and employs the local villagers as chefs, waitresses and guides. The profits from the business are channelled back into the community, specifically agricultural programmes. Support and advice is offered to yield good crops of rice, fruit and vegetables in a way that does not compromise the environment. The "camp" prepares meals for its guests using local produce. This is sustainable conservation and it replaces what went before, namely the relentless destruction of the rainforest.

The guides led me across the mountains and into the villages. Alas they spoke very little French – country folk generally speak only Malagasy (similar to a language spoken in Borneo) – but the walks offered vital exercise and an insight into rural life. I noted the Merina houses were built of clay, mostly two storey with thatched roofs and small, wonky wooden verandas outside the upstairs windows. Indoor wood fires served for heating and cooking but in the absence of chimneys the exterior of every building was stained around the window through which the smoke poured out. There was no sanitation, water would be fetched and carried from one of several nearby wells; toilets where they existed were tiny external enclosures surrounding a hole in the ground.

There was no sign of a cemetery or a burial ground of any sort, disappointing in the light of everything I'd read about the crucial role of death in Madagascar. The dear departed are seen as messengers of the gods and the tombs of those wise and wily ancestors can often be more lavish than the homes of the living. Life savings are, perversely, lavished on death and in the case of the Merina – and one or two of the other tribes – every corpse is buried, exhumed, and buried again. An extravagant ceremony accompanies each process, the first funeral a melancholy occasion (crying and wailing encouraged) whereas the second, always five to seven years later, is a rare old knees-up.

This celebration is known as *famadihana* and is a full day event. The deceased is removed from the coffin and unwrapped from its shroud as family and friends gather round, drink lots of rum, sing songs and have a chinwag with the skeletal remains. Quite what sort of conversation takes place is hard to imagine. "Haven't you lost a bit of weight since I saw you last?"

The escorted walks yielded little in the way of wildlife though back at camp it was a different story. My home at Saha had walls and a ceiling of canvas, a concrete extension for a bathroom and a thatched roof, all of which served me well in terms of protection from the forces of nature. The sounds of the night were a constant reminder that I was outnumbered by several million to one but I felt secure and at peace with my world until woken by the sound of scratching and burrowing. Torchlight applied to wristwatch revealed it to be 2.30 am.

The noise was loud and close, not ever so far from my head. Something was digging away at the thatch, taking the roof apart bit by bit. I could hear loose matter rolling down the slope of the tent; surely it was only a matter of time before Roland was sharing my bed. Could this be the Giant Jumping Rat for which Madagascar is famous? The king-sized rodent with the rabbit ears? And if it was, would I feel any better about it? Would I bollocks.

Think clearly Jenks. Investigate. Put your underpants and flip-flops on and get out there under the moonlight. I did as I was told. The terrain was rough, steeply sloping and demanded more sturdy footwear but nonetheless I gained enough height to peer onto the roof. Where I could see... absolutely bugger all. So I enjoyed a couple of minutes admiring the star-peppered sky and returned to bed.

Scratch. Claw. Burrow. The loudly bawled instruction "Go away you little bastard it's three o' clock in the morning" had no impact whatsoever despite the ferocity of its delivery. Only one course of action remained and a chuckable shoe was quickly located with the help of the torch. The first blow was carefully aimed but lacked any sort of venom, meekly brushing the canvas and descending tamely to earth. A girlie attempt if the truth be known. OK Roland, this is it. I took a deep breath, jumped on to the bed, let out a piercing shriek and hurled the leather weapon upwards with a force that had me wobbling drunkenly on the mattress. The shoe struck the angle of the canvas with a mighty thwack, gathered momentum on impact and hit me so hard in the face I dropped like a stone. My own whimpering was the last sound I heard until Daniel arrived four hours later to take me away.

* * * * *

The greatest, most important Merina king of all time ruled from 1787 to 1810. His name was Andrianampoinimerinandriantsimitoviaminandriampanjaka, some title for a man who stood 4ft 7ins (1.40m) tall, though he was known to his twelve wives and all who loved him as Andrianampoinimerina. His former palace is a sacred site to this day, sitting high on the plateau above the paddy fields and just 21kms from his sumptuous residence in the capital clearly visible in the distance.

I was surprised to find the royal gaff was no more than a dark, wooden shed, the size of a double garage and supported by a thick central pole. Its only features were strategically positioned in the corners according to points of the compass: the door to the south-west, a north-west facing window and, most important of all, raised high in the north-east corner, the king's bed. Across the room at a much lower level was the bed that his wives would share, the twelve usually together at the same time. This had my imagination running amok, posing some very difficult questions. How big

266

was a king-size bed in Madagascar at the turn of the 19th century?

Mr A was an ambitious man whose goal was to "let only the ocean be the limit of the Merina kingdom". His son, Radama I, continued the fight and thanks to arms supplied by Britain, a country always eager to get involved, rival tribes quickly capitulated. Alas Radama died a young man and the fate of the country fell into the hands of his widow, a lady whose favourite hobbies included sexual intercourse, torture and execution. The Wicked Queen, as history has labelled her, was as mad as a box of frogs and throughout her 33 year reign she saw to it that a large portion of the male population was either royally bonked, or bopped off, or both.

The views from the top were worthy of any royal family. I hadn't expected this of Madagascar, had no notion that the country would be so lush and fertile. How could politics make such a mess of a wonderful place like this? Just look at the history. Thirty odd years in the grip of a sadistic nympho, more than seventy under a brutal colonial regime and, following independence in 1960, two decades of Soviet-style stagnation. By the 1980s the economy was paralysed, the people demoralised and the country, re-named from the Malagasy Republic, an almighty mess.

Socialism was dumped only to be replaced by corruption, unrest and ultimately violence. The people took to the streets in 1991 in the face of gunfire and again in 2002 when a stand-off between two would-be presidents resulted in roads and bridges being destroyed and food supplies cut off. Marc Ravalomanana prevailed and under his leadership Madagascar struggled to its feet. He made primary education free, cleaned up the cities, stamped out much of the crime and won international respect – and funding – by designating vast areas as protected land. Many would argue that the country was moving in the right direction but it was not to be a happy ending. Another military coup in 2009 saw Mr R exiled to South Africa and a puppet president installed in his place. The new man, Rajoelina, was well known to everybody – he used to be a DJ on the radio.

Returning to the capital I was left in no doubt as to what Daniel thought of the current situation. A country in limbo, funding stopped, contracts suspended, people losing jobs left, right and centre. This was supposed to be an interim government but who had voted it in and who could get it out? The Malagasy people had no say in anything, just like the days they were being screwed by the French. Aaagh the bloody French – for all we know they were probably behind the latest coup!

My landlady in Tana painted a similar picture of a people so downtrodden that a sense of resignation had long since set in. Nonetheless Aina was giving it her best shot against the odds, a divorced lady running her own business in a macho world, pioneering a B+B concept she had picked up from time spent in France. A charming lady whose elegance was reflected in every detail of her home, in the beautifully presented food and in the intelligent conversation she offered with every meal.

We talked about divorce though it hit a raw nerve. If a man wants to move on that's fine, normal, very straightforward but if a Malagasy woman seeks to break free, no matter how violent her husband, she will bring shame on her family and society will cast her out. Hence thousands, perhaps millions, of females elect to suffer in silence until the torturer leaves or one of them dies. A tragic story though sadly not a new one, no different in fact from much of the rest of the developing world.

It does, however, seem ironic given the lengthy process a Malagasy man has to go through to earn his bride. Every tribe has its own rules but one common to all is that in asking for the lady's hand the would-be groom must hire an orator to present his credentials to the bride's father. The future father-in-law will also contract a family member or even a professional negotiator and the two hired hands must battle it out for several hours, like lawyers in a courtroom, to decide whether or not the marriage can proceed.

I learned a lot from chatting with Aina, albeit that my limited French made it hard work. She introduced me to traditional Malagasy food which invariably consisted of rice, vegetables and the seemingly ever-present, highly-prized zebu. A strange cow with a hump on the neck and considered to have mystical powers, this animal plays an important role in local life. A man's wealth is measured according to the number of zebu he owns and in some tribes he must prove himself worthy of a bride by stealing a few for her father. It is also the main source of tender, tasty meat.

Aina's was an ideal base for exploring Antananarivo (a capital with four A's in a country with four A's, an unparalleled phenomenon) and I walked the streets for the best part of two days. Orientation did not come easily. Tana is in a steep basin with the main boulevard, Avenue de l'Independance, in the flat section at the bottom and the other areas of the city clinging to the hillsides at varying levels. Bridges, tunnels and numerous flights of steps link the different sections together and the geography (though little else) reminded me of Luxembourg City. It was crowded, chaotic and extremely colourful.

At no point did I see another white face. This made me something of a target for beggars and vendors in the core of the city but in the outlying suburbs the atmosphere felt completely relaxed. In one such area I changed money at the bank and at 3000 Ariary to £1 emerged onto the street with a substantial bundle stashed in a pocket just above the knee. Common sense dictated a swift return to the safety of my room so twenty minutes later I was back Chez Aina – staring in disbelief at a razor slit where my shorts had been slashed! I'd be done but, incredibly, I hadn't been robbed. The thief had failed to lift his prize and my money and passport remained untouched, poking out through the gap in the fabric.

Aina's team soon had my shorts fixed but the sense of violation diminished my already minimal enthusiasm for wandering around. So on receiving an e-mailed invitation to a local language school I jumped in one of the many ancient Renault taxis and agreed a fare that was the equivalent of £1. Whereupon the delighted owner drove on to the forecourt of the adjacent filling station and purchased a single litre of fuel.

The MD of the school was the wonderfully-named Lova (though pronounced Luva) and I was surprised to find she was only in her twenties. Her role was to teach English to young people whose parents, in the main, had not had that same opportunity and the long-term goal was to attract pre-school children who could enjoy the fun of kindergarten whilst absorbing a third or even fourth language (some clients were second generation Chinese and Indian, the main ethnic groups). Lova explained that for her and her friends, as middle-class teenagers fifteen years earlier, the language of choice would have been French; Malagasy was not considered "cool" to young folk with eyes on first-world Europe. But today there is a greater sense of pride in speaking the native tongue, and although most people in the city are fluent in French, it is English that people now aspire to. "Maybe one day French will be our third language, I certainly hope so," she signed off with a lovely big smile.

* * * * *

It took half a day to reach Andasibe, another A-town, this one due east of Tana. The countryside was every bit as spectacular as it had been to the north with gushing rivers, shady glens and fields of rice, beans, manioc, cabbage, sweet potato, banana and pineapple to name just those I can remember. We also passed a couple of abandoned train carriages, set back from the road, away to the left. Why were they there?

There is a railway line through Andasibe that links the capital to Tamatave on the east coast. After years of closure it has recently re-opened to provide a weekly service to tourists but the two carriages stand in the field to commemorate an important part of the nation's history. They relate to an event in 1947 when the Malagasy in the east of the country took to the streets to make a case for independence; WWII had ended and sixty years had passed since the French had taken their island by force. The colonists, angered by the temerity of this protest, responded with an act of sheer brutality. Up to 80,000 innocent people were gunned down, among them 140 defenceless men who had been detained in rail carriages in the town of Moramanga. The bodies were removed but the carriages have remained there ever since.

It left me cold. My happy jaunt into the beautiful countryside had been sullied by a story of human evil, a grotesque act of violence proving once again that humans are no less primitive than animals of the jungle when it comes to protecting what they consider to be their own. I resolved to put this slice of history on hold but to find out more about the Malagasy Uprising.

I was heading for the Andasibe-Mantadia National Park, one of at least twenty in the country. There are also as many "special reserves" and in total, thanks to ex-Pres Marc R, Madagascar has dedicated close to 10% of its land to the protection of the wildlife and its diverse habitats. The island hosts a plethora of animal species that are found nowhere else on earth but it is the lemurs that have long since captured world attention. Over a hundred variants have been identified, the list continues to grow, and – as I was shortly to discover – they differ greatly in size, diet and behaviour.

The lemurs that feed on insects are active at night, the nocturnal species slightly greater in number than their daytime counterparts. My plan was to get out on safari soon after sunset so after checking into the lodge, changing into clothes that covered every bit of flesh and spraying myself in poison (let the lemurs have the insects) I joined the local guide for a walk in the forest.

My first observation was the size and power of the tool in his right hand, the strength of the Wembley floodlights compared to my pocket torch which, I realised, was only good for lighting up a pocket. But as events would unfold, it mattered not. Even in broad daylight I'd struggle to spot a London bus parked in a tree so no amount of technology was going to have me track down a hairy-eared dwarf lemur in the pitch darkness.

"Psst. David." Voice lowered, arm outstretched. "There it is, on the branch, just over there." He had seen the hairy-eared chap where all I could see, despite the beam, was trees. A period of intense staring followed. I finally focused on the little bundle of fur. It was about a foot long, sitting quietly, seemingly unperturbed by the human attention or several thousand megawatts lighting up his immediate surroundings. The big eyes and the cute little face gave him an air of friendliness whereas the body, I'm sorry to add, could easily have belonged to a rat.

Except that these guys are not rodents, they are primates. One of us.

They are at the bottom of the list of which man is top with monkeys and chimps and gorillas occupying the middle order. But this is Madagascar and there is no middle order. The stronger and smarter monkey families never made the move from the African mainland hence the lemurs that would not have survived against the fittest have thrived in the country's isolation.

The mouse lemur, the tiniest of all, was betrayed by his stary eyes. He (if he was male, not sure how you tell) was on his own, as these odd little chaps usually are and wouldn't have to move very far to collect enough insects to see him through the night. We stood there in the trees in absolute silence and watched him for quite some time; how could a creature small enough to fit in a tea cup belong to the same animal group as an orangutan?

Having been lucky enough to see the smallest of the lemurs the plan for the next day was to go in search of the largest. I rose soon after the sun was up and as I took a walk by the river a series of strange, high-pitched calls emerged from across the valley. It was the Indri, those large black and white panda-like lemurs performing their morning ritual. One or two at first, reminiscent of the sound of dolphins, then other families joined the chorus from several miles away. The valley was filled with a weird but glorious sound.

I followed my own morning routine of fresh fruit and scrambled eggs and met the guide as arranged at the entrance to the park. The modern building doubled as an information centre and the wall-mounted boards explained that until man's intervention some lemurs had been the size of gorillas and weighed up to 200 kilos (a daunting sight, no doubt, to little chaps arriving in boats from Indonesia). Today the Indri and the Sifaka are as big as they get but in kilo terms they barely make it into double figures.

It didn't take long to find the first family since the guides monitor their movements on a daily, even hourly, basis. Fortunately for us they were easy to access from the main path and once we'd reached the spot even I couldn't miss these real life teddy bears with their big round ears and startled faces. There were five or six leaping around in the trees, predominantly black with flashes of white, and unlike other species of lemur, without tails. We settled down to watch the circus and the cuddly performers were more than willing to put on a show.

It was to be the first of three troops of Indri we encountered at close quarters that morning yet the biggest treat was still to come. The Diademed Sifakas, a little smaller than the Indri, have grey bodies, black and white faces and striking orange limbs, a quite different colouring from all the other lemurs and widely regarded as the most attractive of them all. As with the Indri they live in the trees and feed on fruits and leaves; no need then to work the night shift. Their existence, as with many other creatures, has been threatened by the chopping down of the rainforest but neither the Indri nor the Sifaka run the risk of being killed for their meat: eating them is considered *fady*.

Fady is usually translated as "taboo" and it's a concept that plays a huge part in Malagasy society. Every tribe has its own and *fady* covers all aspects of life from what must never be eaten to what must never be done: a man wearing shoes while his father is alive, a pregnant woman milking a cow or eating fish, a funeral on a Tuesday, children sleeping in the same house as their parents, pointing at a tomb....the list goes on and on. A visitor to a new region, whether Malagasy or not, should avoid the risk of offence or confrontation by seeking out the chief to verify the local *fady*.

I spent the afternoon walking the few potholed streets that make up the town of Andasibe. In sharp contrast to the plush tourist lodges here was the reality of life in the third world: houses cobbled together with whatever material was available, jobless men sitting around on their doorsteps, women feeding babies from formidable chocolate brown nipples (hopeless at spotting animals but rarely does a nip pass me by). I watched the children playing in the dust with the only "toys" that were available to them – the object of the game to flick one bottle top as close as possible to another.

There were small open shacks that served as shops and a few with tables bearing *hotely* signs indicating that food and drink (but not accommodation) was on offer. All that separated it from a million other communities of the developing world was the abundance of fresh food piled up in the market and the animal that was moving glacially along the stone wall at the side of the main street. The chameleon was perhaps a foot long with an arched back and a tail like a Catherine wheel and as I watched it progress in peculiar slow motion I swear it changed from a mottled green to the same grey as the stone beneath it. The chameleons are the best of all to watch, they never run away, though to many Malagasy they bring a message of foreboding from the ancestors and must be quickly chased away, or even killed.

The railway station of Andasibe has been smartly renovated and looks far too grand to receive just one train a week. It hasn't always been so. Until 1994 there was a regular service from Tana but the cyclone that year was far more devastating than anything that had gone before; the sea and river levels rose from the east and the land where trees no longer stood gave way to the raging torrents. The water moved as far inland as Andasibe, some thirty miles from the coast, and to the horror of the local folk even brought crocodiles into the town. The monsters were harpooned to death, the railway line rendered unusable.

The rains of Madagascar fall for several months a year, most frequently and most heavily in the east. The downpours typically start late in the day so Saturday April 9th was running true to form as the skies turned black and the heavens opened with impunity. The timing could not have been worse; it was just approaching 6pm, the hour that any self-respecting alphabet traveller prepares for his evening cocktail. Or bottle of Three Horses.

The storm was ferocious, bordering on frightening, and any thoughts of a quick dash to the bar were banished as soon as I ventured onto the veranda. I would have to wait it out patiently and rely on radio to maintain contact with the outside world. A few gentle twiddles on the shortwave dial had the BBC World Service crackling into life, not with the second half football commentary I'd expected but the Grand National, live from Aintree, and the dulcet tones of Cornelius Lysaght (the only

Cornelius I know). With the volume turned up full to compete against the lashing rain and the angle of the radio constantly adjusted I was able to enjoy the full nine minutes of frantic, demented, breathless commentary as Ballabriggs prevailed over Oscar Time and Don't Push It. Three horses, just not in a bottle.

* * * * *

The RN7 links Tana, in the centre of the country with the city of Tulear on the south-west coast. The longest road by far, it follows Madagascar's mountainous spine due south for 400 kms and on reaching Fianarantsoa, the second city (perhaps on account of its four-A status) changes direction to run a further 550 kms to the ocean. It promised to be quite a trip, and geographically speaking, a journey of two halves.

Antsirabe, three hours in, was a good choice of stopover. The spa town of 200,000 people was instantly likeable and exuded a sense of importance with its *quartier* of colonial style villas and the once-magnificent Hotel des Thermes set in vast and splendid grounds. The coolest place in the country, a tropical Buxton, you might say, with a happy, chaotic bustle and 8000 rickshaw (pousse-pousse) wallahs ready to jog across town with customers aboard their hand-pulled chariots. I was easily persuaded to take a ride and enjoyed seeing the town from my royal chair (rather more appealing than Dhaka in the rain) but how sad that in the 21st century a barefooted man should be selling his sweat, and his soul, in this way. Was I helping him or merely perpetuating a dreadful, ill-disguised form of slavery?

He dropped me as requested at the entrance to the main hospital and smiled graciously when I paid more than he asked. How long would I be, he wanted to know, should he wait for me to come out? It was a question to which I had no answer. This was the first time I'd ever visited a hospital on a mission of this sort.

It was Lonely Planet that had started me off. The authors of this dependable guidebook had aroused my curiosity with a story of how the town had been founded by Norwegians over a hundred years earlier (they too were on a mission) and that to this day they are still in Antsirabe and "running the hospital". How utterly bizarre, don't you think? It had to be checked out, hence my now opening the metal gate, entering a world of heavily pregnant women and people who looked even more confused than I was.

Convinced all eyes were upon me I resolved to walk quickly and purposefully towards a door marked "administration". If only it had said "Ageing Scandinavians". Gathering of thoughts and a short rehearsal had been the rough plan but both were denied when a stern looking chap in a white coat caught me off guard at the entrance:

"Vous voulez quelque chose monsieur?"

"Er....oui. Les chefs. Norwegiennes." Made up, but it had to be something like that.

The man looked confused. What part of 'I want to see the Norwegian bosses' could he not understand? Then he smiled, which made things a lot better and he explained that the only Norwegians he knew of were student nurses. And they were at the "other" hospital.

Another rickshaw, another hospital, another embarrassing conversation. No Norwegian bosses here guv, or words to that effect, just five student nurses from Oslo. Would you like to meet them? I took a deep breath and paused but only to contemplate how Messrs Sid James or Benny Hill might have handled the question. What is "Caaaaw not 'arf"...in French anyway?

The five young ladies were happy for a diversion from their work and to answer as many questions, in perfect English, as I could put to them in questionable Mancunian. The hospital was run by local people and had been for many years but there was an ongoing nurse exchange programme and Norwegian church groups still helped the cause by sending funds to Madagascar. Their own little team would stay for three months, have a couple of weeks' holiday and then the next batch of nurses would come out to take their places. They loved the town, were looking forward to seeing more of the country and their long-term hope was that one day they would each receive a copy of The Ten-Letter Countries. I had seduced five Scandinavian women.

Feeling childishly pleased with myself I walked past an ambulance with Stavanger (Norway's fourth city) on its doors and headed for L'Avenue de l'Independance. As in the capital, the city's principal thoroughfare was an elegant boulevard enhanced by lawns, trees, monuments of significance and a handsome building at one end that had once served as the railway station. The pousse-men followed but were often content to chat when no business was forthcoming; this was a relatively hassle-free stroll.

The taller of the monuments, a vertical, rectangular piece of art comprised eighteen separate engravings depicting each of the country's tribes. They were named and listed in alphabetical order and I suspect few people will have noticed that the first ten began with the letters A and B. At the far end of the wide street the large mounted slab was in the unmistakeable shape of Madagascar, its east coast so straight it could have been cut with a guillotine (another tool of French law enforcement). An impressive memorial, it stands as a mark of respect to those who were killed during the bloody uprising of March 29th, 1947.

With an hour left before moving on I ordered a Coke from the "Buffet de la Gare", sat in front of the old station and enjoyed the views along the magnificent boulevard. The parallel rows of trees gave it an added dimension and even the lines of pale blue benches in the colours of water sponsors Eau Vive contributed to a setting of which Antsirabe could be proud. The other person in the café, making an early start on the Three Horses, must have read my mind.

"It's a lovely city, isn't it," or words to that effect in French. "My first time back here for 15 years."

He lived in Tamatave on the east coast, had retired from the (much more expensive) island of Réunion and held a French passport having served the country's army.

"I'm from Algeria," he added ... "and I won't be going back."

* * * * *

Time spent on the move in Madagascar is not time wasted. Far from it, the long journeys along the plateau will be remembered as highlights, not only for the magnificent scenery but for the higgledy-piggledy houses and villages that add the colour and the wonderful people who bring their charm to the roadside. The smiling children who clamour round every stopping bus in the hope of collecting an empty plastic bottle to take back to their parents. The ladies with babies strapped to their bodies, selling souvenirs and woven baskets at makeshift stalls. Even at the roadblocks, where the daunting rows of metal spikes jut out into the road, the policemen who always seem to have a ready smile. Poor it might be, politically shambolic without doubt, but this is one friendly, welcoming country.

The plateau seemed to roll for ever, steeper and yet more dramatic as we headed south. The rice fields filled the floors of the valleys where the geography would allow, otherwise in neatly contrived terraces on the hillsides. This was no longer Merina country, it was the home of the Betsileo, a people renowned for its ability to yield three rice crops a year where two is considered the norm. This the most crucial commodity in Madagascar, the staple food of the country (most people eat rice three times a day) and despite the best efforts of the Betsileo yet more has to be imported to meet the massive demand.

After many hours heading south along the RN7 something very unusual happened. We turned left. One more hour on a narrow road took us across a hilly, forested landscape to the edge of Ranomafana, perhaps the country's most important national park. It covers the area of a small English county, attracts 2000 visitors a month and, thanks to the dedication of Dr Patricia Wright, an American conservationist, it hosts a research centre for scientists from all over the world.

The park opened in 1991 with just one hotel to support the tourist trade. Today there are fourteen and mine was the imaginatively-named Hotel Nature. Built in the style to which I was happily becoming accustomed, each room was a small bungalow set high up on the mountain with the added treat of a veranda and sweeping views of the rainforest as far as the eye could see. A feast of colour by day, the sounds of the tropics and the infinite stars of the southern sky by night.

The guides of Ranomafana work as a team; one group goes off ahead to track down the wildlife, the rest await directions by mobile phone. So when the tourists turn up they are quickly delivered to a frolicking troop, a system that has obvious advantages but feels only one step removed from a Dial-A-Lemur service. Nonetheless we had a good morning's walk through the forest and the Golden Bamboo lemurs put on an unforgettable display of munching. One branch after another, to the delight of the jostling photographers, they devoured the bamboo as though there was no tomorrow. But why, of all the different lemur species, does only this one eat the stuff? The likely answer is that it contains large quantities of cyanide and most other creatures, man included, would be dead within a day. That the Golden Bamboo lemur can ingest and survive all that poison is a mystery yet to be solved.

The walk along the road from the park entrance brought me into contact with two men bashing their zebu with sticks. They smiled and posed for photos (the men, that is) and explained they were heading north; their job was to walk to Tana, four hundred kilometres away! I later learned that it's common practice to transfer cattle in this way from the south of the country, about seven weeks being the normal delivery time. In the final week the zebu owners make the trip by minibus, meet their herders with the animals up in the city and pay the wages from the proceeds of the sales. The men then have the option to return south by bus but more often choose to keep the money in their pockets, or spend it in the bar, and walk back home.

By contrast I had covered half the country from the luxury of a window seat with an air conditioning system to control the temperature and a curtain to fend off the glare of the sun. A pampered existence that was set to continue as we boarded the bus once again to follow a more westerly course, to drop down from the rich and rolling landscape of the plateau towards the hot, flat and infinitely less fertile terrain of the mid-south.

The world of predominant dark green was to change with the passing of every kilometre marker. The rainforest was no more, in its place a random scattering of spiky trees on a bone dry carpet of dust and granite. Though the Malagasy vehemently resist any cultural connection to the big continent this was very much an African landscape and inhabited by a people, I noticed, far darker and more African in appearance. The Bara, the zebu herders.

We reached Isalo, a region of odd-shaped rock formations and deep gorges, sacred to the locals and today protected as a national park. The Bara are no longer permitted to live within its boundaries but they retain the right to bury their loved ones upon this notoriously wild terrain. Their custom, as with the Merina, is to return five to seven years after death to exhume and wash the bones of the deceased, sometimes even coating them in honey (spare ribs?) prior to re-internment in a different tomb. Again, it's the most important ceremony of all, a lavish, joyous celebration, at the end of which four very drunken men (most likely the sons) will be nominated to transfer the sticky but newly-wrapped skeleton to a permanent place of rest.

The most sought after graves are in the crevices high up on the rock face, as close as possible to the gods. Thus tradition dictates that, upon attaining a satisfactory level of inebriation, the four chosen ones with their special package will follow a path to the top of the mountain, attach themselves to ropes and attempt to abseil down to a suitable opening. Not surprisingly, a further death will often ensue (at which point the crowd stops cheering) but according to Bara folklore a man who falls does so at the behest of the deceased.

I had expected the trek through the park to be physically challenging but the footpaths were undemanding and the wide open spaces brought a welcome breeze. This was a cowboy movie setting, a breath of fresh air in every sense and a world apart from the sticky, enclosed rainforests of Andasibe and Ranomafana. The highlight of the day was undoubtedly the "Grand Canyon", a wide crater surrounded by immense sandstone rocks, a geological phenomenon that had evolved over millions of years. The only vegetation, the bushes and wild flowers, were species designed to survive the climatic extremes.

My treasured memory of that day is sitting atop a boulder, the wind cooling my sweat, binoculars capturing miles of rugged countryside. The sheer rock faces dominated the immediate surroundings and my field specs further earned their keep by picking out a small pile of stones at the entrance to a cave, no more than a dimple high up on one of the vertical walls. In keeping with Malagasy tradition the simple cairn had been left to denote a burial site; in keeping with Bara tradition the grave would only be accessible to the birds and the gods.

* * * * *

Continuing coastwards the plains became harsher, hotter and more arid; a land upon which it seemed only the baobabs had found a way to prosper. The weird trees with their fat, branchless trunks are another Malagasy speciality – six of the world's eight varieties are exclusive to the island – and here their strange form brought the only vertical dimension to a horizontal landscape.

The unique wildlife of Madagascar attracts visitors from all over the world though it's not the reason they come to Ilakaka. The ramshackle settlement just south of Isalo is the new centre of the sapphire trade and a place to which the good, the bad and the ugly have been drawn. Inevitably it is society's most ruthless that have taken control and are winning the battle of the greedy versus the needy: killings are commonplace, violence is a way of life, gambling and prostitution form the mainstay of the local economy. A horrible mess, the hotchpotch of shacks generates a human stench in every sense and another example of the government's failure to manage its valuable resources.

This seedy encounter seemed entirely at odds with the wholesome life of Madagascar and it left behind a sour taste. But, as always, a pleasant surprise was just around the corner. I was at the roadside, discreetly shedding a tear for Nelson, when I spotted the finest gecko ever seen. Lying diagonally on the back of a road sign it was about eight inches in length with a lime green head, a dark green body and a crazy black pattern throughout. It was later identified as a Standing Day Gecko (to admire when standing and taking a leak) and will forever remain my favourite lizard.

The high spirits returned, the greenery oozed back into the landscape and with 24 kms still to run I glimpsed the Mozambique Channel for the first time since the day I landed. The city of Tulear was not yet in sight but its strange, isolated mountain, more flat-topped and table-like than even that of Cape Town, would dominate the last of many hours spent aboard the bus.

* * * * *

Tulear was the end of the road but it wasn't the end of the journey. A zebu cart at the jetty would take over to haul passengers and bags across the beach and deep enough into the water to reach the mooring of the waiting boat. My final TLC destination was the beachside village of Anakao, an hour to the south.

The owner of the only lodge, a formidable lady from Geneva, stood barefoot in the sand to greet her guests as they paddled ashore through the lukewarm water. With true Swiss efficiency pleasantries were exchanged, mealtimes explained, food orders noted and keys issued – her organisational skills clearly undiminished by twelve years in the land of *mora mora*, that much-loved Malagasy term for "take it easy, chill out, no hurry..."

Everything about the place was exactly as I had hoped. Simple, no modern frills, just a row of huts in the sand and enough technology to ensure a well-chilled Three Horses at sundown. The staff replenished buckets of cold water twice daily for "showering" and the maid arrived each morning to fold the bed sheet and sweep the veranda. All I had to do was sit and enjoy a few days of quiet contemplation.

Sleeping, reading, writing…. one hour was much the same as the next until a menacing-looking visitor appeared at my neighbour's door. Well over six feet, he was a swarthy, powerful individual and by far the largest snake either of us had ever seen in the wild. The Madagascar Boa is the biggest in the country and this particular chap, with an ornately patterned black and brown body the girth of a human leg, was content to curl up on the veranda and stay there for most of the afternoon.

My own brush with nature was rather less exotic. The first large cockroach made his dash as I picked up the toothpaste, the sudden movement in the silence and the semi-darkness a shocking alternative to a loud "Boo!" Instinct was to grab the first available weapon – a can of deodorant heavy enough to pin and crunch – but as I lifted it another of the vile creatures scurried into action. Again I was startled. Rattled even. But before I could strike the two scuttled frantically round the back of the washbasin and took up positions behind toilet bag and shaving gel respectively. The waiting game they so enjoy.

With *Sure Active* primed in right hand, I sent *Gillette Pure & Sensitive* (how very apt) flying with my left. I should have known better. This time two more family members emerged and, sensing I was in a mean mood, darted off swiftly in opposite directions. How many there were I could not be certain, nor did I really want to know. For sure, with or without *Sure*, total eradication would be impossible; my only hope was to take one of them out purely as a symbolic gesture.

The proposed victim was duly selected and the rat-attack shoe brought back into service in preference to flimsy cosmetics. I launched in, a madman on the loose, arms flailing, toiletries rolling and crashing to the floor. And how he ran, the grotesque little critter, taking cover behind anything still standing until his cunning attacker had upended every single item in the bathroom. So what you gonna hide behind now, chum?

There was no answer because cockroaches do not talk. (Long may that remain the case.) What they can do with great efficiency is slip into a crack in the wall and lie as flat as a sheet of paper, knowing full well you can see them but that no amount of shoe bashing will expose them to risk. At that point they know they have won, they have survived again, as so often they do. And as the final act of impudence, just to really piss you off, they poke out that creepy, wiry antenna and wave it slowly up and down.

Cockroaches prevail everywhere on the planet and some even grow wings to add an extra level of torment. They are disgusting and utterly pointless but I resolved to calm down, accept defeat gracefully and regard their presence as an inevitable fact of life (like marzipan on a Christmas cake). I was privileged to be in a beautiful country with a fascinating wildlife and it was time to get things into perspective – why should one behave like a spoilt child just because some animals are prettier than others?

* * * * *

There could be no more calming influence than the soothing motion of the tide and my view by day of the fishing boats with their makeshift sails, wooden canoes with lateral extensions like sidecars on motorbikes you see in old wartime footage. And looking out further, across the channel, the island of Nosy Ve, inhabited only by birds, the last slither of land before the African coastline several hundred miles beyond. Yet again the vagaries of alphabet travelling had brought me to the shores of the Indian Ocean.

She looked beautiful, calm and relaxed, the friend I'd remembered from the Seychelles and those gorgeous little islands in the north of Mozambique. Incredible to think that just a decade earlier she had turned into a monster, risen up and claimed the lives of almost a quarter of a million people. Madagascar survived that tsunami but the ocean remains an ever-present threat to the island folk; cyclones return to the region every year and – just as in Bangladesh – death and destruction invariably follows in their wake.

The adventure had come full circle, quite by chance, from the city of Dhaka on the Tropic of Cancer to the beach of Anakao, almost swimming distance from the Tropic of Capricorn. Madagascar had truly delivered. Not just in terms of its interesting people and amazing wildlife but in its subconscious gathering of all that is wonderful in the world of the ten-letter countries: the paddy fields and rickshaws of Bangladesh, the multi-tiered city of Luxembourg, the stunning mountain scenery of Montenegro, the reefs and beaches of the Seychelles.

A common ground that extends way beyond the geography. Consider the spread of Islam that extended as far as the coast of Madagascar and the deserts of Mauritania, pushing the religion to its southern and western boundaries. There's the conflict of local language versus that of the former colonist as we encountered throughout Central Asia and, most significantly of all, the trauma of the bloody battles for independence as the Mozambicans also suffered at the hands of their European masters.

Madagascar has so much to offer and one day I hope to return. I'll head out on the train to Tamatave, up the remote north-east coast through the vanilla plantations and over to the island of Sainte Marie where the whales cruise by. I'll find remote beaches and trek across national parks and who knows, I might even go in search of the elusive Aye-Aye, that scary species of lemur with rabbit teeth and spooky claws.

It is often said there are places in the world you must try to get to during your lifetime. But what they forget to mention are those you need to visit at least twice. There must be a book in there somewhere.

ALPHABET TRAVELLING:
THE RECIPE FOR ADVENTURE

Ingredients: 1 bag Scrabble letters
2 dice
1 atlas

Method: Pick a tile from the bag, throw the dice, then locate a
country with that initial and the corresponding number of
letters. This is your destination.
If you pick an X or throw a 2, stay at home, paint the house,
and try again next year.